W9-CMM-129

DAILY LIFE IN PERU

DAILY LIFE SERIES

Daily Life in the Time of Homer
by Emile Mireaux

Daily Life in Florence in the Time of the Medici
by J. Lucas-Dubreton

Daily Life in Carthage at the Time of Hannibal
by Gilbert and Colette Charles-Picard

LOUIS BAUDIN

DAILY LIFE IN PERU

Under the Last Incas

TRANSLATED BY

WINIFRED BRADFORD

ILLUSTRATED

New York
THE MACMILLAN COMPANY
1962

Translated from the French

LA VIE QUOTIDIENNE AU TEMPS DES DERNIERS INCAS

First Printing
Printed in the United States of America

Library of Congress catalog card number: 61-8261

To my South-American Friends

PREFACE

WRITERS of 'daily lives' are fortunate who have at their disposal documents compiled by those who are the object of their studies. We cannot avail ourselves of any such facilities in recalling the life of the Indians in Inca times, for writing was then unknown. We are obliged to limit ourselves to consulting archeologists, folk-lore experts and chroniclers.

Archeology permits light from the past to filter through haphazard, by means of discoveries. Mythical sculptures, stylized designs, and hieroglyphic signs suggest hypotheses rather than supply solutions, and sharpen our curiosity rather than satisfy it.

A wealth of folk-lore lengthens echoes to which we listen with some satisfaction, for we know that the Indian environment has changed little through the centuries. But however slow this evolution may have been, it existed none the less, although its full impact escapes us.

An added difficulty is that the contributions of the pre-columbian society of Peru are often mingled with those of the Vice-Royalties and the Republic in an inextricable whole.

There remain the writings of the Spaniards which were certainly numerous, indeed too numerous, a chaotic mass of information—political, economic, social, military, religious, anecdotal, and scientific, generally badly presented, sometimes contradictory, rarely impartial. We must stress the difficulty which even the best-known chroniclers experienced in appraising the facts and the institutions, and in shedding their memories of classical antiquity and their Mediterranean prejudices, especially their political and religious ones. Garcilaso de la Vega praises the Incas excessively, Sarmiento de Gamboa pours scorn upon them, the secretaries of the conquerors lose themselves in military details, missionaries are bogged down in interminable sermons. Poma de Ayala is fashionable today amongst historians because he was an Indian, his manuscript has only recently been discovered, and his text is intermingled with artless drawings, but he shows little evidence of culture or objectivity.[1]

[1] R. Porras Barrenechea: *El crónista indio F. Huaman Poma de Ayala,* Lima, 1948.

We have scarcely any reliable sources at our disposal, and we are bound to exercise the greatest prudence in the handling of documents; nor have we even the advantage of being helped in our task by the atmosphere of grandeur and beauty which the poets of classical antiquity were able to provide in the Mediterranean world. No master of phrase or verse has celebrated the Indian heroes.

Under these conditions our contemporaries may be excused for having little knowledge of the Incas. For an overall view of this civilization the reader's attention may be drawn to our own work, *L'Empire socialiste des Inka* (Paris, Institut d'ethnologie, 1928), and better still, if he understands Spanish, to the third edition of the revised and complete translation which appeared in 1953 at Santiago de Chili (Libreria Zig-Zag). He will find in these volumes an abundant bibliography which will permit a considerable reduction in the notes in the present book, which are limited to a few essential references. The hurried reader will be interested to glance at the brochure, *Les Incas du Pérou* (Paris, 3rd edition, 1947), and also at *Vie de François Pizarre* (Paris, 1930).

We must also warn the reader that in order to avoid a pronunciation which might at times appear ridiculous, we have written the Quichua words in French[2] and not in Spanish. This procedure presents no inconvenience for this language was only a spoken one and there was no question of spelling in the days of the Incas.

Our only ambition, in the following pages, is to recount as accurately as possible the life of the Indians during one of the most extraordinary, yet least known periods of the history of the world. We shall be happy if we succeed in drawing the attention of our fellow-countrymen to these magnificent Andean countries. They are as inspiring on account of the remains they hide as for the hopes they arouse—for the mysteries of their past as much as for their promises for the future.

[2] English here. Translator's note.

CONTENTS

ILLUSTRATIONS

COLOMBIA
ECUADOR
BRAZIL
SELVAS
BOLIVIA
CHILE
Cali
Rio Magdalena
R. Guaviare
R. Patia
Pasto
R. Mira
Esmeraldas
Ipiales
R. Esmeraldas
Otavalo
Pichincha
QUITO
Bahia de Caraques
Latacunga
Ambato
Riobamba
GUAYAQUIL
CAÑAR
Puna I.
Tomebamba
Tumbez
Vilcabamba
Ayabaca
Payta
R. Piura
Huancabamba
Piura
Sechura
R. Marañon
Rio Napo
R. Putumayo
R. Japura
R. Javary
R. Ucayali
R. Jutahy
R. Jurua
R. Purus
Cachapoyas
Coyor
Cajamarquilla
Eten
Cajamarca
Huamachuco
R. Huallaga
Trujillo
(Chimu)
Mocha
Huaylas
R. Santa
R. Marañon
Chavin de Huántar
Huaraz
Huanuco
Recuay
Cerro de Pasco
R. Urubamba
Paramonga
Huacho
Lake Chinchaycocha
Tarma
Chancay
Canta
Acobamba
Ancon
Jauja
LIMA
Rimac
Matucana
Pachacamac
Lurin
Huanta
Chilca
Mala
Huancavelica
Machu Picchu
Ayacucho
Ollantaytambo
Cañete
L. Choclococha
Cangallo
R. Apurimac
CUZCO
Chincha I.
Pisco
Andahuaylas
Racche
Paracas
Abancay
Yannoca
Ica
R. Pampas
Vilcañota
Ayaviri
Nazca
COLLAO
L. Titicaca
Puno
Acora
Koati I.
Arequipa
Chucuito
Copacabana
LA PAZ
Desaguadero
Quilca
Tiahuanaco
Illimani
R. Desaguadero
Cochabamba
R. Madre de Dios
R. Beni
Arica
L. Poopo
International Frontiers
Mountainous Region
Miles
0
250

PART ONE

THE SETTING AND THE INHABITANTS

CHAPTER 1

THE COUNTRY

THE RULE OF NATURE

THE INTER-ANDEAN HIGHLANDS
LAND OF FEAR

IN South America, it is impossible to speak of man without first considering nature, for she holds sway—she always has done and always will. Nothing here is on our scale. Rivers, mountains, forests—everything is a hindrance, everything is hostile. Man does not seem to have been provided for in the plan of creation of this continent, he is accidental.

This circumstance produces first shock, and then fear. The framework of the region on which we shall focus particular attention, where desolate plateaux alternate with unconquered peaks, is conducive to the maintenance of 'original fear.'[1] The superhuman becomes inhuman. This is the country which the Spaniards formerly called 'High Peru,' contained between the two Corderillas, but which stretched north and south, far beyond the limits of the actual country of Peru, for it extended as far as Ecuador, Bolivia, and the north-west of the Argentine. The Andes rule there as imperious and deceptive mistresses. The geographers[2] say these mountains are young and of a simple structure, without geological faults, and they are indeed defensive walls whose breaches lie at an altitude of 12,000 feet. They seem to have been thrown up at the dawn of time, and are still without erosions or smooth surfaces. They are unfurrowed by wind or water, and present a continuity which, in Europe, is comparable with the Pyrenees, and even then they only bear a faint resemblance. These are living mountains, for they pursue their slow evolution regardless of

[1] H. de Keyserling: *Méditations sud-américaines,* French translation, Paris, 1932, chap. 1.

[2] *El Perú en marcha,* Lima, 1943 (an anonymous and well-documented work, published by the *Banco de crédito del Perú*).

man, pierced here and there by active volcanoes, and shaken at times by disturbing earthquakes.

Fear is further aggravated by isolation. To the west, after crossing the Corderilla, there appears, almost at once, one of the greatest oceans of the world; Polynesia is 5,000 miles away and Australia 7,500 miles. Eastward, beneath the mountains, lies the Brazilian forest, more difficult to cross than the sea. This land has lived withdrawn into itself, and it is well known what efforts have had to be made to reach it.

The inter-andean zone just described is one of those which to-day form the group of so-called Pacific States; the other two zones are the coastal and forest areas. This zone is the most important for us, since it was the cradle of the Inca Empire, and we shall begin with a description of it.

It can be seen from the map that the Corderilla which forms the western boundary of this long, narrow corridor, is pierced by only one large river, the Santa. The other watercourses flow eastwards through the eastern Corderilla. This peculiarity added to the mystery. The Amazon and several of its principal tributaries rise on the Peruvian plateau, and the Indians did not know towards what inaccessible ocean flowed the waters which irrigated their lands.

The two parallel Corderillas are joined by transverse ridges or nodes, lower than themselves, forming natural frontiers between the drainage basins. The largest of these is occupied by Lake Titicaca, imposing amongst its circle of snowy giants; it is here that the tableland reaches its maximum width of about 600 miles.

To the north of this country, so renowned in the ancient history of South America, there stretches another area no less famous—the region of Cuzco, capital of the Inca Empire. Here the two ranges are only 200 miles apart, and the ridge of Vilcañota is the southern boundary. Stretching to the north, the corridor contracts to a width of 150 miles, and the alternating series of ranges and ridges continues to the borders of the Republic of Ecuador.[1]

The landscape seen by the traveller, and which first impresses

[1] The isolation is such that, according to legend, the tribes did not think it of any use to build prisons because nature kept men prisoner in the place where they lived.

him, is that of the Peruvian *puna,* identical with the *páramo* of Ecuador. This is an immense grassy wilderness, situated at a height of between 9,000 and 15,000 feet, stretching out of sight to the north and south. Not a living being, not a tree, not a sound; it is a country of silence, monotony and sadness. Here and there rocks have been hurled about, split by volcanic action, with zigzag fissures cracked open by earthquakes. The flooding light of the tropical sun succeeds the icy cold of night at these high altitudes, without the mitigating gentleness of dawn and twilight.

However, the tableland at times descends as low as 6,000 feet, and the traveller delights in the pleasant valleys with a warm climate and fertile soil. Here are situated centres of population on volcanic cones, fertilized by alluvium from the watercourses flowing down from the Corderillas. These are the cultivated, as distinct from the pasture areas.

The reaction of Europeans to the inter-andean plateau, which the Peruvians call the *sierra,* differs enormously according to individuals, and it reveals their mentality. Some are filled with admiration for this savage grandeur, this primeval atmosphere; to them it recalls the early ages of the Earth, and they sense the presence of God. Others only see emptiness and sadness, masses of rock and earth which only produce boredom. To apprehend the feeling of this countryside, one must go far beyond the domain of the senses. The *sierra* is something beyond human experience, and is an instrument of choice among men, now as in the past.

THE COAST: LAND OF DROUGHT

The second region of Peru, the coast, forms a narrow stretch of land between the ocean and the western slopes of the Andes, slopes which are harsh and stony, and seldom watered by rainfall. This coastal plain presents two quite different characteristics. The area to the north of the Gulf of Guayaquil is humid and wooded, the other to the south is dry and sandy. The sea currents are the cause of this. Flowing from the Antarctic in an easterly direction, 150 to 170 miles wide, is the Humboldt current. This mass of water, more than three degrees centigrade colder than the surrounding atmosphere, slashes the blue sea with a band of grey-green, and hurls itself against the Chilean coast. It then flows along the coast northwards to the region of Payta (northern Peru), where it encounters the Niño crosscurrent, whose warm blue waters have come from the tropics. This current causes the Humboldt current to deviate from its course and turns it towards the open sea in a westerly direction. Its relatively low and constant temperature produces a lesser degree of salinity, which is favourable for the production of plankton. For this reason it is the home of a considerable number of fish of excellent quality, which in turn attracts multitudes of birds, whose excrement form mountains of *guano,* rich in nitrogen.

Thus, to the south of the Gulf of Guayaquil, the Peruvian coast remains dry and desert-like, for it lies between the Corderilla which holds the clouds coming from the east, and the Humboldt current which cools the winds from the sea, so that they provide no humidity at all. The light clouds which obscure the sun do at times bring a light drizzle, the *garrua,* which the people of Lima emphatically call rain. But this is very rare, and when it does come it brings disasters in its train. Nothing is prepared for it; it washes away the seeds, the little houses of dried earth, and even the mud-brick (adobe) walls of the ancient cities. In 1945 this happened at Chimu, the old capital of the realm of that name, to the great disappointment of archeologists and tourists.

It is easy to see how the Humboldt current hinders life on land and increases it in the sea.

The coast, like the plateau, is extremely isolated; it is geologically young, rectilinear, and without bays and large ports. The centres of population are on the banks of rivers, at some distance from the sea, in the midst of country on which they depend, and they are separated from each other by deserts of sand. Only a few fishing villages are situated near the ocean.

So, in Peru, the sea was not put to the service of man. The Indians were agriculturalists and not sailors. Certainly there was a certain amount of navigation in earlier times. The first inhabitants of the Inca Empire whom the Spaniards met were on the open seas off the coast of Ecuador. They were sellers of fish from Tumbez, and were sailing on a raft.[1] But in the

[1] J. de Sámanos: *Relación de los primeros descubrimientos de Francisco Pizarro y Diego de Almagro,* in *Colección de documentos inéditos para la historia de España,* t. V.

interior of Peru the only means of communication were the roads, and one of these actually ran along the coast.

It is possible that there were contacts between the inhabitants of South America and those of Polynesia. We shall see that such movements of population were even probable, but they were limited, although it is likely that they were carried on in both directions, east to west and west to east. The sporting exploit recently achieved by a team of Scandinavians who crossed the Pacific Ocean on a raft on the pre-columbian model, by making use of the Humboldt current, has taught us nothing new in this respect.[1] But the chronicler Sarmiento de Gamboa recounts that the Inca Tupac Yupanqui, after conquering the provinces along the Peruvian coast in the fifteenth century, was told of lands to the west, far beyond the horizon, whose existence had been revealed by travellers who had arrived in ships. It was said that far to the westward were islands which were inhabited and rich. The king at first did not pay much attention to these rumours, but he was intrigued by the information and by the insistence of those who brought it. So he consulted a sorcerer who confirmed the truth of these tales.

Urged on by his adventurous spirit and conscious of his power, the Emperor had built a fleet of rafts which set sail from Tumbez carrying a veritable army into the unknown. The chronicler gives a figure of 20,000 fighting men, and lists the names of the captains. The voyage lasted nearly a year, and the proof of this long absence is provided by the events which took place in the capital during this time, when it was thought that these foolhardy navigators would never return. We shall come back to them later. For the moment it is enough to know that the Peruvian armada certainly reached some Polynesian island, because certain objects were brought back and placed in the fortress at Cuzco, where the Spaniards saw

[1] Thor Heyerdahl: *The Kon-Tiki Expedition*, London, Allen & Unwin. The correct name of the Peruvian god is 'Tiqsi'; it therefore differs from the name of the Polynesian god. The reader will find a severe but fair criticism of the scientific claim of the Scandinavians in an article by a qualified expert, A. Métraux: *Le Voyage du Kon-Tiki et l'Origine des Polynésiens*, in *Revue de Paris*, July 1951, p. 119, and another no less searching in that of Professor R. Heine-Geldern: *Heyerdahl's hypothesis of Polynesian origins: a criticism*, in *Geographical Journal*, London, December 1950.

them. A dignitary of the imperial family was charged with their care, and Sarmiento gives us a description of this booty, but it was rather strange, for he records gold, a brass chair, a horse's skin and jawbones, and even some Negroes! [1]

The most astonishing thing about this expedition was not that the Emperor's men reached such distant lands—imitators in the twentieth century did so also—and won themselves fame equal to that of Christopher Columbus, but that they returned. These fragile craft were not wrecked on the Marquesas, and they achieved a gigantic round trip across the Pacific.

THE EASTERN FOREST: LAND OF MYSTERY

The third zone of Peru, the virgin forest, was not suitable for the development of a civilization. The upper courses of a great river such as the Amazon were too enclosed, swift-flowing, and broken by rapids to serve as a communication route. As a whole, the natural setting was against the establishment of an Andean Empire.

Not only were enormous areas unsuitable for cultivation, but the difference in altitude prevented the dweller in one region from becoming acclimatized to another. For this reason the Inca armies, descending from the tableland towards the sea, stayed half-way down for a time before continuing their journey.[2]

On the map, the population appears as a series of islands separated by empty stretches—a human archipelago. That such dispersal of strength was effective was due in olden times to an extraordinary organization—that of the Incas—and in modern times to an extraordinary invention—that of the aeroplane.

The unity of a nation, in the Pacific States, is the outcome of human will. If the foreign observer is at first discouraged

[1] P. Sarmiento de Gamboa: *Segunda Parte de la Historia general llamada índica*, Berlin, 1906, p. 90; M. Cavello de Balboa: *Miscelánea antártica*, French translation, Paris, 1840, chap. 7 (in French under the title, *Histoire du Pérou*).

[2] It is known that Bolivian soldiers from the high plateau suffered, during the Chaco war, from having to fight in the plains at a low altitude.

by the apparent hostility of nature, he can take confidence from studying the activities of man. History corrects geography.

Man in South America pitted himself against nature, and already, by the fifteenth century, he had succeeded in overcoming her by creating the Inca Empire.

THE RESTRICTED ANIMAL WORLD

If nature has not changed much between that time and ours, the landscape is no longer the same. Except in certain privileged valleys it is not very pleasant, even today, but it was formerly much less so. Only llamas were to be seen in the pastures where today the cattle multiply, and the eucalyptus, now so common, did not shade the pathways. If the twentieth century tourist is filled with admiration for the wild grandeur of the *sierra,* it is easy to imagine the impressions of the Spaniards, 400 years ago.

The llama has been mentioned, and it should indeed be mentioned first. Its wild brothers the *guanaco,* which seems to be the oldest of the family, and the *vicuña,* justly famed for its beauty, became comparatively rare after the Spanish Conquest, but the llama itself, and its near relative, the *alpaca,* have remained the faithful companions of the Indians. The llama is well known to all children who frequent zoological gardens, and to all postage-stamp collectors, for it appears on the Peruvian coat-of-arms. It is worthy of its reputation. This animal, with a long neck and fine head, is elegant and distinguished, yet it will carry light loads, but it would die where it stands rather than carry an excessive burden. It will scornfully spit a long jet of saliva in the face of anyone who annoys or ill-treats it.[1] This abstemious beast is most useful, for it is able to go without food or water for several days, eats grass and produces useful wool and dung, though not meat, for after the age of three years its flesh has a bitter flavour, due to

[1] P. de Cieza de León: *Segunda Parte de la Crónica del Perú,* in *Biblioteca hispana-ultramarina,* t. V, Madrid. 1880, chap. 111; J. D. von Tschudi: *Contributiones a la historica, civilizació y lingüística del Perú antiguo,* in *Colección de libros referentes a la historia del Perú,* t. 9, p. 226.

the vegetation on which it feeds. Above all it appears to harmonize with its surroundings in the Andes, and its familiar outline was described by the Spaniards as that of a big sheep or small camel.

The beast and the man are truly made for one another; both are sober and disciplined, both are dreamers, pursuing their quiet and slow-moving existence in a grey countryside, and through uneventful days. It is easy to understand the story of the llama who began to pray, and converted his wondering master to the Christian faith.[1]

The native dogs and the little Indian pigs, which in olden days made up the family livestock, were of secondary importance. On the coast, certain tribes had domesticated the falcon.

THE DIVERSE VEGETABLE WORLD

In the vegetable world, maize held an eminent position, comparable with that of the llama in the animal world.[2] Since it grew at high altitudes and on poor soil, it provided both food and drink. Another cereal, *manco,* formerly grew as well as maize, but has completely disappeared since the white man introduced wheat.

For us Europeans, the most remarkable of the pre-columbian products is the potato, since it came to us from Peru. It had two rivals, *oca,* the sweet potato, and *jiquima* which disappeared after the Conquest, like *manco.*

Amongst vegetables, the most common in early times was *quinua,* the small rice of the Spaniards, and an annual. There were three varieties growing in the *sierra* whose grain was edible. The stalks, when dried, were used as fuel, and the ashes were included in the preparation of *lipta,* which was mixed with *coca.* Also eaten were *cañahua,* which had the advantage of growing at a height of more than 1200 feet, *achita* in the temperate zones, and all kinds of beans, which appear in the designs on Chimu pottery, and above all *agi,*

[1] Ventura García Calderón: *Vale un Perú,* Brussels, 1939.

[2] Some archeologists have recently discovered in South America some agricultural civilizations without maize. W. C. Bennet: *A Reappraisal of Peruvian Archeology,* in *American Antiquity,* v. 13, 1948; W. C. Bennet and J. B. Bird: *Andean Culture History,* New York, 1949.

'the Indian pepper,' a usual condiment added, sometimes excessively, to most meat dishes.

In the tropical valleys, there was a more varied flora, and many fruits: tomatoes, guavas, *guabas, chirimoyas,* pineapples, *paltas* (avocados, alligator pears, wild pears of certain chroniclers)—a wide choice was available to the discerning. Add to these *yuca,* renowned for its flour, *chicoma* or *ajipa,* whose roots were edible but which no longer exists, and *mañi,* an herbaceous plant cultivated for its seeds which were used for starch and as a condiment, and from which was pressed a yellowish oil.

A great number of plants could be classed as industrial in pre-columbian times. Even the grass of the plateau (*ichoa*) was used as fodder for the llamas, as a basic roof covering, and as a strengthening material in brick-making. *Algarrobo* was sought for its sap which was sticky, and for its branches for use as fuel; *opuntia,* the ordinary tree cactus with red fruits and menacing spines provided prickles for use as needles. For colouring matter, *artemisca* or *malco* were used, also *achiote* with its red grain, and *jagua* with its black sap. *Totora,* the reed which grows on the shores of Lake Titicaca, is well known to tourists because it is used in the making of the picturesque boats whose photographs adorn all books relating to this part of the country. The most useful of the textile plants was *maguey* or *cabuya,* still widely found in several districts of the high tableland.[1]

We shall learn about medicinal plants in the section devoted to healers.

Trees were rare on the plateau; the ornamental willow provided its white wood, the *ceyba,* which grows to a height of 24 feet, was common on the banks of the Apurimac, and was used because its wood was impervious to water. The sorb-apple reached a height of 45 feet and was used in building Cuzco. In the tropical forests more beautiful kinds of wood

[1] The best documentation on this point is given by Father B. Cobo: *Historia del Nuevo Mundo,* Séville, 1890–1895, v. 1, book 4; L. Parodi: *Relaciones de la agricultura prehispánica con la agricultura argentina actual,* in *Anales de la Academia nacional de Agronomia y Veterinaria,* 1937, v. 1, Buenos Aires; L. Valcárcel: *Historia de la cultura antigua del Perú,* v. 1, vol. 2, Lima, 1949, p. 68; G. F. Carter: *Southwestern Journal of Anthropology,* February 6, 1950; G. R. Stonor and E. Anderson: *Annals of the Missouri Botanical Garden,* 1949.

were found; the *lucumo* was sought after by workers in ebony, and in some places the cedar grew to a height of 60 feet.

Compared with the enormous number of animals and plants at our disposal nowadays, the Indians of olden times seem to have been at a disadvantage. But they could not picture an abundance such as ours, and they were grateful to the gods for the rare products they showered upon them. Riches are psychological rather than economic, and consist of the moderation of desires rather than the accumulation of good things.

CHAPTER 2

THE TIMES

THE ASCENDANCY OF THE PAST

AFTER THE BACKGROUND, THE TIME

LET us imagine ourselves in the reign of Huayna Capac, at the end of the fifteenth or the beginning of the sixteenth century. This is a solemn moment, for the Empire has reached its zenith. The rulers recognized that the social system had passed beyond man-made standards; 12 to 15 millions of Indians scattered through a territory five times that of France were under a uniform and rigorous regimentation. To govern such a state was not impossible but it seemed foolhardy. There is an optimum size for Empires as for other undertakings. The Emperor decided to divide his lands between two of his sons, and so made two brothers into mortal enemies and sowed the seeds of civil war. This civilization had now reached its peak, the hour when destiny changed its direction, when the gods, who until then had been favourably disposed, abandoned their worshippers.

The average Indian was certainly not aware of the tragedy of this moment. His geographical knowledge was limited to the narrow region of his birthplace. He knew that the Empire was immense without any clear idea of its extent. He knew that it formed his world and that savage tribes surrounded him, against whom wars were waged in which he himself had taken or would take part. His historical knowledge was lacking in objectivity and exactitude, for he was compelled to listen on feast days to stories recounted by official story-tellers. In this way he learned an expurgated and doctrinal history, designed to glorify the ancient rulers and entangled with legends where often gods, animals, and men intermingled. Myths of a particular locality were also handed down from generation to generation and at times introduced a discordant note into this strange symphony.

BEFORE THE INCAS THERE WAS NOTHINGNESS

It is not easy to discover an underlying theme in so many variations, and it is still more difficult to position correctly in the past facts which for the most part are described as going back to the creation of the world, and which show few signs of connection between themselves. However, one acknowledged fact must be underlined. It appears that all the legends relating to the origin of the Incas were devised so as to form a starting point for the official history. The Spaniards allowed themselves to be caught in this deceit, which they could have easily unmasked, and they believed that before the Incas there was on the plateau only *behetrias,* that is complete anarchy. The presence of the ruins of Tiahuanaco alone, which they knew and admired, should have been enough to undeceive them. Many of them remarked that these remains were inexplicable without even attempting to find some explanation.

Let us follow the course of the centuries, beginning with the alleged origins of the Incas according to the official recorders. The first inhabitants of Peru, indeed of the world, said these early historians, lived like animals in isolated groups and worshipped different idols, such as the mountain tops, plants and wild animals. Fear and admiration inspired the form of worship; the puma was venerated for its strength, the condor for its imposing grandeur, the bat because it could see by night, and the owl for its bewitching eyes. No animal escaped becoming a divinity somewhere. Everything, too, which served a useful purpose was made an object of worship; earth, fire, even the air, maize, fish, llamas. Human sacrifices were frequent, for they enabled the soothsayers to foretell the future by examining the lungs and heart of the victims. The Antis, dwellers in the great virgin forests of the east, had a reputation for cannibalism second to none, according to the facts established by certain modern explorers.

In prehistoric times men lived entirely naked in the tropics, wearing only a belt, and the women a 'cache-sexe'; these are still commonly worn in many districts of the Amazon. On the plateau they were accustomed to clothe themselves with animal skins and to make coverings of wild hemp.

In this way the historians of the Inca period described primitive man to audiences who marvelled that they themselves were so remarkably civilized. They passed over in silence, not only all the civilizations previous to the Incas, but also the whole history of the races subdued by them. Outside this dynasty, there was nothing because there could be nothing.

THE DIVINE ORIGIN OF THE INCAS

But the Incas did appear from somewhere. It was impossible to neglect completely the places which had, in effect, been the cradle of the civilization preceding their own, that of the Aymaras. According to Indian legends, there appeared on an island in Lake Titicaca a man and a woman, both created by the Sun.[1] This beneficent heavenly body gave them a gold stick and ordered them to go wherever seemed best to them, but to settle permanently in the place where the stick disappeared from view when they struck the ground with it. The Sun ordered them to teach the wild inhabitants who peopled the land to worship him, to give them laws, to teach them to till the soil, care for their herds, and to build houses and towns. The Sun directed them to exercise their power with justice and kindness in the same way that he himself exercised his by giving them light and warmth, and he established them as rulers of the whole earth.

These two left the shores of the lake and set out towards the north. Each day they struck the earth with the magic wand, but in vain. Then they settled for a while at Pacaritampu, a short distance from the Cuzco valley. And here a second legend was grafted on, though independent of the first, according to some accounts, for here arose Tampu Tocco, which means 'the house with windows,' identified by some writers as the actual ruins of one of the most important dwellings in Machu Picchu. This looks out on the canyon of the Urubamba through three fine windows—it is a marvellous viewpoint and unique of its kind. They say that from these

[1] A. de Calancha: *Corónica moralizada del orden de San Agustín en el Perú,* Barcelona, 1638, book 1, chap. 14.

windows there came forth the 'original' four brothers who conquered the whole country. Sometimes their wives are named, and ten *ayllus* (or communes) obeyed and followed them.[1]

The first version tells us that the royal pair continued their journey and that when they reached the hill of Huanacauri in the Cuzco valley, the magic stick disappeared into the ground at the first blow. At this time the area was covered with forests, and the people lived in a state of extreme misery and degradation. The prince and princess shared the task which had been assigned to them, the one travelling north and the other south, gathering together and teaching the natives. For their part, impressed by the sumptuous clothing in which the Sun had clad his children, which in no way resembled their own, and attracted by the promises made to them of a happy and easy life, the natives took these divine emissaries for chieftains and obeyed them. Order was established quickly and an age of prosperity reigned in the valley where the city of Cuzco was founded. It was divided into two parts as a tribute to the princely pair—the first mythical explanation of a division which has remained a mystery up to our own time.

It was during this period that the Indians learned to till and irrigate the land, and the Indian women to weave and spin. They were also instructed in the art of war and subdued the neighbouring tribes.

These are clearly legends and call to mind the conquest of high Peru by the Incas and the conquest of the earth by the cultivators. The first has the second as foundation, for the eras of great wars are often the outcome of technical and economic evolution. The golden stick which vanished into the ground indicated the most fertile soil where the primitive spade could be wielded without difficulty, and the four brothers who came from Tampu Tocco symbolized, one may believe, the taking possession of the soil by the edible vegetation. There was also mention of the shrub called *coca,* described as the vegetal incarnation of a woman from heaven with a message of consolation for men who work and suffer.[2]

[1] Garcilaso de la Vega: *Primera Parte de los Commentarios reales,* Madrid, 1723, book 1, chap. 18; P. Sarmiento de Gamboa: *op. cit.,* chaps. 13 and 14.

[2] R. Porras Barrenechea: *Mito, tradición e historia del Perú,* Lima, 1951, p. 25.

The Indian found in the innumerable variations of these tales something to feed his memory and his imagination. The memory of those wretched forbears who once wandered in the Cuzco valley in search of nourishment that was all too scanty made him feel the weight of the debt he owed to the Incas. The presence of the desert site where stand the ruins of Tiahuanaco plunged him into a world of legend and mystery.

It is surprising that in this latter setting of drought and height, the appearance of the first sovereign at the dawn of time is credited with having succeeded a disastrous flood—a disaster described at times with amusing detail. For instance the shepherds who had taken refuge on the highest points reckoned, with understandable relief, that the mountains grew taller as the floodwaters rose! All these stories about a deluge, set in the American 'roof of the world,' are too closely copied by the chroniclers from the biblical tradition not to be suspect. The Indians, after the Conquest, transposed the accounts of the missionaries, helped too, very often, by apostles of the Christian faith who used unscrupulous methods, so as to build up a sacred history of the New World. They even went so far as to pretend that the four brothers of whom we have spoken, and their four wives, were saved from the flood, and that the windows from which they stepped forth were those of the Ark, and that the prince who appeared at Tiahuanaco was Noah. Garcilaso de la Vega, recording these tales which he had heard in his youth at Cuzco, is himself doubtful and excuses himself by saying that he did not wish to take sides, but he was simply recording what he had been told—he invited his readers to make up their own minds.[1]

On the central theme of the apparition and installation of the first Inca, usually called Manco Capac, a number of fantasies have been embroidered. One of the most amusing of these refers to a common deception; the mother of this first monarch was a woman of remarkable intelligence, gifted with a spirit of initiative rare amongst the Indians; indeed we may say she was extremely astute. She worked for a long time preparing for her son a rich garment covered with gold panels, and a head-dress of brilliant feathers. She then sent him to a

[1] Garcilaso de la Vega: *Commentarios reales, op. cit.,* book I, chap. 18.

grotto situated on the side of the hill overlooking Cuzco. She waited for a grand feast day, and then, under the rays of a summer sun which made his costume glitter, she made the young hero, handsome as a god, walk forward towards the astonished and admiring crowd. The bold impostor declared that he was the son of the Sun and he was proclaimed Emperor.[1]

This legend is curious, for it is not compatible with the majesty of the Inca, and the belief in his divine origin. It bears witness to the childish and opportunist character of the people who liked to hear and repeat it. Rarely in these legends of the past are there sombre dramas, assassinations, or violence. The deities are often familiar and smiling, poetry reigns supreme; the fox who loved the moon mounted two thick ropes to reach her and remains attached to her luminous disc; the comets take refuge on the snowy summits after dazzling the world with their fiery wings; the stars are crumbs fallen from celestial banquets.[2]

ECHOES FROM THE COAST

THE POLYNESIAN ENIGMA

Let us picture now the period preceding the Inca domination in the light of some of the strange myths recorded by the chroniclers. It is tiresome to state that we are no longer concerned with Lake Titicaca, where one would have expected the Aymara civilization to have provided an inexhaustible source of stories, whether true or not; it was by sea and on rafts that the first Indian chiefs arrived.

The still savage natives of the northern coast of Peru, situated between Tumbez and Chimu, saw a great number of rafts arrive bringing whole families, and led by a chief called Naymlap.[3] Father Cabello de Balboa, telling this story, avers that the displaced tribes came from the farthest extremity of Peru, which is illogical and improbable. Had this been so they

[1] A. Ramos Gavilan: *Historia del célebre santuario de Nuestra Señora de Copacabana*. Lima, 1621, p. 5.

[2] R. Porras Barrenechea: *Mito, tradición e historia, op. cit.*, p. 23.

[3] M. Cavello de Balboa: *Miscellánea antártica, op. cit.*, Part 3, chap. 17.

would have landed at Tumbez, as did Francisco Pizarro, for rafts follow the line of the shore and could not have missed this attractive port after the endless virgin forest which lined the coast of Ecuador. So the rafts must have come from the west. Let us hold to that conclusion. Naymlap ruled over a nation already well-organized, for he was attended by a great number of concubines, servants, officers and other undefined personnel. He settled himself inland, built houses and palaces, and had a long and prosperous reign about which we have no information whatsoever. When he felt the hour of his death approaching, he asked his close companions to bury him secretly in the room where he had lived. This was done, and it was announced publicly that the king had decided to leave his people and that he had taken wings and flown away. It was thought that in this way a halo of glory would be added to the memory of the vanished sovereign, but the subjects of this model state were so dismayed at the news that they in their turn left the country and scattered in all directions in search of their ruler—the unforeseen and tragic consequence of a lie. Only those born in the country remained behind, for they were still relatively young.

The account lists the names of a series of successors to Naymlap, but without any other information, which deprives the names of interest. It seems that the narrator had hoped to hide by means of a useless list of names the total absence of information about the lives, environment and times of these personalities. Unfortunately it is from these that we can often draw conclusions. The native chroniclers thought they had told everything by giving these Christian names, which stand like milestones along a desert road.

And so we reach a certain ruler called Fempellec, about whom we know nothing except that he had the misguided idea of ousting the idol brought by Naymlap. Taking advantage of this strange circumstance, an evil spirit took possession of a very beautiful woman, who seduced Fempellec. Punishment followed swiftly; heavy rains fell, causing a flood—a deluge—followed by a period of drought and famine. The people accused the debauched ruler of being responsible for these disasters and threw him into the sea, bound hand and foot. So ended the direct dynasty of Naymlap.

After this dramatic event, the powerful ruler of the Chimu nation, a neighbouring country to the south whose history is unknown, conquered the peoples of the coast. Once again the list of Christian names appears in the account, but not for long. We are now approaching the moment in time when the Incas advanced across the plateau and threatened the coastal nations whom they eventually subdued. The most puzzling and most interesting part of the story for us is its beginning; the arrival by sea of an already civilized people. This fact is confirmed by Father Anello Oliva who insists that he obtained the explanation from a keeper of the knotted cords named Catari. He was well esteemed for his knowledge and is also mentioned by other writers.[1] His explanation was that the tribes driven out by the flood reached the coast of Ecuador, and one of them, led by a chief called Tumbe, settled on the southern shore of the Gulf of Guayaquil and founded the town called after the name of their leader. Quitumbe, a son of this hero, in order to escape an invasion by giants who had captured his brother, crossed the Corderilla and reached the tableland, where he founded the city which has borne his name ever since—Quito.

Quitumbe, in his hurried flight, omitted to take his wife with him and abandoned her completely. The deserted wife resented this bitterly. She asked the gods to punish the faithless husband, and so as to solicit their goodwill, she resolved to sacrifice her son. Happily a condor appeared at the moment when this cruel act was about to take place, seized the child and carried him away to a Pacific island. When he was grown-up, strong and handsome, the young man built a raft and reached the mainland, where he was imprisoned by savages. The daughter of the barbarian chieftain became enamoured of him; she secretly sent him an axe with which he killed his guards and escaped to an enchanted place where he lived an idyllic existence with the lady who had delivered him.

The legend of destruction by water, which the chroniclers inevitably linked with that of the Flood, was finally explained by F. López de Gómara, who describes the change which came over the Peruvian coast which had now become dry and

[1] J. Anello Oliva: *Histoire du Pérou,* French translation, Paris, 1857, chaps. 3 and 4.

sterile. The first god to appear on Pacific shores was Kon (or Con), who created men and women and gave them fertile lands in which to dwell. But these creatures behaved wickedly, and to punish them the angry god forbade rain to fall. Then Pachacamac, a new god, arose, drove out Kon and changed the first men into animals and created a new human race. These people showed their gratitude by building the celebrated temple on the Peruvian coast whose ruins still bear the name of their divinity.[1] However this benefactor forgot to make the rain fall again, and the coast has now become a sandy waste.

All these accounts, incomplete and often strange, are difficult to link up with each other, but they are none the less informative. They confirm, curiously enough, the present-day hypothesis of the annihilation of a country situated between the New World and Australia, where a civilization developed whose remains are to be seen in the statues on Easter Island and the monolith on the island of Fiji.[2] This agrees with the idea that a crumpling of the earth's surface may have raised up the Andes and made part of the Peruvian-Bolivian plateau (Collao) cold and sterile, and may have caused a crack in the earth along the whole Pacific coast where the seas are now very deep. This would explain the isolated burial grounds along the shore, like the huge necropolis of Paracas, which were the cemeteries of the buried cities. It would also explain the many representations of steps on monuments and artistic objects, such as the one displayed in the courtyard of the museum at Cuzco, which is a symbol of the ascent of the Andes by a people in flight.

There is little doubt that in early times there were contacts between the natives of Polynesia and those of South America. There is abundant proof in the objects which appear on both sides of the Pacific; the propeller, the Pan's flute, the blowpipe, and the knotted strings. There are striking resemblances between the Maori tongue and the Quichua (or Quechua) language. Certain words have the same meaning. *Apay* means

[1] López de Gómara: *Historia general de las Indias,* in *Biblioteca de autores españoles,* t. 22, Madrid, 1852, p. 232.

[2] The hypothesis of a catastrophic earthquake is rejected by J. Imbelloni: *Las Tabletas parlantes de Pascua,* in *Runa* (Buenos Aires), vol. 4, 1951, p. 93.

'to carry,' *makay* means 'to strike,' *muku* means 'stained,' *mutu* means 'mutilated,' *pucara* means 'a fortress,' and *turnu* means 'frightened.' A great number of words obviously have a common origin and have only undergone slight modifications.

QUECHUA	MAORI	MEANING
ajsu	*ahu*	clothing
curaca	*cura*	chief
chuki	*kuki*	lance, pointed stake
illa	*ira*	light, to shine
inca	*inca*	emperor, warrior
ipu	*ipu*	fine rain, cloud
kaka	*kaka*	bastard, descendants
kara	*kiri*	skin
karu	*koroa*	absence
kuru	*kutu*	worm
papi	*papi*	humid, muddy
raku	*raku*	snow, clear colour
tipa	*tipa*	needle, tattooing
unu	*unu*	water, to drink water

Plants, too, provide further telling proof; the American sweet potato is found in Polynesia, the cultivated American cotton with 26 chromosomes seems to be the result of a cross between the Asiatic cotton with 13 chromosomes and the wild Peruvian cotton also with 13 chromosomes. Several Hawaiian plants seem to have been imported from America in very early times.[1]

Finally, archeologists have recently discovered in the northern regions of Peru funerary villages situated on the slopes of high cliffs and consisting of houses containing statuettes; experts have observed similar customs in Celebes.

This last evidence may also be the result of west-east as well as east-west migrations; the voyage of the Peruvian fleet during the reign of Tupac Yupanqui showed that this was possible.

Since the Indian delighted in recalling the past, it is all the more difficult to distinguish the real from the imaginary in this mass of stories. His dislike of change, his fundamental desire to remain in familiar surroundings, and the absence of

1 J. Imbelloni: *La Esfinge indiana*, Buenos Aires, 1926, addition by E. Palavecino, p. 335; R. Cúneo-Vidal: *Historia de la civilización peruana*, Barcelona, s.d., p. 85.

writing, gave him a taste for stories, whether true or not. A modern historian has remarked that the Quechua language contained a great number of words connected with narration, and that different words were used in the recounting of an event, or a fable, and different again when relating imaginary and wonderful deeds, or the words of a song, etc.[1]

THE GLORY OF THE CHIMUS

After all these legendary tales, let us now turn to a neglected history—that of the conquered peoples about whom the conquerors kept no records, a history which survived only in the memory of the conquered, and from which it was effaced little by little by mingling with legend. The Incas so completely absorbed the races whom they subdued that they even despoiled them of their own past. We can only find accounts of these things amongst those chroniclers who were sufficiently far-sighted to study regional history by questioning the Indians belonging to other than Inca tribes.

The oldest civilization, that of Chavin, does not appear in the chronicles; it is only shown to us by the remains left in the *sierra* and on the coast of central Peru. These gigantic walls and the sculptured representations of geometrical monsters tell us nothing about the lives of the men who conceived them. Experts fix this civilization approximately at the opening of the Christian era, from the fourth to the seventh century.

As for the Manabi civilization, on the coast of present-day Ecuador, we cannot even fix the century to which it belonged. The only important clues are some basreliefs, and seats shaped like a U, all carved from stone.

By contrast, we do know that the Chimu king had conquered the north coast of Peru as far as the boundary of Ecuador, and we know from the official accounts of the Inca period that prolonged and difficult struggles led to the submission of this race and its integration into the Empire. But between the periods of legend and history there is a hiatus which contemporary scholars are trying with great difficulty to fill, by collating the modern discoveries of archeologists, ethnologists, anthropologists, and linguists.

[1] R. Porras Barrenechea: *Mito, tradición e historia, op. cit.*, p. 21.

The Chimus spoke a language of which certain words remain, notably in the dialect spoken in the port of Eten, and which raise an insoluble problem: was the language written down? Father Montesinos, whose bold assertions have often been found to be correct, holds that writing existed in former times in Peru, and that it had been banned by the Inca rulers.[1] This prohibition, which the reader may interpret according to his own conception of life or his personal experience, as a proof of wisdom or folly, could be explained by the fact that writing did not originate on the plateau but could have been brought there by the Chimus. When the masters of Cuzco subdued this nation which was hostile to them for so long they may have desired to efface all records of their previous history. This explanation is not very convincing however, since the Incas did not hesitate to borrow from the peoples they conquered any institutions which appeared to them capable of perfecting their own system or of contributing to their prestige. It appears that in this way they adopted from the Chimus the idea of relays of runners for the transmission of official messages.

On much of the pottery attributed to the Chimus there are delineated Indians running through a desert of sand-dunes dotted with cactus—a characteristic of the coastal region. They carry llama-skin bags containing beans, a piece of quartz used for making lines on these seeds, and a white powder which made the lines thus hollowed out more easily visible. The beans are often drawn separately like decorative motifs; they bear designs which are not a reproduction of those with which nature sometimes decorated them, but they often look like blobs or points. The link between the beans and the messengers is underlined by the presence of each of them in the same settings, and by the odd connection which is sometimes stressed in the form of beans with two legs also running across the landscape.[2]

Sometimes the messengers have the head of a fox, which is an animal renowned in both the New and the Old World for its astuteness. Was this an allusion to the skill which the runner

[1] F. Montesinos: *Memorias antiguas historiales políticas del Perú,* in *Colección de libros españoles raros o curiosos,* Madrid, 1882, t. 16, chap. 4.

[2] R. Larco Hoyle: *Los Mochicas,* Lima, 1939, t. 2, chap. 5.

must display in completing his task, or did it allude to the skill which the official in charge of the interpretation must display? This man also appears on ancient vases, holding a pointed tool in his hand, but we do not know whether he used it to trace out the signs or to classify the seeds. Even today, in certain districts on the coast, the herdsmen count their beasts by means of beans in a small bag which they always carry with them; the colours of the seeds correspond to the various kinds of animals, cows, calves, and so forth.

In a few cases the messengers are represented as holding in their hands objects similar to the backbone of a fish, apparently made up of strings attached to a central cord. No doubt this was the ancestor of the knotted cords of which the Incas made such wonderful use, as we shall see.

THE MANY FORGOTTEN NATIONS

Another great nation which history, as taught by Cuzco, left in oblivion, was the realm of the Caras, situated to the north of the Empire.

According to an Ecuadorian writer,[1] the name Cara came from a chief called Caran who may have landed, at some time impossible to specify, on the north coast of Ecuador at the spot now called Bahia de Caraques. Again we find an indication of an arrival by sea, on rafts. There is also a confused story of an invasion by giants in a rather more southerly part of this same coast of Ecuador. There is no doubt that an early civilization did exist in these parts.

The Caras climbed the Corderilla and clashed with the scattered tribes there and subdued them. They took Quito as their capital and built two temples, one to the Sun and one to the Moon; they also set up a social system with a king and nobility. They had no messengers or knotted strings, but had a method of counting for keeping their records. A rectangular flagstone was marked out in divisions; these divisions, which were placed at the two extremities of a diagonal, jutted out, sometimes with two storeys. Pebbles had different values according to the compartment in which they were placed, and as in all mnemonic instruments, their colour indicated the nature of object being counted.

[1] J. de Velasco: *Historia del Reino de Quito,* 1841–1844, 3 vol.

The Caras were clever weavers and tanners, and above all skilful workers in precious stones, for they had at their disposal the emeralds which gave their name to one of the coastal provinces of Ecuador. Their civilization more resembles that of Colombia than Peru. A very aggressive race, they succeeded in spreading towards the north, but finally, when advancing southwards, they clashed with the Puruhas, a warlike people who used spears and slings. However, by means of alliances and marriages they succeeded in extending their kingdom where force of arms would only have led them into prolonged warfare. Moreover, they were threatened by a danger far greater than any other, and were obliged to conserve their forces to meet it. Little by little the Inca Empire was reaching out towards them, and before long, battle was joined.

Other nations, too, had prospered before being absorbed by the conquerors from Cuzco, and that at a relatively recent date, in the thirteenth and fourteenth century of our era. The realm of Cuismancu was in the coastal valleys of Lurin and the river Rimac; it was of great religious importance, for the temples were particularly numerous and some of them celebrated, such as Pachacamac. The town situated near this sanctuary was in two parts, of which one was reserved for pilgrims. In the Rimac valley, where Lima now is and from which it takes its name, the idol of Rimac Tampu (where today is the airport of Limatambo) was famed for its oracles.

About 18 miles from the present-day capital of Peru, was Cajamarquilla, a town inhabited by a small mixed group of tillers of the soil, shepherds and fishermen—all humble folk. Protected by a small fort, it contained a great number of 'cave-dwellings,' according to present-day expressions; that is to say a big cave whose use seems to have been to act as a shelter for the living and not as a burial place for the dead. The walls were of dried mud, bricks, or lumps of beaten earth, and each house had its small llama paddock. The narrow doorways showed an erosion of the sides of the entrances on account of the constant rubbing of the garments of those going in and out.[1]

Still in this same district, the site of Ancu, nowadays a

[1] Varii Auctores: *Lima precolombina y virreinal,* Lima, 1938, p. 49.

beach much frequented by the people of Lima, was once an important centre. The many objects found in the graves, of which it is estimated that there are about 35,000, belong to three different eras, Chavin, Chimu and Inca. The presence of original articles from the Peruvian plateau are proof of the manifold exchanges between the coast and the interior.[1]

To the south of the Cuismancus' lands were the valleys of Chilca, Mala, and Huarcu, whose ruler was named Chuquimancu. Owing to an intensive agricultural system these valleys were rich in spite of a total absence of rain. The cultivators used a high-grade manure made from sardine heads, which they buried with maize seed in deep holes in the ground. In addition, they irrigated by means of canals. Garcilaso says he was amazed when he travelled through the country.

So as to defend the valley of Huarcu (today called Cañete), a huge fortress was built which stopped the inland nations from invading them, and later on, it held off the Incas for a considerable time.

Continuing south along the coast, we find the war-like Chinchas, who were always fighting their neighbours. In this region, in the towns of Ica and Nazca, was one of the biggest centres for the making of pottery in pre-columbian America. There, too, remains are still to be found. At Tambo Colorado there are the ruins of a palace and of an Inca fort, where the soldiers of the high plateau lived for a time so as to become used to the tropical climate before going down to sea-level. The Chinchas put up such a formidable resistance that it took several years of war before the Incas triumphed over these formidable opponents. Once again the men of Cuzco carried the day by a clever ruse which had nothing to do with fighting courage; they destroyed the irrigation canals which brought water from the *sierra,* and by this means threatened their enemies with famine.[2]

Farther south still, the fishing tribes remained backward peoples. But we must now return to the plateau. About the tenth century of our era, there appeared a civilization whose centre was situated at Tiahuanaco and which bears the same

[1] R. Carrión Cachot: *Ancón,* Lima, 1951.
[2] H. Urteaga: *Tambo Colorado,* in *Boletín de la Sociedad geográfica de Lima,* 1939, p. 85.

name. In this high place are strange and mysterious ruins whose extent point to the existence of a town. The most remarkable of these are at Acapana, a sanctuary where there are standing stones, undoubtedly the remains of an enclosure; also a fallen statue called by the natives the 'Brother,' a monumental stairway of flagstones, and finally the Gateway of the Sun. The lintel of this building is a monolith, and on it is represented a god holding in his hands, which have only four fingers, on one side a sort of propeller, and on the other a kind of quiver holding two arrows. On the two sides of this central figure, 24 individuals turn towards the centre and seem to hasten in that direction. The doorway is relatively low and a litter could never have passed through it; but the monument seems to have been for show and meant to crown a building. From this it can be deduced that to discover the ruins of the temple it is only necessary to dig in the terrace which supports these ruins. Here and there on the plain are the remains of walls, some of which are pierced with small holes where golden-headed nails were placed.

Besides these remains this civilization has left us its language, whose admirable qualities we shall have occasion to admire in a later chapter.

The Aymaras were supreme on the high plateau from the tenth to the twelfth century, and one finds traces of them in many districts, but nothing is known of their history.

After the Tiahuanaco era there comes an intermediate period about which we know nothing. The first Incas then appeared, surrounded by legendary glory; we shall meet them again when describing the life of these Emperors. (Part 2, Chapter 1.)

THE INDIAN SOCIAL UNIT

The Indian was generally too localized in space and too careless of time to take any interest in the exploits of his distant ancestors. His world was his own community to which he and his parents belonged and were supposed to belong from the beginning of time; the *ayllu*.

No doubt this name is derived from a native social unit which has been modified in the course of history, but this grouping has always kept as its main characteristic the solidarity engendered either by the kinship, real or fictitious, of its members, or by communal tilling of the soil. This latter element infers that the natives were no longer nomadic, and that is why it appears, logically, in second place.

The *ayllus* differed according to the relative importance of these two factors. In the same way their composition varied according to whether they mingled or not with the village communities. Of course, in the large centres of population there were several *ayllus*.

At the time of the first Incas the *ayllu* retained its original triple character—religious, family, and economic.[1]

The *ayllu* had an ancestor, real or imaginary, in the totem, *guarqui,* which took the form of an animal, or inanimate object, or natural phenomenon, such as a puma, a rock, or lightning. This confusion of worlds is perfectly indicated by the representations of a stylized bird or quadruped with a human head, on pottery or textiles.

It will not be surprising that we shall often have occasion to draw attention to this unified and all-embracing conception, taking no account of elementary or obvious classifications.

Alongside this first principle of the group there appeared their particular deities, the *conopas*; these were very varied, and were usually represented by statuettes of men or animals made of baked clay, or even just simple stones of an unaccustomed shape. These were placed in niches provided for them in the walls of the cottages.[2]

When speaking of the family character of the *ayllu,* it must be understood that this term is used in its widest sense. To begin with, the Indian did not separate himself from his surroundings, his personality was based on his background, which overflowed the family unit and extended to the whole group of blood relations making up the *ayllu.* This in its turn formed part of a brotherhood or *parcialidad* (*suyu* or *saya*) usually coupled under the names *hanan* and *hurin,* that is the high and the low.

[1] J. Mendoza del Solar: *La evolución social y política del antiguo Perú,* Arequipa, 1920, p. 65; H. Castro Pozo: *Del ayllu al cooperativismo socialista,* Lima, 1936; F. Cosio: *La Propiedad colectiva del ayllu,* in *Revista Universitaria del Cuzco,* 1948, 1; J. A. Fonvielhe: *L'évolution juridique de l'Indien du Pérou,* typewritten thesis, Bordeaux, 1952. The German sociological school of H. Cunow departs from this principle that the whole organization of pre-columbian Peru rests on the *ayllu.*

[2] P. J. de Arriaga: *Extirpación de la idolatría del Perú,* Lima, 1621.

The *hanan* were considered to be superior to the *hurin,* but we do not know exactly why. Perhaps the latter were the new arrivals, the immigrants, or on the contrary they may have been the original occupants who had been subdued by the conquering *hanan.*[1]

There is to this day a Bolivian village, almost inaccessible, which is hostile to the white man and mindful of tradition. It offers us an excellent example of ancient Indian groupings; it is called Collana, and is situated 40 miles from La Paz, facing Illimani, at a height of 11,400 feet. Until 1946 the inhabitants kept the right of maintaining their own organization and their own rule of law—Spaniards could not live there, not even missionaries. A priest from La Paz spent a day there once a quarter, and the village headman was the only one who spoke Spanish.[2] The central square is divided into two unequal parts by a great transversal line; these divisions are the *sayas* which are still respectively called *manan* (high) and *aran* (low). The first of these 'partitions' is the more important, and each section is itself divided into two parts, each one assigned to an *ayllu.* There are four *ayllus,* though once there were ten; they bear the names of the places from which their occupants originally came—Tiahuanaco, Viacha, Huaque, and Pukarani. The square is marked out in this way so that on the occasion of a great festival the inhabitants know exactly where to stand. The village itself is divided in the same way, and llama bones, placed upright, indicate the boundaries of the *ayllus.*

There are other examples. At Sechura, on the coast, there are divisions which correspond to inhabitants born in the area, those born outside, and strangers from other regions. Each group occupies an angle of the square on feast days.

At Chincheros, on the tableland, 20 miles from Cuzco,

[1] Controversies on this point are lively and confused, especially with regard to the two brotherhoods at Cuzco. See especially F. Montesinos: *Memorias antiguas historiales, op. cit.,* chaps. 1 and 6; B. de las Casas: *De las antiguas gentes del Perú,* in *Colección de libros y documentos referentes a la historia del Perú,* Lima, 1939, chap. 17; Sarmiento de Gamboa: *Historia general, op. cit.,* chaps. 8 and 9; J. de Matienzo: *Gobierno del Perú,* Buenos Aires, 1910, chap. 15.

[2] J. Vellard: *Un village de structure précolombienne en Bolivie,* in *Annales de Géographie,* July 1943, p. 206; McBride: *The agrarian Indian communities of highland Bolivia,* New York, 1921, p. 14.

the inhabitants still live in these *ayllus* or communes.[1]

The cell or central core of the family was originally the mother, since maternity alone was indisputable in establishing descent amongst a promiscuous primitive people. The father asserted his authority and became head of the family when the nomad *ayllu* was transformed into a settled group working on the land, and the children thus became the instruments of toil—a position they still hold in Peru. Patriarchy was thus substituted for a matriarchy and traces of this still lingered in the days of the Incas.[2] The parents of the male line were the foundation of the *ayllu*,[3] and the wife, falling into second place, became the property of the husband, as she still remains in the Andes.

At the same time sexual taboos were instituted. Marriage within the group was forbidden, and a wife had to be found outside, either by combat, kidnapping or collective agreement. However, the supreme Inca seems to have been the exception to this rule, for he married one of his sisters; but it may well be argued that we are mistaken about this, for the word sister did not have the same meaning for the Peruvian Indians as it does for us. The masculine *Ego* gave the name of father not only to the author of his days, but also to that author's brother (that is his uncle); and he called brother not only those whom we understand as brothers, but also the sons of his father's brother, that is, his cousins. For this reason there is some confusion among historians.[4] The taboos disappeared only through

[1] M. Kuczynski-Godard: *El pensamiento arcáico mítico del campesino peruano,* Lima, 1948, p. 33; A. Miro Quesada: *Costa, sierra y montaña,* Lima, 1947, p. 400.

[2] Especially on the north coast of Peru.

[3] The wife, on marriage, joined her husband's *ayllu.* A. Sivirichi: *Derecho indígena peruano,* Lima, 1946, p. 221.

[4] Garcilaso de la Vega: *Comentarios reales, op. cit.,* book 4, chap. 8; Vaca de Castro: *Discursio sobre la descendencia y gobierno de los Incas,* in *Colección de libros y documentos referentes a la historia del Perú,* t. 3, Series 2, Lima, 1920, p. 24: J. Mejia Valera: *Organización de la sociedad en el Perú precolombino,* Lima, 1946, chap. 4. For C. Levi-Strauss the assertion that incest was forbidden marks a moment of extreme importance in the history of humanity. It indicates evolution from the order of nature to the cultural order, from submission to free-will—the arrival of a new order, for it corresponds to the first formation of a rule independent of the commands of nature. This rule is not arbitrary, it obeys the principle of reciprocity. I give up my sister and my daughter, and my neighbour must do the same so that I can take a wife from his family. From this exogamy was established. (*Les structures élémentaires de la parenté,* Paris, 1949.) It is not necessary for us to examine here the very obscure problem of out-and-in-breeding amongst the Incas. Usually

force of circumstance and without in any way affecting the basic principle, as when feasts were prolonged for several days and ended in drunkenness and general debauchery.[1]

Finally the economic aspect of the *ayllu* was altered; the link which derived from kinship was replaced by one deriving from that of land, so that when a group settled in a district it became an agrarian community. This arrangement, which preceded Inca times, has survived to our own day and remains the most solid institution of those which have flourished in the Andes. It respected the autonomy of the family by integrating it with the group by means of a tripartite division; woods and pastures were worked communally, the house and paddock belonged exclusively to the family, and cultivated land was periodically redivided amongst the family units. It was rather an ordinary system which seems to correspond to a necessary stage in human evolution, for it is found in all continents.[2]

The cohesion of the community remained strong. The links with other groups were established peacefully by means of gifts which ensured to the donor a magic ascendancy over the recipient, a hold which he endeavoured to counteract by a reciprocal donation. This process was the origin of the method of barter. In the same way, the individual acquired prestige when the importance of the gift was such that the debtor never managed to override its effects, and in this way a chief established himself.[3]

So we picture the fifteenth Indian as a dependant of the territorial community whilst remaining closely linked with his family. To ask what kind of ownership was his makes no sense. He had a wife, clothing, and certain personal belongings; did the rest belong to the community, the king, or the gods? The Inca as sovereign ruler decided these things, and

marriage is exogamic through being linked to the totem group, and endogamic through being linked to a political group. (C. Bouglé: *Essais sur le régime des castes,* Paris, 1908.) On degrees of parenthood, see H. Cunow: *El sistema de parentesco peruano y las comunidades gentilicias de los Incas,* Paris, 1929.

[1] It is actually so on feast days in Bolivia today.

[2] L. Baudin: *L'Empire socialiste des Inka,* Paris, 1928, p. 84.

[3] In the town of Ayacucho recollections of *Potlatch* are recalled by the imposition on two families each year of a burdensome feast which lasts several days. (M. Kuczynski-Godard: *El pensamiento arcáico, op. cit.,* p. 32.) Inversely social contempt breaks the solidarity of the group—he who steals from a neighbour has to leave. (J. Delgado: *Folklores y apuntes para la sociologia indígena,* Lima, 1931.)

the judicial problems posed by the Spaniards did not arise.

We have seen that at Collana each *ayllu* lived in a designated part of the village. Thus it was everywhere else. Often the *ayllu* lived in a block of buildings made up of a series of cottages surrounded by a wall. At Machu Picchu the groups of dwellings differed from each other by the arrangement of the rooms or by some architectural characteristics, for example in the way the stones were cut.[1] At Cuzco each house was assigned to an *ayllu* and not to a family.

The *ayllu* was truly the social unit of the pre-columbian society of Peru.

[1] H. Bingham: *Lost city of the Incas,* New York, 1948, p. 186.

CHAPTER 3

SOCIETY
THE DUALIST PRINCIPLE

AMONGST the ethnic groups which composed the people of the Inca Empire, we are able to recognize the Chimus, the Urus, the Quechuas (or Quichuas), and the Aymaras, and these all spoke different languages.

FOUR TYPES OF INDIANS

There is little to say about the first two groups. The Chimus, who have already been described, were conquered by the Incas in the fifteenth century. The ruins of their capital city, the designs on their pottery, and the woven materials found in their graves, showed them to be a highly civilized people.[1]

The Urus appear amongst the last of the dolichocephalic peoples of the South American continent, and seem to have been of very ancient origin. Because of their methods of catching fish, they are thought to have come from the region of the Amazon. The *totora,* the tall reed from Lake Titicaca, was used for building their miserable hovels and their graceful canoes. A very primitive people, they live to-day on the banks of the Desaguadero, which serves as an overflow canal for Lake Titicaca. They are on the way to complete extinction. The lowering of the waters of the lake has deprived them of their means of livelihood by causing the reeds to disappear, and the raising of the water since 1946 came too late. But at the time about which I am writing in this book, they were still sufficiently numerous to populate the slopes of the Andes from the lake to the Pacific.[2]

The Quechuas and the Aymaras live up on the plateau and

[1] E. G. Squier: *Peru, incidents of travel and exploration in the land of the Incas,* London, 1877, chaps. 7, 8, 9; O. Holstein: *Chanchan, Capital of the Great Chimu,* in *Geographical Review,* 1927, p. 36; R. Larco Hoyle: *Los Mochicas,* 2 vol., Lima, 1938.

[2] J. T. Polo: *Indios Uros del Perú y de Bolivia,* in *Boletín de la Sociedad geográfica de Lima,* 1901, p. 445; E. Palavecino: *Los Indios Urus de Iruito,* in *La Prensa,* Buenos Aires, November 18, 1934; J. Uriel

exhibit common characteristics. Their colouring is a sallow brown and they are short and broad in stature on account of the height at which they live. Their extremely white teeth contrast with their very black hair, and they have slits of eyes equally black. Europeans find them ugly on account of their large broad heads, their large noses, bulging foreheads and prominent cheekbones, but they admit that they have character and relate them to the Mongols.

The Quechuas, by far the most numerous, constituted the greater mass of the subjects of the Inca Empire. The Aymaras, who lived in the areas to the south and to the east of Lake Titicaca, were the founders of the empire of Tiahuanaco—earlier than that of the Incas.[1] They both have the same physical and physiological characteristics,[2] but the Aymaras are more primitive and more reserved than the Quechuas, whose expression is nobler and more lively.

It is the Quechua Indians whose way of life we are describing. But were the Inca rulers themselves Quechuas? Legend holds that they came from another race, but there is no justification for this belief.[3] It is, no doubt, an expression of the desire to differentiate, which we shall now put into perspective, for it shows itself in a fundamentalist dualism.

THE NOBILITY AND THE COMMON PEOPLE

It is likely that the first division into categories of peoples was simply that of which all history provides examples—that between conquerors and conquered, rulers and ruled. But in Peru, little by little, the division took on a singular pattern, assuming an extraordinarily national character. The links between the two classes as they were constituted were inspired by logic and not by a blind force, and no unscaleable barrier was erected between them. So we can make no comparison

Garcia: *Pueblos y paisajes sud peruanos,* Lima, 1949, p. 54; J. Vellard: *Contribution a l'étude des Indiens Uru,* in *Travaux de l'Institut français d'études andines,* Lima, 1949.

[1] A. Posnansky: *Tihuanacu,* New York, 1946. There were possibly several successive Aymara civilizations, and controversy on this subject has been very lively. See J. Imbelloni: *La esfinge indiana, op. cit.,* p. 45.

[2] G. Rouma: *Quichuas et Aymaras, Brussels,* 1933.

[3] Garcilaso de la Vega maintains that the Incas had a special language different from Quechua, the use of which was forbidden to the common people. (*Comentarios reales, op. cit.,* book 8, chap. 1.)

with a caste system, and we come to speak of the nobility and the common people.[1]

This dualism extended to all fields without exception, material as well as spiritual. In a curious way it even applied to the past. For we know that the Indian people were only acquainted with an expurgated history, but the members of the nobility were fully aware of the shadows hidden in this way. On his accession, the Emperor chose several Indians with specially trained memories as the historians of his reign; a special word exists in Quechua to indicate them—*Pacariscap Villa*. These specialists were charged with the duty of remembering all the events which emerged from the records of the knotted strings, and with composing accounts destined for the members of the ruling class alone.[2] Moreover, the Inca Pachacutec, the great reformer whose initiative we shall often have occasion to mention, summoned to the capital Indians renowned for their knowledge of the past. Their accounts were recorded on painted tablets placed in a suitable building near Cuzco, where no unauthorized person was allowed to enter. It is interesting to note that this kind of investigation, instituted by the King, was repeated in the sixteenth century by the viceroy Francisco de Toledo.

The imperial archives, thus brought into being, were cared for by special curators and interpreters.[3]

History destined for the mass of the population was established on the death of each sovereign by a council of high officials and scholars, who examined the events which had taken place during the reign and decided which were suitable to be recorded. Storytellers and singers were advised upon the themes which could serve as outlines for their stories and poems. For example, the defeat of the Inca Urco by the Chancas was passed over in silence.[4]

[1] For distinctions between the nobility and the common people, see L. Baudin: *L'Aube d'un nouveau Libéralisme*, Paris, 1953, chap. 8.

[2] A. Oliva: *Histoire du Pérou, op. cit.*, p. 22; L. Baudin: *La Formation de l'élite et l'enseignement de l'histoire dans l'Empire des Incas*, in *Revue des Études historiques*, April 1927, p. 107.

[3] M. de Morua: *Historia del origen y genealogía real de los reyes Incas del Perú*, Lima, 1925; C. de Molina: *Relación de las fábulas y ritos de los Incas*, Lima, 1916; F. Montesinos: *Memorias antiguas, op. cit.*; R. Porras Barrenechea: *Quipu ye quilca* in *Mercurio peruano*, January 1947.

[4] P. de Cieza de León: *Crónica del Perú, op. cit.*, chap. 44.

How can we know, under these conditions, what was the true history of the Incas? We shall try to recount the order of the reigns in spite of the omissions and distortions, whether voluntary or not, of the native historians, and despite the lack of understanding and inadequacies of the chroniclers. In order to conjure up the life of the Indian, it is indispensable to know how he himself described the past when his membership of the nobility permitted him to know it accurately.[1]

THE TRUE STORY OF THE INCAS

Official history began with the first Manco Capac, who, they say, settled in the Cuzco valley. In reality he dispossessed the original inhabitants, but the names of their totems or characteristics remained associated with the different quarters of the growing town; for example, the humming-bird quarter, the weavers', the tobacco, and the mixed quarters. The sovereign lived in the temple of the Sun; consequently he belonged to the lower part of the town (*hurin*), thus securing priority for this fraternity.

Manco Capac was a mythological name applied to a whole dynasty and not to one person. In Indian chronology he was followed by Sinchi Roca, about whom we can say the same, for the term Sinchi indicates a chief elected to conduct a war. The need for a unified command was the first sign of unity amongst scattered tribes—it is easier to understand 'against' than 'for.' The grouping of age-old communities, that is to say of *ayllus,* sprang from this imperative need for self-defence. And so there arose leaders who asserted their power and who were grouped in this category. After Manco Capac, who led a tribe and a restricted community, we come to Sinchi Roca, who directed a confederation of tribes.

It was usual for a leader to be chosen by common agreement amongst the allies. This is proved by the evidence of the chroniclers that the eldest son of Sinchi Roca did not succeed his father. We assume, therefore, that in the domain of power there was no hereditary vocation for a ruler's descendants.

[1] P. Ainsworth Means: *Ancient Civilizations of the Andes,* New York, 1931; M. R. T. de Diez Canseco: *Pachacutec Inca Yupanqui,* Lima, 1953. This latter work is excellent and has proved especially helpful.

During the era of the Sinchis the conquered territory consisted only of a few valleys near Cuzco, and did not, in the south, reach farther than the ridge of Vilcañota.

After Sinchi Roca came Loque Yupanqui who seems to have been a real personality, for he exhibited a very special individuality which perhaps entitles him to be singled out from his ancestors and his successors. He was a peace-loving ruler, and maintained the confederation by a series of alliances. However, he was obliged to undertake several wars, but he entrusted his son with the command of his troops. To sum up, his reign was a time of consolidation rather than of the expansion we shall hear about later.

Maita Capac, the fourth son of Loque Yupanqui, was, in spite of his youth, destined for war. Although a premature baby, he was of remarkable strength. He crushed the confederation of the Alcabizas, invaded Collao, and reached the shores of Lake Titicaca which he crossed by canoe. In the west, for the first time, the warriors from the high plateau descended the slopes of the Andes and reached Arequipa.

How Capac Yupanqui came to power is shrouded in mystery. Historians believe that he killed his brothers, or at best compelled them to stand down in his favour. He it was who built the great suspension bridge across the Apurimac, which became the gateway to new conquests. He allied himself with the Andahuaylas (or Andanaylas) who welcomed him favourably. This prosperous people who were, unfortunately for them, neighbours of the Chancas, a war-like and powerful tribe, willingly joined the Cuzco confederation in order to defend themselves.

Thanks to another and equally celebrated bridge, the reed bridge thrown across the Desaguadero, the overflow from Lake Titicaca, the Cuzco armies penetrated the area south of the lake towards the regions which now form part of Bolivia, towards Lake Poopo and the Cochabamba valley.

This Emperor was the first great architect of conquest, thanks to his organization of transport, roads, and bridges, and thanks also to the *mitimaes,* whose nature and set-up we shall describe, but which consisted of transferring population in order to further the general welfare of the Empire.

THE DYNASTY OF UPPER CUZCO

With Inca Roca there began a new period in the Inca story. For this monarch belonged to Hanan Cuzco, that is to say to the brotherhood of Upper Cuzco. How did this change come about? It is difficult to say exactly, for dramatic happenings at court naturally do not figure in popular history, and the curators of the knotted cords—those truly documentary records whose nature and purpose have already been described—did not willingly inform the Spanish investigators of such events. It is possible that the capital was the scene of some sombre family tragedy, for a woman described as a concubine of Capac Yupanqui is later described as the wife of Inca Roca. Did she succeed in placing a Hanan Cuzco on the throne by poisoning the Hurin Cuzco Emperor as Father M. de Morua alleges? We are reduced to guesswork.

Whatever happened, the title of Inca was henceforward applied to the ruler. Since he could no longer live in the lower part of the city, he had a palace built for himself in the upper part, and it is from this reign onwards that each new Inca had a new dwelling. The temple of the Sun was sacred to worship alone. It is possible that at this time there came about the separation of the civil and religious elements of the hierarchy, the separation of the high priest from the Emperor, for up to this time one and the same person held the two titles.

Following the same sequence of ideas, Inca Roca may be regarded as the first Emperor who was forced to enlarge and beautify the city, and to him are owed the schools in which scholars were able to exercise their profession.

This enterprising ruler, who came to power by a *coup d'état,* first had to enforce his authority on his own ground, by defeating the supporters of the Hurin Cuzco and of a number of heads of *ayllus* who sought to profit from circumstances and seize their independence. Then he was obliged to face up to the Chancas who also thought the time was ripe to brave their rivals at Cuzco and brought the Andahuailas into subjection. Inca Roca drove the Chancas back westwards and freed the Andahuaylas, who were in the dangerous situation of being the buffer state between the two most powerful federations of the Andean plateau—the Chancas (Ayacucho) and the Incas (Cuzco).

These exploits did not prevent the sovereign from enhancing the ceremonial with a character and magnificence which remained for long afterwards; dances and banquets amidst singing and flowers added prestige to celebrations as well as to triumph of arms, and both bore witness to present prosperity and confidence in the future.

However, confidence in the days to come was scarcely justified. The confederation rested on links whose solidarity had not been truly tested. Following some obscure and sentimental rivalries and a rebellion, one of Inca Roca's sons was threatened with death. On hearing this, it is said, he began to weep, but the executioners record with terror that these were tears of blood. Left alive the young man fled, aided by a concubine of one of his abductors. He reached Cuzco and, according to custom, became co-ruler with the king under the name of Yahuar Huacac—he who weeps blood.

Singled out by fate in this way, this ruler seems to have remained weak and unable to defend himself. Popular history passes over him in silence and his death remains a mystery. There are two versions; according to one of them he was assassinated at a feast given by tribal chieftains when he was preparing to leave for a campaign against the Collas. For this reason the keepers of the knotted strings, the repository of true historical events, may, with natural delicacy, have sought to hide the facts when interrogated by the Spaniards. According to the other account, the Chancas attacked the Incas, and panic broke out at Cuzco where nothing of this kind had been anticipated. The Emperor himself had to evacuate the capital, whilst his son, hastily gathering together his troops, marched against the invaders who were forced back. After this victory father and son quarrelled violently, and the former was constrained to retire to a distant place where he quietly lived out his sad life, and the son ascended the throne under the name of Viracocha.

At the time of this change of régime the outstanding problem was the invasion by the Chancas. This formidable confederation in which were grouped the Indians of the Ayacucho region, Vilcas, Cangallo, Huanta, Huamanca, and Huancavelica, was similar to the confederation of Cuzco. The tribes included in it said that they too came from a lake region—

Lake Choclococha ('the maize ear lake,' a name connected with a local legend). These tribes were perhaps more loosely linked together than those of the Inca confederation, for their divisions marched into battle led by their own chiefs. They were also more primitive and more cruel than their rivals, but they did not yield to them in pomp and ostentation. Important people wore sumptuous clothes made from vicuña or llama wool, ornamented with designs of animals or monsters. But above all it was in their faces and hair that they differed from the men of Cuzco. Above their eyes they drew lines of red ochre and vermilion obtained from mercury found at Huancavelica. They wore caps or turbans or went bareheaded; sometimes their heads were shaved, and sometimes they allowed a moustache to grow.

The check to their plan to conquer Cuzco discouraged the Chancas for a time, but did not diminish their desire for power. Viracocha, thanks to his success, had no difficulty in dealing with the palace quarrels which were not lacking at the time of his accession. The people of the Hurin Cuzco always sought to profit from a change of ruler in order to regain power. Since they exercised religious functions and lived in the temple of the Sun, the conflict ran the risk of taking a serious turn. Viracocha applied himself to appeasing the spirits, but it was his successor who resolved the problem by reforming the worship of the Sun.

Viracocha took care not to attack the Chancas again, but extended his hold in other directions so as to ensure recruitment to his army and consolidate his position before embarking on a new venture. Each Inca, when he ascended the throne, began by making a tour of the whole of his territory so as to renew the links existing with the different tribes, and so as to prevent certain of them from rebelling in an attempt to regain their independence. Viracocha next turned towards Collao, where the threat of his imminent arrival was sufficient to induce the principal chieftains to submit without fighting a very unequal battle.

The son chosen by Viracocha to reign with him, according to custom, was Inca Urco. But when the aged Emperor retired to his country home, Urco abandoned himself to pleasure and vice. Cieza de León, who is particularly reliable,

shows him as a drunkard and a debaucher, and even stresses annoying and crude details. To crown all, this unworthy monarch was a coward. The Chancas, well-informed as to the situation, judged that the moment to act had arrived.

PROVIDENCE INTERVENES

Viracocha, weakened by age, decided to leave with his court, but once again a man providentially appeared in the guise of one of the king's sons, Cusi Yupanqui, better known by the name he was to take later—Pachacutec. It was he who put himself at the head of the troops, organized resistance, and induced several neighbouring tribes to join him. Thus history curiously repeated itself at the beginning and at the end of the reign of Viracocha—attack by the Chancas, flight of the Emperor, appearance of the hero who crushed the invader and took the sceptre in his turn. But this time it was complicated by the presence of Urco, the legitimate sovereign named by his father, who, as a monarch aware of his power and infallibility, could not admit that he had been mistaken in his choice.

The Chancas, confident in their strength, were deceived by Viracocha, who received their envoys, declared himself ready to surrender, and disowned his son's preparations for resistance. They thought they would easily get the better of a young upstart repudiated by his own family. But the future Pachacutec organized a spy system which enabled him to learn of the movements of his enemies, placed his soldiers in the most favourable positions, and after offering sacrifices inspired his troops by telling them of a vision he had experienced; the Sun himself had promised his help in gaining the victory.

The Chancas, descending the hill of Carmenca which overlooks Cuzco, made a confused attack, brandishing their lances and shouting with joy at the prospect of the rich spoils which they promised themselves from the city lying stretched out at their feet. Their faces were painted red and black, their hair oiled and curled. But the attackers found their adversaries ready to receive them, replying to their arrows with slingstones, and to their spear thrusts with bludgeon strokes. Many fell into gigantic holes which had been prepared in advance and carefully hidden. Then, whilst they were struggling in the city suburbs, Prince Cusi, his head covered with a puma skin, and followed by the cream of his warriors, hurled himself on the flank of the invading army, directing his attack towards the idol which the Chancas had brought with them to lend encouragement and to be present at their victory. Indians from neighbouring tribes, long awaiting the opportunity for this meeting, were massed on the slopes and waited until the god of battles had decided the issue, so that they could enter the lists in a cowardly manner on the side of the conquerors.

After long hours of uncertain struggle, Prince Cusi managed to seize the idol, whilst the defenders of Cuzco still held out on the outskirts of the town. To the cries of the Incas were added the shouts of the spectators who considered that the Chancas had lost the day, for their deity had abandoned them, and so they joined forces with the men of Cuzco, and there followed a great slaughter of the invaders.

The prince, according to custom, presented himself before his father Viracocha with the enemy idol, and with clothing, jewels and hair taken from the conquered, and did homage to him. The Emperor, with incredible obstinacy, insisted that the same homage should be paid to his son Urco, whom he still wished to be treated as ruler. The young prince refused. One chronicler goes so far as to claim that his own compatriots laid an ambush for the victor on the route of his return to the city, but that he escaped owing to the vigilance of the captains in the prince's suite.

The news of this victory over a people regarded as the most formidable in the Andes spread throughout the plateau, and a great number of cities submitted to the Incas of their own free will.

However, the Chancas were not wiped out. Prince Cusi gave them no time to re-form their army, but attacked them in open country, pushed them back, and pursued them without respite or rest as far as the region of the Andahuailas.

On his return he repaired to his father, who this time received him according to tradition, trampled on the enemy spoils, and declared his intention of taking as his heir-apparent the man who had given so many proofs of intelligence and courage.

For their part, the people of the Empire decided to depose the useless Urco and to refuse him entry into the city. Even the wife of this unfortunate man abandoned him and went to Cuzco. Urco made an effort to reunite some partisans in the Yucay valley, and to stir up a conspiracy, but he died a violent death shortly afterwards, either in attempting to bring about his own project, or in battle at Collao.

The Empire was at last established and its founder, Pachacutec, bathed in glory, became a god to the majority of his subjects. On the Carmenca hill, where the first battles we have described took place, the heads of the Chanca chiefs were fixed to the tops of long pointed stakes, while their skins stuffed with straw and ashes hung beneath; these bore witness to the authority of the monarch, and, far better than any recital of facts, made clear to newcomers to the imperial city the necessity of total submission.

THE WORLD REFORMER

The accession of Pachacutec took place at the beginning of the fifteenth century. At this time the Indians, according to the writers, were aware of the grand outlines, at least of the more glorious ones, of the history we have just been retracing. The military chief and the high official incorporated in the imperial hierarchy drew from it vanity and enthusiasm. The Emperor himself thought everything was possible and wanted to do everything. The huge framework, administrative, military and religious, which we shall examine in detail, was built up under his direction with the materials gathered by his ancestors through the ages, and was approved by the whole population. Factual history now takes second place.

However, there were continual wars. Carried away by enthusiasm, the chosen people threw themselves into the business of conquering all the neighbouring lands, but they did so with caution and after detailed preparations designed to avoid risks—ordered planning was to be seen throughout. Towards the north the Andahuailas, already often mentioned, the Soras and the Rucanas fell under the sway of the Cuzco confederation, and hustling aside the Chinchas, they reached the ocean. We know how the Indians from the high plateau succeeded in acclimatizing themselves little by little to coastal conditions by staying in camps built half-way down the Corderilla, and how they overrode resistance by cutting off the irrigation canals and destroying the harvest.

Chuquimancu resisted for a long time, sheltered by its fortresses, Cuismancu surrendered without a fight, and the great temple of Pachacamac fell to the Inca might.

However, on the plateau, neighbouring nations were still threatening. The Collas, dwellers on the shores of Lake Titicaca, were divided into prosperous tribes, jealous of their independence. They were ruled by princes, some of whom, notably the princes of the Hatun Colla and of Chucuito, were able to raise large numbers of troops and could even have stood up to the Incas had they allied themselves to form a common army. Their soldiers were, for the most part, Aymaras, and were particularly tough and war-like.

These lands had already been conquered, but because of the great distances the reins of bondage were slack and, with each change of ruler at Cuzco, the princes regained further liberty. Pachacutec crushed the lord of the Hatun Colla in two battles which gave him possession of the city, and the lord of Chucuito surrendered of his own will.

Then the Emperor set forth against the northern peoples. The historian has the impression that he struggled to obtain what he considered was his due, striking first on one side and then on the other. The undertakings were usually hard and dangerous, for his enemies lived in what the Incas considered a state of savagery and lacked neither cunning nor cruelty. The Huanca tribes in the region of Jauja burned their prisoners and kept shreds of skin as trophies; they loved dogs, eating their flesh with pleasure, and making their skulls into trumpets which they used as an accompaniment to their dances or to encourage their warriors in battle.

Pachacutec applied to the conquered Huancas the rule of high politics which was worth more to him and was more durable than invading armies. He did not kill off his prisoners, but set them free; he did not destroy the villages, but had works of general benefit to the community put in hand as we shall see. In this way he assured himself of the support of his former enemies.

General Capac Yupanqui, Pachacutec's brother, who commanded the imperial army, advanced to Lake Bonbon (Junin), but he made two serious mistakes; he passed on a secret message to a concubine, and he exceeded the Inca's orders by conquering the country of the Conchucos, although he had not received orders to do so. In spite of his victories he did not escape punishment and was put to death. This pitiless sentence throws a garish light on the rigidity of the military defence of the Empire; we shall comment on this later in trying to explain the spirit of the organization and the mentality of its directors.

Freed of enemies to the south, north and west, in the east the Empire remained frustrated by forces which up till now it had been unable to overcome—the forest lands. Pachacutec made an attempt in this direction, but nature was a greater enemy than man, and the imperial troops, decimated by the climate and by wild animals, were obliged to return, shamefaced, to the plateau.

The Emperor then led his troops in person. He had reached the threshold of the forest when he was recalled to Cuzco. Some prisoners from Colla had escaped, returned to their own country, and were stirring up a revolt.

In accordance with custom, Pachacutec chose one of his sons to share authority with him, Prince Amaru, the eldest son of his legitimate wife. They both set out southwards, threw back the Collas, and the Emperor then returned to the capital, leaving his son the task of bringing this enterprise to completion. But the prince was timid and inept, and his brothers and generals led the soldiers to victory. Pachacutec, duly warned, reconsidered his choice and replaced Amaru by Tupac Yupanqui.

During this campaign part of the army again entered the virgin forest in the hope of rolling back still farther the boundaries of the Empire in this direction also. But nothing more was heard of them, and the Emperor knew that the great Pachacamac definitely forbade his people to uncover the mystery which lay hidden in this hot, humid land of greenery and mud, stretching to infinity towards the sacred country from which the Sun departs each day to visit the earth.

It was during the condominium of Pachacutec-Tupac

Yupanqui that the latter attacked the realm of the Chimus. The subjects of Cuismancu and Chuquimancu brought him effective help, for they were traditional enemies of their powerful northern neighbours, with whom they had had many a conflict in former times, and they were accustomed to the coastal climate. On their side the Chimus had at their disposal imposing defence lines, but their leaders, softened by a life of luxury and pleasure, had lost the war-like qualities of their ancestors. The king decided to give battle, but his advisers persuaded him to treat with the enemy, whose troops were perfectly trained, and who were known to be forbearing in victory. The Inca certainly treated his new vassal generously; he kept him in power, and had his sons trained at Cuzco in conformity with the skilful political organization he had set up.

THE LAST INCAS; THE ZENITH OF THE EMPIRE

After the death of Pachacutec, and thanks to his many reforms, the Empire was united. There were no more attempts at revolt at each change of ruler. Roads were constructed between towns, messengers carried directives and reports, statistics were drawn up; inspectors ensured the exact application of the rules, directors held in their hands the controls of this immense economic and administrative machine. Henceforth, to the eye of the observer, the nation appeared a homogeneous whole, more and more centralized and uniform, with a militarized zone prudently sited along its frontiers.

The individual Indian of the people acquired the mentality which was to become his definite characteristic, resembling the llama lost in the herd who obeyed the orders of a distant and invisible shepherd. The more the Empire extended and strengthened itself, the more the individual withdrew into and effaced himself.

Wars were now waged on the outskirts of the civilized world, and many days of marching were necessary before the soldiers reached the place of battle. Outside the Empire, too, the only nations left were backward and poor, with a few exceptions, and it was these who must be discovered and subdued so that the Inca peace could reign over the whole world.

Beyond the sheltered and picturesque valley of the Urubamba, quite near Cuzco, there stretched the menacing, haunting forest which had wearied the tireless Pachacutec. From time to time bands of wild Indians came forth from their jungle lairs, and quickly reaching the plateau, operated profitable forays when they were able to slip through the small fortified positions on their road. Tupac Yupanqui conducted carefully prepared expeditions which reached the great Amaru river (called today the Madre de Dios), where they used canoes to descend the stream in the direction of Beni. It was impossible to subjugate the inhabitants of these immense areas, but the passage of the troops who killed a great many of these primitive people bold enough to oppose the invaders, spread fear and made the incursions of the forest people into the Andean valleys less frequent.

The Emperor came upon another kind of resistance when he adventured into the extreme south. He had to cross the formidable Atacama desert and found some war-like and well-organized tribes, the Araucans, who were very jealous of their independence. He threw them back, but he recognized that he could not subdue them, for the farther he advanced the more fierce and successful was the resistance he met. Since he was already far from his bases, he definitely fixed the Rio Maule as the southern boundary of the Empire.

The Emperor then turned his attention towards the north. The realm of the Caras, established on the plateau, formed the natural extension of Peruvian territory, and reports of its prosperity offended the sovereign of Cuzco. It was separated from the Inca Empire by lands occupied by the Cañaris, renowned for their bravery, cunning and ferocity.

Tupac Yupanqui made sure of his departure bases by establishing himself first of all in the upper valley of the Amazon, and at Cajamarca; then he subdued the people living to the east towards Chachapoyas where once again the forest put an end to the expedition; then he turned west towards Piura and reached Tumbez and the Gulf of Guayaquil. Then he set forth to conquer the Cañares. In fierce battles the enemy chiefs were slain or taken prisoner, but the Inca showed himself magnanimous and sought to attach the vanquished people to him by courting their favour. He caused roads to be built, and temples, palaces and public stores, and even deigned to reside in their capital Tomebamba which he made a large and wealthy city. In this way the Cañares became the most loyal subjects of the Inca, even to the point of providing the monarch's personal bodyguard.

This city became the base of operations against the realm of the Caras. This was one of the longest and bloodiest wars the Incas had ever undertaken, and the men of Cuzco passed through some critical times; they failed at Mocha, and lost the whole province of Puruha with the town of Latacunga. In the end they made a triumphal entry into Quito, the capital, which became the great rival of Cuzco.

Again the Inca marched northward and ended his journey at the river Ancasmayo which became the most northerly frontier of the Empire.

Descending the eastern slopes of the Corderilla he found again the green barrier of the forest defended by the savage Jivaros, so turning to the west of the western Corderilla, he reached the sea, but only encountered a few scattered tribes for whom he did not consider it worth delaying his march.

In some parts of the Cara kingdom the people appeared so wretched that the Inca envoys only exacted one tribute—a certain number of lice, of which they appeared to have plenty.

It was at this time that the Emperor's journeys along the north coasts of Peru were undertaken, and also the great maritime expedition alluded to at the beginning of this book. These give a precise idea of the boldness, even the temerity of these men, who did not hesitate to entrust themselves on an unknown sea, without any of the information and material at the disposal of the young men who recently astonished the world by accomplishing only half of this round voyage.

It is not surprising that such a voyage lasted nearly a year, and that the people of the capital showed some anxiety about the fate of the sovereign and the soldiers who accompanied him, estimated at about 20,000 men. It is said that a general, in order to calm the people, let it be understood that he had received good news of the expedition. This opportune deceit was not at all to the Emperor's taste when he heard of it, and its author was condemned to death.

Tupac Yupanqui's return was made slowly by the coastal

route and permitted a close inspection of the countries through which he passed. The monarch fasted for a fortnight to prepare for his triumph. His father came to meet him with 30,000 warriors. The two armies met in mock combat, and the Emperors entered Cuzco to preside over the victory ceremonies and feasts.

Pachacutec died soon afterwards at the height of his glory. Tupac Yupanqui followed exactly the plan of his father, and completed the pacification and organization of the Empire. When he felt the first onset of his final illness he withdrew to a country house set in the midst of gardens.

His successor, Huayna Capac made visits throughout the Empire, and realized that one single monarch, however inspired, could no longer control a territory which was, in fact, as big as France, Italy, Switzerland, Belgium and Holland all put together. He established himself at Tomebamba and then set forth to subdue the people of Quito who had rebelled. These redoubtable adversaries held him in check for some time. He reached Quito, but clashed, to the north of this city, with the Caranquis who defeated him and forced him to retreat. The Emperor's brother was defeated and killed at the siege of Otavalo. There was no peace until the ruler of Cuzco married a daughter of the king of Quito named Paccha Duchisela.

As much from choice as necessity, Huayna Capac settled himself at Quito and at Tomebamba, deserting Cuzco, which he left to his son Huascar. By Duchisela he had another son, Atahualpa. When he died, appreciating the extent of the Empire, he left it divided between the two sons—a decision which was logical but at the same time unwise. The two brothers became enemies, and there was rivalry between Quito and Cuzco which became fatal to them both. For at this time, messengers had already made known the appearance on the northern costs of bearded men and centaurs who could control lightning.

Here we reach a period later than that of the Indians whose daily life we are describing. We now realize what the common people and the nobility knew of their own history, and we understand that in hearing these events recounted, even when not expurgated for the needs of popular information, they experienced a feeling of legitimate pride.

CHAPTER 4

INDIAN PSYCHOLOGY

DIFFERENTIATION between the two categories of population was pushed so far that the members of the nobility were considered by the common people to be the spokesmen or representatives of the gods. In order to understand this extreme application of the dualist principle, we must study the native psychology more deeply.

THE FLUID AND OVER-CROWDED INDIAN WORLD

The entire life of the Indian was bathed in an atmosphere of unreality. All-powerful nature can only rule when it becomes spiritualized. In Peru everything was alive. The smallest object had a soul; the llama and the potato, the rock and the individual.[1] But this soul could be collective, an invisible spirit which animated a multiplicity of representations; today we should describe it as the spirit of a species, a usual and creative principle. The world itself had its own principle, the egg represented on a gold panel above the altar in the temple of the Sun at Cuzco.

With the blind and deaf ignorance of the white man, we think the plateau is deserted. But this solitude is full of presences and of sound. Thousands of beings lie in wait for us, apparently inanimate, but who think and feel as we do, who are good and bad, who exhibit wills and passions. If we are conscious of this life it is not isolation we fear in the Andes, but the loosing of this multitude.

It is up to us to seek the favour of these entities whose attitude and behaviour obey the same pressures as our own. The cosmic unity is perfect. There are no barriers in space any more than in time. The sorcerer knows this well, for he can, at will, change instantly both time and place, descend or re-ascend the road of time, assume the form of a stone, plant or animal. His body has no precise outline and can be

[1] P. J. de Arriaga: *Extirpación de la idolatría del Perú, op. cit.*, p. 16.

divided. Hair and nails continue to be part of him after they have been cut, and that is why they are carefully preserved, for the malicious who may get possession of them would be able to gain an ascendancy over their original owner. The sorcerer is able to detach his limbs from his body and to order his head to leave his trunk. We shall find these essential aspects of the Indian mentality again in connection with religious conceptions and practices.

In this Indian world, ever-changing[1] and over-populated, each word, each gesture risked setting in motion infinite repercussions on every plane, whether visible or invisible. The individual, the social, material and moral were narrowly interdependent. An illness was a disorder and a sin.

Behind the passivity of the peasant, the shepherd, the artisan, lay a constant mental tension; friend and foe were everywhere and constant attention had to be given to the smallest details which might pass unobserved and produce reactions. It was prudent not to upset the established order of things, and to mistrust everything abnormal. From this came worship of the *huacas* and of all things impressive in their grandeur, strength, beauty or originality—the great cats of the forest, the snowy summit, the strangely shaped rock.[2]

It is understandable that the meaning of a word could be stretched infinitely and that in the end it was used to mean the worship of the things themselves—the idol, the sanctuary, the tomb.[3] It is also clear that the multiplicity of these objects compelled the Indians to submit to equally numerous and always imperious rites which prepared them for subjection to the social discipline instituted by the Incas.[4]

THE TWO RELIGIONS

To these ancient religious conceptions were grafted the teachings brought by the conquerors from Cuzco, and the set-up was then completely changed. Not only were the religious con-

[1] Compare Levy-Bruhl: *L'Ame primitive,* Paris, 1927, p. 134.

[2] J. Tello: *Wira-Kocha,* review *Inka,* Lima, 1923.

[3] J. de Arona: *Diccionario de peruanismos,* in *Biblioteca de cultura peruana,* no. 10, Paris, 1938, p. 233.

[4] If in olden times myths absorbed reality, sometimes there may be today a tendency to hold on to the myth and escape the reality. (M. Kuczynski-Godard: *El pensamiento arcáico, op. cit.,* p. 9.)

ceptions of the masses different from those of the ruling class, they were used by them for a political end, and they became an instrument in the hands of the leaders. In order to unify the Empire, the Incas showed respect for the beliefs of the nations they subdued, adopted their idols, and limited themselves to imposing on them only one superior and incontestable god—the Sun. At the same time they stressed the divinity of the Emperor who represented on earth the heavenly body whose son he was, and in this way invented the most formidable method of domination. The man-god of Cuzco had a direct influence on the consciences of all his subjects.

The monarch and the ruling class had very different conceptions from the common people. Dualism appeared in this domain also. According to this new spiritual plan, the divinity of the sovereign faded and another deity appeared, a deity who was abstract, inexpressible, unique, a god so similar to the Christian deity that writers as well-informed as Garcilaso de la Vega and Bartolomeo de las Casas had no hesitation in saying that the Incas worshipped the true God, and that the Indians had come very near to basic truth.[1]

The Incas went much farther than the Spaniards along the path towards super-eminence, for they only built two temples to their supreme god, one at Cuzco and one at Racche; they reasoned that since their deity was present at all times and in all places, it was not very intelligent to establish him in one place. They even refrained from making offerings to him, under the pretext that it was impossible to offer him anything he did not already possess, since he possessed all things. We know nothing of the special worship offered to this deity for the two temples are in ruins, and the ceremonies were secret. The Spaniards, for the most part, did not understand the importance of investigating in this field.[2]

[1] Garcilaso knew very well that he would shock his contemporaries by expressing himself in this way, but he did so in no uncertain terms. *Comentarios reales, op. cit.*, book 2, chap. 6. Las Casas adds that the Indians had a greater knowledge of God than the Greeks and Romans: *Apologética historia sumaria,* Madrid, 1909, t. 1, chap. 126. See also W. Prescott: *Histoire du Pérou,* French translation, Paris, 1861, t. 1, p. 98; P. Ainsworth Means: *Ancient Civilizations of the Andes, op. cit.*, p. 429.

[2] Nothing could have been more foreign to the Spaniards than a dualist conception of religion. A. Bandelier considers that there still exist secret societies in high Peru: *The Islands of Titicaca and Coati,* New York, 1910, p. 123.

The god of the nobility bore different names, in particular those of Pachacamac and Viracocha, the one borrowed from the religion of the coastal peoples, and the other from the Aymaras. The origin of this double naming is reported by the chroniclers. The Inca Tupac Yupanqui, after invading the region where Lima stands today, found himself in front of a famous temple sacred to a powerful idol, which he dared not attack. He spoke with the priests and learned that their god Pachacamac was a manifestation of the supreme invisible god.[1] He was already called Viracocha on the plateau, since he created the world at Tiahuanaco, and he had conferred the insignia of power on the first of the Inca Emperors, Manco Capac, and then vanished into the sky.[2]

In several chronicles we find a curious story. The famed Inca Pachacutec, at a meeting of priests and soothsayers, is reputed to have asked which was the most powerful of the gods, and they replied that it was the Sun. The king then made an important speech, explaining that the Sun, who was obliged to toil each day like a worker at lighting and heating the earth, found his efforts thwarted by clouds and falls of rain, and thus could not be the 'Lord of Creation.' He ended by asserting that the supreme creative being was Viracocha.[3]

Perhaps we may see here an attempt by this great king to initiate the priests of the Sun into certain secret beliefs held by the ruling class.

After this meeting Pachacutec seems to have had two statues of Viracocha carved in solid gold, and had them placed in the two temples mentioned above.[4]

We know that the Emperor spoke to the Sun as to a member of his family, whilst to Viracocha he addressed himself with the marks of the most profound respect.

[1] B. Cobo: *Historia del Nuevo Mundo, op. cit.,* t. 4, p. 47; M. Uhle: *Pachacamac,* Philadelphia, 1903.

[2] B. Cobo: *Historia del Nuevo Mundo, op. cit.,* t. 3, p. 124.

[3] B. Cobo: *Historia del Nuevo Mundo, op. cit.,* t. 3, p. 156; J. de Betanzos: *Suma y Narración de los Incas,* in *Biblioteca hispano–ultramarina,* Madrid, 1880, chap. 11; C. de Molina: *Relación de los fábulas y ritos, op. cit.*; M. R. T. de Diez Canseco: *Pachacutec Inca Yupanqui, op. cit.,* p. 136.

[4] These statues had a human face and wore clothing. Such a representation of an abstract god is surprising. There are many things which are obscure in the narratives of the chroniclers.

PSYCHOLOGICAL ANTIPATHY BETWEEN THE COMMON PEOPLE AND THE RULING CLASS

The essentially mystical character of the Indian, to whatever class he belonged, influenced in different ways the common man and the ruling class.

The constant presence of entities which we call supernatural, the exigencies of a background usually harsh for man, all induced the Indian to adapt himself without rebellion and, also, by a lively reaction, to identify himself with his surroundings in order to survive under these conditions; leading a miserable and always insecure existence, he tended to appreciate men and things for their immediate and direct usefulness. Thus, at the same time as a passivity, with its happy corollary of resistance to grief, we find a communal spirit, generator of the idea that an individual act affects the collective group to which the individual belongs, an idea to which we must return in order to understand the practice of 'confession.' There was also the unsentimental character of the family tie which remains, even today, strictly utilitarian. Sentiment is not lacking but it plays a minor part.[1]

Modern commentators generally describe the man of the commune, *llacta runa,* as being under a rigorous discipline, whose time was divided between work in the fields and the profession of arms, and who was overwhelmed with melancholy and boredom. No doubt his over-riding characteristic was melancholy, and this still strikes the observer today. The Quechua language has a series of words to describe the different shades of meaning of this affliction. We must also admit that the Indian was a great follower of tradition, and that he liked order, harmony and good balance. From these come the characteristics seen in his art; geometrical lines, repetition of the same motifs, and symmetry of design. From these, too, stem his dread of nature with its freaks, want of proportion, and boundless space. From these grew the huge structure of this society, also geometrical, which we shall study, and whose exact and well-defined proportions ensured equality amongst the common people, the hierarchy of their leaders, and the permanence of the whole.

[1] See farther on in this book, 'The Family Life of the Common People.'

However, in the midst of this social structure the Indian did not maintain an immovable, set countenance. Certainly he remained a fatalist, resigned to the caprices of innumerable powers, supernatural and human, which surrounded him. '*As!*' he exclaimed at each stroke of fate, 'it has to be so!' But he did not renounce for ever all valid judgment; he appreciated, admired, scorned, and even retained a certain sense of ridicule, which today gives to the faces of the more intelligent an enigmatic yet mocking expression which modern artists have at times been able to portray.

In contrast with the common people, the ruling class, strong in their divine mission and endowed with a spirit of initiative and foresight, were active and calculating. Responsible for ordering an immense Empire, they showed themselves hard and even cruel to those who resisted them. Something of the savage still dwelt in them. Atahualpa, even at the time of the Spanish conquest, had Indians hanged at the roadside, and had a drum made from his brother's skin and a cup from his skull. There is no doubt but that such would have been the fate of Francisco Pizarro had he been defeated.[1]

But history and folk-lore prove that sentiment did exist in this class of the society. The only Inca drama which has come down to us, *Ollantay,* has as its theme the passionate and thwarted love of a captain for a princess, and the sombre events of the Spanish conquest have been lightened by the charming and true romance of Quilacu and Golden Star.[2]

The almost unlimited power at the disposal of a member of the ruling class over his inferiors, gave him a pride which was prejudicial to him, and a nobility which struck the admiration of the Spaniards. It was because he thought himself the invincible master that the supreme Inca rashly allowed Pizarro's band to cross the Corderilla and reach him, when he could easily have stopped them in the passes, and it was because he was conscious of his superiority that he appeared so great, even to his conquerors.[3]

[1] R. Porras Barrenechea: *Las relaciones primitivas de la conquista del Perú,* Paris, 1937, p. 51.

[2] L. Baudin: *La Vie de François Pizarro,* Paris, 1930, p. 91.

[3] R. Porras Barrenechea: *Una relación inédita de la conquista del Perú,* Madrid, 1940.

PART TWO

THE LIFE OF THE RULERS

CHAPTER 5

THE LIFE OF THE SUPREME INCA

THE MAN-GOD

IN a highly organized state it is logical to approach social analyses by commencing at the summit of the hierarchy, and in Peru this means starting with the ruling class of which the supreme Inca was the head.

Whoever dared to glance at the man-god retained the memory of a glorious vision. The sovereign wore a sleeveless tunic reaching to his knees, trousers of striped material, and a long, wide cape, decorated with geometrical motifs, which was thrown over his shoulders. The two ends were attached across the chest or passed under the left arm and knotted on the right shoulder so as to leave both arms free. His clothes were made of fine vicuña wool, and his feet were shod with sandals of white wool. A ribbon encircled each leg above the knee, and another encircled each ankle. The insignia of authority, the *mascapaicha,* consisted of a many-coloured braid wound several times round the head above the forehead, and from this hung the *lautu,* a red fringe with red tassels fixed to little golden tubes. A large tuft set above the braid carried at its highest point three small black and white feathers of the sacred Curiquinque bird. The hair was cut short and the ears were elongated under the weight of huge discs of precious metal.[1] Some members of the nobility had the right to wear the *lautu,* but not a red one, and their earrings were smaller. An embroidered bag carrying *coca* hung at the monarch's side.

At solemn ceremonies the supreme Inca held in his hand, according to the occasion, a gold sceptre as long as a halberd and surmounted by tiny feathers, and sometimes, at very special ceremonies, by the *mascapaicha,* whilst he himself was

[1] Our description is inspired by the drawings of Poma de Ayala, and especially by the one which represents Pachacutec (p. 108). These drawings may be seen in the Paris edition of 1936, or in that of La Paz, in 1944, which is easier to handle. The manuscript of Poma de Ayala is entitled *Nueva Corónica y buen gobierno.*

adorned with a war head-dress, and carried either a club with a golden head shaped like a star, or a copper shield decorated with the imperial coat-of-arms.

On this escutcheon each Emperor had his personal sign. Sinchi Roca had a falcon; Loque Yupanqui had geometrical motifs, as did Maita Capac; Capac Yupanqui had a quadruped in the upper part, a bird in the middle, and a snake on the lower part; Inca Roca had a bird; Yahuar Huacac had geometrical figures and Pachacutec a rainbow and two snakes; Inca Yupanqui seems to have had nothing and his shield remained empty. Tupac Yupanqui and Huayna Capac both had geometrical figures, but about Huascar we know nothing. Atahualpa, on the contrary, had a whole mass of designs, with a falcon between two trees, two snakes, and a puma under a rainbow.

The emperor's name was always laudatory, and for this reason we often find the same words in the kings' names, but in different combinations. *Capac* means 'Lord'; *Yu* means 'memorable,' and *Huayna* means 'young.'

For certain ceremonies the sovereign fixed on his breast the golden disc of the Sun. He sat on a carved wooden chair covered with fine cloth, or on a throne of solid gold. He ate from gold and silver dishes, and slept on a cotton mattress with woollen blankets.

Whoever obtained an audience, even if he was a victorious general, advanced with eyes lowered, feet bare, and a load on his head as a sign of obedience.

THE SISTER-WIFE AND THE HEIR

The Empress wore a tunic of blue, pink, yellow or orange reaching to her feet, and girdled with two bands of decorated material, one, usually red, round the waist, and the other of various colours round the lower part. A cloak was thrown across the shoulders, crossed over the breast and held by a pin with a large wrought head. Sandals of white vicuña wool covered the feet, and a fine veil fixed on the top of the head fell freely down the back and over the hair, which was long.

The supreme Inca married his eldest sister say the chroniclers, and maintained an endless number of concubines. His *ayllu* could not be a portion of land since his territory was the whole Empire itself—it remained one of blood relationship. This was sub-divided because of the great number of his descendants, due to polygamy. Each new Inca founded an *ayllu* on his accession. For this reason he was the inheritor of the throne and not of property, which remained in the possession of the members of the *ayllu* of the dead monarch. At the beginning of the sixteenth century there were eleven royal *ayllus* in Cuzco.

The Emperor designated his successor, usually chosen from one of the sons of his legitimate wife. Some writers reproach the Inca code of laws, so complete in other respects, for having omitted to indicate a rule for the succession to the throne. The sovereign wished to keep entire freedom of choice, although this was rather unwise, for there were difficulties at times if the monarch died suddenly.[1]

A very wise arrangement completely mystified the genealogists until it was understood by modern historians. The designated successor had to share the power with the reigning sovereign before exercising it alone. Thus the reigns are set in periods of condominium, each monarch serving an apprenticeship with his father, and afterwards inviting one of his sons to do the same with him. The complication was still more aggravated, as we have seen, by the fact that the Emperor replaced an heir who proved to be unsuitable by another of his sons, when he thought it necessary or was constrained to do so by force of circumstance. This was the case on several occasions at the beginning of the fifteenth century. Inca Viracocha took as his assistant his son Urco, of whom we have already spoken, and later replaced him by another son, Cusi. He, when he became Emperor under the name of Pachacutec, appointed his son Amaru as his successor, but he in his turn was obliged to yield his place to another son, Tupac.

[1] Such as was the case on the death of Huayna Cupac: at this time doubts were raised as to the legitimacy of the accession to the throne of Huascar, who was designated heir by his father on his death-bed without an official proclamation having been made. This was one of the causes of the civil war between the two brothers.

THE GREAT EVENTS OF A REIGN

The Emperor's accession was marked by a ceremony which involved great crowds of people, and the chiefs of many provinces arrived at Cuzco bringing gifts. There were shells for the sacrifices, many-coloured pottery, cotton materials from the coast, woollen garments, arms, and sandals made from aloe fibre from the dwellers on the plateau; materials made from bird feathers, *coca,* and aromatic plants from the eastern forests. This colourful crowd filled the great square at Cuzco where, on a platform, were set statues of the gods and the mummies of dead Emperors. The heir to the throne, who had endured ten days of fasting and prayer in his palace, took his place in the midst of this great multitude, whom the grandeur of the place and time had reduced to a respectful silence. The reigning sovereign then arrived, took off his own head-dress with the *lautu* and placed it on the prince's head, giving him the new name which he was to use. He then paid him homage by drinking a cup of *chicha,* a drink made from fermented maize, and by kneeling before him.[1]

Before and after the ceremony, many sacrifices were offered in the temple of the Sun; shells, *coca,* llamas, and even children chosen from amongst the most beautiful. All the idols, all the sacred places, and all the *huacas* received blood from the victims. Some dried blood was even sent by means of slings in the direction of the summits of neighbouring mountains.

The Inca's marriage, that is his union with his sister, took place in the temple of the Sun on the same day as his accession. From the moment that the day had been decided, the bride-to-be was treated as the daughter of the Sun, and from him the new Emperor asked for her hand. The ceremony varied in ostentation according to the circumstances. The Inca Pachacutec, after having made his request in the temple of the Sun, went to the house of the young girl with a numerous suite, passing through alley-ways decorated with carpets and hangings. His father, the Inca Viracocha, awaited him with his betrothed, who on seeing him, pros-

[1] J. de Betanzos: *Suma y Narración de los Incas, op. cit.,* chap. 17; C. de Molina: *Fábulas y ritos, op. cit.,* p. 35; De Diez Canseco: *Pachacutec Inca Yupanqui, op. cit.,* p. 107.

trated herself. The bridegroom raised her, presented her with rich apparel, and begged her to put it on. Then he took a sandal richly ornamented with gold and placed it on her right foot with his own hands. The old Emperor then rose and embraced the new Empress. Pachacutec followed suit, offered the princess 100 women as serving maids, gave her his hand, and asked her to go with him to the temple of the Sun. The high priest awaited them with two bowls of *chicha,* and this the Inca poured on the ground as an offering; then two white llamas were sacrificed. The festivities which followed lasted for three months and the chiefs returned to their provinces loaded with gifts.[1]

The funeral ceremonies of an Emperor were no less imposing than his coronation, if one can so describe the assumption of the *lautu.* When the Inca Viracocha died, his body was placed in a litter and paraded through the streets of Cuzco, accompanied by soldiers in war array. The son of the dead monarch, the heir to the throne, wearing garments of white and grey vicuña wool, was chief mourner. The women followed, their hair cut short, their faces blackened, weeping, lamenting, and beating themselves with plants, and sounding drums.

The monarch's body was embalmed, and the mummy was clad in the finest wrappings, and the *lautu* was placed on the head. Meanwhile there was a series of sacrifices in the temple of the Sun; many llamas were sacrificed, but also women, servants, or friends who wished to follow the Emperor into the beyond, and even some children. For a whole year, on certain suitable days, the mummy visited the capital at the head of a long procession of mourners and high officials, accompanied by the lugubrious sound of drums, interrupted at times by the sad call of flutes and by songs which recalled the deeds of the dead man.

The succession of the Supreme Inca obeyed the principle of distinction between power and possessions. The power passed to the son of the legitimate wife chosen by the father before his death. This was a wise arrangement which has already been described, but which at times provoked the

[1] M. de Morua: *Historia, op. cit.,* book 3, chap. 31; J. de Betanzos: *Suma y Narración, loc. cit.*

resentment of the sons who were passed over, and who were unwilling to be thought inferior to the others. A daughter could not succeed to the throne.[1]

Property remained at the disposition of the dead man. The mummy continued to reside in his palace as in the past, surrounded by his weapons and his artistic treasures and his servants. The heir to the throne had another dwelling built for himself, and that is why there are at Cuzco remains of as many palaces as there were kings, each one bearing the name of an Emperor.

The man-god was supposed to live for ever.[2]

THE EMPEROR'S MARVELLOUS ENERGY

To appreciate the life of the ruler, one must add to the foregoing events the constant wars which he himself was obliged to direct, and the very considerable work of planning and control in the economic field. It is extraordinary how much Pachacutec, for example, managed to achieve during his reign. He rebuilt towns, reformed the army and religion, unified the language, and organized a detailed and unified economic structure. He transformed a confederation of tribes into an Empire, and brought several long and difficult campaigns to a successful conclusion. Even when we realize that his work may have been exaggerated by the historians who were quick to attribute to him that which should have referred to his predecessors, one cannot help admiring such energy.[3] There must also be added to this list his hunting trips and his travels.

Game was abundant because no one but the Inca and the nobility was allowed in certain districts in wild animal preserves, such as the province of Huamachuco. Hunting only took place in any particular area at intervals of at least four years. It was done in this way. Several thousand Indians surrounded a certain area and advanced steadily towards

[1] F. de Santillán: *Relación del origen, descendencia, política y gobierno de los Incas,* in *Tres relaciones de antigüedades peruanas,* Madrid, 1879, para. 18.

[2] B. Cobo: *Historia del Nuevo Mundo, op. cit.,* book 12, chap. 20.

[3] L. Baudin: *L'Inca Pachacutec, réformateur du monde,* in *Annales de l'Université de Paris,* April 1953.

each other, aiming at a central spot. All the time they made a great uproar and in the end encircled the terrified beasts.[1] Harmful animals were killed, the vicuñas and *guanacos* were shorn, and the females set free. All this was duly registered in the records. For a great number it was one of the rare occasions when they ate meat.

In the region of Nazca, on the coast, the chiefs hunted with falcons. The designs on their pottery show the natives holding arrows in one hand and in the other an *estólica* on which a falcon was perched, and sometimes they appear to be watching the sky, as if to follow the flight of these birds of prey.[2]

The sovereigns' journeys often lasted several months, and sometimes more than a year. The Inca was carried in a litter, where he was seated with his wife when she accompanied him. A light framework built above the seats supported a roof, and from it fell hangings pierced with openings so that the illustrious travellers could see without being seen.

Traditionally porters were provided by the Rucana tribe, who lived to the west of Cuzco. When they ascended the mountain slopes, they rested their burden on platforms arranged for this purpose. They took great care not to stumble, for this would have been a bad omen, and so as to minimize this risk, the chiefs of the districts through which the roads passed arranged for these to be carefully swept and levelled before the procession passed along. Several thousand warriors always accompanied the Emperor.[3]

THE PART PLAYED BY WOMEN

The Empress was not without influence over her husband. The legitimate wife of Pachacutec ruled in Cuzco on several occasions when her husband was absent, and she organized help for the victims of one of the most violent earthquakes

[1] Cieza de León: *Crónica del Perú, Primera Parte,* chap. 81. The Austrian *Kreisjagd* is, on a much lower level, analogous to this Peruvian method of hunting.

[2] E. Yacovleff: *Los Falconidos en el arte y en las creencias peruanas,* in *Revista del Museo Nacional de Lima,* 1932, no. 1, p. 56.

[3] F. de Jerez: *Verdadera Relación de la conquista del Perú,* in *Biblioteca de cultura peruana,* no. 2, p. 59; F. Montesinos: *Memorias antiguas, op. cit.,* chap. 22.

Arequipa ever suffered. It was the wife of Tupac Yupanqui who obtained the favour of the Indians of the village of Yanayacu, as we shall hear. However, they always remained lower in rank than the Emperor; for instance one wife prostrated herself before her husband whenever he showed irritation, and remained in that position until he asked her to rise.[1]

The Empress and the ladies of the court spun and wove and busied themselves over their toilet. They plucked their eyebrows and rouged themselves with vermilion extracted from the Huancavelica mines or with the red berry of the *achiote*. The hair seems to have been the object of particular attention in all classes of the population and to have been held up as a criterion of beauty. The Indian woman wore her hair long and parted down the middle of the head, except in a few regions where it was plaited, or in a case of mourning when it was cut short. The hair was combed with a row of thorns closely set between two wooden sticks; it was washed with water in which she had steeped bark and beans, and with certain herbs she made it 'Blacker than jet.'[2]

The Indian chronicler, Poma de Ayala, has sketched the portraits of the Empresses who succeeded one another on the throne of Cuzco. This picture gallery is somewhat quaint. Some were beautiful, others ugly; they were gay and sad, healthy and sick; some loved flowers, others birds; several were helpful and kind, many took pleasure in feasts and banquets, one of them took to drink, and another was something of a witch.[3]

THE IMPERIAL CITY

The Inca and his family lived at Cuzco (the Quechua word for navel), a town geometrically laid out, and situated at an altitude of 10,500 feet. Pachacutec had the city entirely rebuilt on a sound plan, so that it should be the centre and the epitome of the Empire. It was arranged in such a way that everything started from the central square where public feasts took place. The importance of the dwellings, from the

[1] Poma de Ayala: *Nueva Corónica, op. cit.,* p. 136.

[2] Lope de Atienza: *Compendio historial del Estado de los Indios del Perú,* Quito, 1931, p. 58.

[3] Poma de Ayala: *Nueva Corónica, op. cit.,* pp. 120 sqq.

(*photo:* Grace Line)

1. Machu Picchu, Peru—terraced mountainside

2. Street scene, Cuzco

(*photo:* G. H. S. Bushnell)

The city of Cuzco today, photographed from the air, with the fortress of Sacsahuaman in the foreground

stone palaces to the mud and thatch cottages, decreased the farther one went from this centre. The status of the inhabitants corresponded to that of the houses, and one found in these dwellings the whole gamut of social strata, from high officials to humble workmen. In addition the town was divided into four sections, north, south, east, and west, and the Indians who came from the provinces were obliged to reside in the section corresponding to the geographical situation of their place of origin; those from the east lived in the eastern section, and those from the west in the western part. Rationalism never surrendered its rights.[1]

It is said that 50,000 Indians took twenty years to rebuild this 'capital of the four quarters of the world,' and 200,000 people dwelt there when the Empire was at its zenith. Its prestige was such that the Indian who was going to Cuzco always stood aside when meeting an Indian coming from the city. It was as if the traveller brought with him something of the majesty of the capital.

The general plan of the city was like a chess-board. The streets crossed at right angles and were paved and narrow; their greatest drawback was that they were divided lengthwise by a gutter.[2] The great square itself was crossed by one of the two streams which flowed through the town, but this was covered over.

The imperial *ayllus,* situated in the centre of the city, were themselves divided into two parts, *hanan* and *hurin,* in accordance with tradition. The districts on the outskirts bore quaint or poetic names, for example, *cantut* flowers (pinks), puma's tail, salt granary, the speaking place (where the Emperor's ordinances were proclaimed), the silver serpent (an allusion to the two channels of clear water which flowed through this area), the gate of the sanctuary, etc.[3] The palaces were built, like the rest of the town, according to previously constructed clay models, and as soon as these buildings are mentioned it is impossible not to enthuse over their walls which still amaze

[1] Uriel Garcia: *La Cuidad de los Indios,* El Cuzco, 1922; R. Larco Herrera: *El Cuzco precolombino,* in *Revista Universitaria de Cuzco,* 1929, p. 224; S. Hagar: *Cuzco, the celestial city,* New York, 1902.

[2] Pedro Sancho considers that this channel left just room for a rider to pass on either side. *Relación para S.M.* in *Biblioteca de cultura peruana,* no. 2, Paris, 1938, p. 177.

[3] Garcilaso de la Vega: *Comentarios reales, op. cit.,* book 7, chap. 8.

the traveller of today. The stones are joined with such perfection that the projections and angles are adjusted to the last fraction of an inch. One of these blocks has no less than twelve angles, as if the architect was making light of the difficulty.[1]

In the shelter of the surrounding wall were the different rooms, all open to the interior courtyard which was adorned with bowls of flowers. Hangings served as doors, animal skins were thrown on the floor, and niches were arranged in the walls. These displayed, to delight the eyes, a harmony of yellow, brown and black pottery, the gold of artistic treasures, and the grey of images.[2]

ONE OF THE MANY PALACES

As an example, let us consider the beautiful palace designed to receive the court,[3] and erected during the reign of Pachacutec at the entrance to the valley of Cañete. The Indians of the plateau did not succeed in pushing back the troops of Chuquimancu and so reach the coast, so the Inca, displeased and obstinate, decided to remain in this place. He ordered hills to be levelled and a miniature Cuzco arose from the ground, with its inhabitants, its sanctuaries, its storehouses, and its houses for the 'chosen women.' The principal building was the Inca's palace. In front of it was a great terrace, 480 feet long and from 250 to 650 feet wide; in the middle of this was placed a stone altar and a space for sacrifices, both raised on a platform reached by steps.

The front of the palace was divided into two equal parts separated by a small stairway and raised above the terrace. On one side were the rooms used for lodging the bodyguard and the priests who were not on duty, and on the other side was another small platform. Along the wall behind this were spaced

[1] Architectural experts never cease their praises in this connection, for ex. Fergusson: *Handbook of Architecture,* London, 1865, book 3, chap. 3; H. Vellarde: *Arquitectura peruana,* Mexico, 1946, p. 44.

[2] For the palace of Tomebamba, C. Balboa: *Histoire du Pérou, op. cit.,* chap. 11. For the palace of Latacunga, A. de Ulloa: *Voyage historique de l'Amérique méridionale,* Amsterdam, 1752, book 6, p. 387. For the palace of Cajamarca, F. de Jerez: *Verdadera relación, op. cit.,* p. 66.

[3] E. Harth-Terré: *Incahuasi,* in *Revista del Museo Nacional de Lima,* 1933, no. 2, p. 101.

out rectangular pillars which served as supports for a hanging made of vicuña wool and feathers. The opposite side was held up by wooden stakes driven into the ground and encrusted with precious metals. In this way a long, covered gallery was provided which gave shelter to the monarch and his family when they presided at the ceremonies which unfolded before them on the terrace.

Above this gallery, there were storerooms and the apartments of the imperial family; rooms for the Inca, the concubines, servants, captains and guards.

A neighbouring building sheltered the couriers with their wood-pile ready to be set on fire as a beacon, and in the distance, along the road leading to Cuzco, could be seen the line of mountain tops on which the messengers of the next relays kept watch beside their own beacons. Their posts were fortified.

A short distance from the palace, a collection of buildings was divided into four. In the first section was stored llama wool, in the second food, in the third *chicha,* whilst the fourth was used to house the guardians of these riches.

The courtyards of this building were also set aside for certain purposes. In one *chicha* was distributed, in another the llamas were herded, and it was reached by a very narrow passage so that the animals arrived one by one at the exit. Here stood an official who counted the beasts and registered their number on the knotted strings. The walls of all this part of the building were higher than the rest, for it is well-known that a llama can clear very high obstacles at one bound.

Another very large courtyard contained rectangular divisions surrounded by little walls and evenly spaced. Here were spread out food products so that they could be dried by the heat of the sun and the cold of night. In the middle, and at the entrance to this place, benches were set against the walls, and niches had been made in the walls for the *conopa* statuettes, protective deities.

The little house belonging to the guard was near by and its terrace served as an observation post for the sentries. The only door of the food-store opened on this side for the sake of easy supervision.

The workers took the produce and made it ready, sitting on

the benches and singing. They threshed the corn, washed the *coca* leaves, and so forth, and then carried them to the clamps arranged round the drying divisions. These clamps, once filled, were covered up with a material made of wool and straw. They were emptied when the time came to distribute the produce.

The door of the 'house of the chosen women' opened in a corner, easy to defend. The apartments stretched in a semi-circle round a courtyard with an altar in the centre. The rooms reserved for the matrons had precedence over those for the other women, in such a way as to ensure the best supervision.

The constructional technique of these palaces as well as that of the temples and fortresses presents problems which we shall discuss when describing Peruvian architecture.

The Emperor's daily life went on, sometimes at his Cuzco palace, and sometimes at his pleasure house situated near the capital at Tampumachay. It was there he enjoyed family life with his wife and children.

SELECTED FOODSTUFFS

The food of the imperial family was much more plentiful and varied than that of the common people, about which we shall speak later. Maize was roasted, boiled, or ground into flour in the form of semolina. The grain of *quinua, achita,* and *cañahua* was also made into flour and used as a basis for soup, with other vegetables or starchy foods. Beans and red beans were eaten cooked, roasted and seasoned with salt and pepper. Potatoes were prepared in the form of *chuño,* that is they were exposed alternately to frost by night and heat by day until they were completely dry. All that was then required was to grind them, mix them with water, salt and pepper to obtain a gruel which was very popular in the Andes. *Yuca* and *oca* were treated in the same way. All Indians used the dried condiments, *aji* and *mañi* very extensively. The nobility added fruits from the tropical valleys to this diet, and above all, in contrast to the common people, they ate meat —llamas of less than three years of age and vicuñas less than two years old. We know that at a more advanced age the flesh of these animals is no longer fit to eat.

The Emperor and his family were able to make considerable additions to their diet. These were brought from the different provinces with great speed by runners; excellent wild duck and partridges from the *puna,* mushrooms, frogs from Lake Chinchaycocha, snails, fish and shell-fish from the Pacific, and these were completely fresh in spite of the distance. The whole Empire contributed to the feeding of the sovereign.

As for drink, all classes of the population used and abused the traditional *chicha,* from the monarch to the humblest of his subjects.

At meal-times, three times a day, food was placed on a mat of plaited rushes stretched on the ground. The Emperor took his seat on a wooden chair covered with a fine woollen blanket, and indicated which dish he preferred. One of the women around him presented him with the chosen food, served on a dish of precious metal or baked clay, standing upright and holding the dish in her hands whilst the king ate. Everything the monarch had touched with his hands, and all the remains of the food were put in a container and burned, and the ashes scattered.

The service of the supreme Inca was undertaken, in rotation, by his wives, who lived in the palace and had an enormous number of servants at their disposal.[1]

A clown sometimes amused the man-god, who was obliged to maintain an absolute passivity in front of his people. A special word in Quechua, *canichu,* indicates this personage, charged with the task of making people laugh, and we know that the Indians were not insensible to jokes, or even to farce.[2]

THE LANGUAGE OF THE INCAS

There remains one unsolved problem. Did the Incas have a language of their own, as Garcilaso claims? Carried away by his desire to glorify his ancestors (the mother of this historian was an Inca princess), this famous writer was perhaps guilty of exaggeration. The dualist principle is not concerned here, for there is no question of a language peculiar to the nobility.

[1] Pedro Pizarro: *Relación del descubrimiento y conquista del Perú,* in *Biblioteca de cultura peruana,* Paris, 1938, no. 2, pp. 291, 303, 304.

[2] R. Porras Barrenechea: Introduction to *Vocabulario* by D. Gonçalez Holguin, Lima, 1952, p. 34.

It is understandable that the family of the sovereign may have retained the language of their own tribe and thus secured its domination on the plateau. It is unfortunate that we know nothing about this language. If, for example, it had been Aymara, it would have clarified their whole history. Garcilaso limits himself to quoting a dozen or so words and says he does not know their meaning, which leaves us as uncertain as before.[1]

It is reasonable to think that Garcilaso did not just call on his imagination, and that in the family circle the members of the Inca dynasty spoke the dialect of their original tribe. This was similar to that of other tribes, but sufficiently different to provide grounds for the belief in an original language. It was the same with the Incas as with Napoleon and his brothers when they spoke Corsican.

[1] P. Patrón and C. A. Romero: *La Tribu Tampu y la lengua especial de los Inkas,* in *Inca,* 1923, p. 432.

CHAPTER 6

THE LIFE OF THE INCA NOBILITY

THREE categories of people made up the ruling class. The first was composed of members of the imperial *ayllus,* though not by right, since certain conditions were laid down, as we shall see.

The second category contained the *curacas,* the chiefs who surrendered of their own will or by force and who were integrated into the imperial hierarchy in the position which corresponded to the numerical importance of their tribe. Their link with the central power was assured not only by the usual means of messages, but also by the obligation placed upon them to present themselves at Cuzco once a year, or once every two years, according to the distance they were from the capital. They were also obliged to send their sons at the age of fifteen years for their education, and finally for their marriage to a girl of the imperial family given to them by the Emperor. The sign of their authority was the wearing of their traditional costume and the use of a low stool on solemn occasions.

In the third category were Indians from the common people who had distinguished themselves by some remarkable piece of work, some outstanding deed, or in some other way. Admission to the ruling class was their reward. Garcilaso de la Vega calls them 'Incas by privilege.'

HOW TO BECOME A WEARER OF THE EAR-RINGS

The first of these categories was by far the most important. The condition imposed on those young men who were members of the imperial *ayllus,* and on the sons of the *curacas,* so that they could take their place amongst the rulers, was that they should take a sort of examination which was held at the end of a course of instruction. This lasted for four years and was given in the Cuzco schools. During the first year the pupils learned the Quechua language which was often completely unknown to the children of chiefs who lived in a distant province where a dialect was in general use. The second year was given up to the study of religion, the third to learning about the knotted strings (*quipus*), and the fourth to history. This knowledge was completed by the teaching of ideas relating to less developed sciences; geometry consisted of land survey, geography of modelling relief maps, and astronomy of observing the equinoxes and solstices.

The teachers were well-known scholars to whose lessons the supreme Inca himself sometimes listened. These professors were called *amautas,* which means wise, ingenious, astute, and there was also a special term, *yachapa,* to indicate 'he who taught.' The reason for this was that the *amautas* were not only professors, their knowledge was universal. They were as skilful at directing the building of a palace as at interpreting the law; at the provision of embellishments for the cult of the Sun as at composing a tragedy. But in spite of the authority given to them, they were not allowed to cane their lazy or naughty pupils more than once a day and then on the sole of the foot.[1]

On the day set for the examination called *huaracu,* the candidates, clad in white, their hair cut short, wearing a black *lautu* on their heads, gathered in the great square where they prayed to the Sun, the Moon and the thunder. They then ascended the neighbouring hill of Huanacauri whilst observing the strictest fast, as did their families (clear water and raw maize). They took part in ritual ceremonies and dances and the priests gave them back their slings. Some days afterwards they received tunics of red and white and spent the night under canvas, with their families, in a place near the capital. They again offered sacrifices and took part in a race in the presence of a great number of Indians who encouraged them with shouts.

This race was the chief test. The goal to be reached was this same hill of Huanacauri which was considered to be one of the most venerated places in all the region because, according to legend, one of the brothers of the first Inca had been changed to stone on this hill-top. But before this remarkable

[1] M. de Morua: *Historia, op. cit.,* book 3, chaps. 2 and 4.

transformation took place, he had been given a pair of wings so that he could play the part of intermediary between his brothers and the heavenly deities. The bird which was especially regarded as the friend of the Indians was the falcon, and this race was run, most appropriately, under the symbol of this bird of prey, whose rapid flight had always aroused the admiration of the natives. The language bears witness to this, for the word *huaman* means falcon and also speed. A series of derivatives stems from this root; *huaminca,* courageous, veteran, captain; *huamincachani,* to appoint someone captain, etc.

For the same reason, the name *huaman* is found linked with that of a great number of chiefs and places, such as the fortress of Sacsahuaman, the town of Huamanca, and the Indian chronicler, Poma de Ayala, was himself baptized Huaman.

If the race was a decisive test, if the falcon was admired for the speed of its flight, it was because the rate at which soldiers could be moved was a factor in victory in a country lacking means of transport. Falcon, race, military qualities, all these meanings were linked together. The surname of falcon was a title of rare quality. All the animals formed a hierarchy, from the bird of prey on the mountain top, to the toad who remained at the foot of this ladder of nobility.

On the day of the contest these conceptions took material form. The organizers placed on top of the hill of Huanacauri a series of rough representations of different animals made of salt—falcon, eagle, vulture, wild duck, humming-bird, vicuña, fox, snake and toad. The contestants took possession of these symbolic beasts as soon as they reached the hill-top, the first arrivals taking the birds, and the late-comers taking the snakes and batrachians which were the only ones left. So each man carried a witness to his strength or weakness, and the onlookers knew who should be praised and who should be scorned. They gave the young men, as surnames, the terms corresponding to *huaman,* calling them falcon, *liasuyhuana* meaning wild duck, etc.[1]

Transposed to the plane of the workers' groups, this system

[1] E. Yacovleff: *Los Falconidos en el arte y en las creencias de los antiguos Peruanos,* in *Revista del Museo Nacional de Lima, op. cit.,* 1932, p. 96.

recalls that used in Soviet Russia to stimulate activity and to encourage rivalry, at the beginning of the socialist experiment. Notices were posted in the workshops symbolizing the rate of production from the aeroplane and the locomotive to the tortoise. Under these symbols, the workers praised those who had increased their output, and jeered at the others.

When night came the Indian contestants slept at the foot of the hill in a place called, for this occasion, *Huaman Cancha,* the 'falcon enclosure,' and the next day, at dawn, they ascended a sacred hill where two stone falcons had been placed.

A little later the young men were divided into two groups and engaged in a mock battle. One group had to defend a fortified place and the other to attack it; the following day the positions were reversed and the combat resumed. Although not armed, the contestants brought such enthusiasm to the test that they often seriously hurt one another.

Later there came shooting with bow and sling, and 'character' tests; the candidate had to bear blows without complaint, remain on sentry duty for ten nights on end without sleep, stand motionless without flinching whilst a captain brandished a club above his head and threatened his eyes with the point of a lance. Practical tests completed the examination—the making of a bow, a sling, and a pair of sandals.

The successful candidates were received by the supreme Inca, who presented them with short, fitted trousers, a crown of feathers, and a breastplate of precious metal, whilst he himself pierced their ears with a golden pin. After this the young men had the right to wear the heavy ear-rings which were the most prominent and distinctive sign of the nobility, and which won them the name of *orejónes,* 'wearers of the ear-rings,' from the Spaniards.

If the ear was torn by the weight it was a bad omen. The Inca Atahualpa, who had an ear injured in battle, was forced to hide it with his cloak.

In between or after this solemn ceremony—it is impossible to be explicit because of the contradictions in the chronicles—other ceremonies took place; the dance of the pumas which the candidates executed to the beat of drums and dressed in the skins of these animals; the snake dance to which we shall refer later, the ritual bath, and the return of his weapons to each young man by the oldest member of his family. Finally there was a banquet in the main square at Cuzco and the clearing of a plot of land. It is understandable that the members of the nobility retained an imperishable memory of these days.[1]

THE RIGHT TO INDIVIDUAL PROPERTY

The status of the nobility recruited in this way was inferior to that of the Inca, but much higher than that of the common people. But when the latter became socialized, as we shall see, the nobility became more individualist. It was not that the Inca wished to operate an economic and social principle, but quite naturally, in making wise use of opportunism, he adopted the custom of rewarding the *orejones* who had shown particular ability with gifts of women, lands, llamas, clothing and artistic objects, and at the same time awarding certain privileges, such as those of having a seat at ceremonies, travelling in a litter, and wearing certain ornaments. The gifts received in this way became the property of the recipient. It could not have been otherwise without them losing their meaning—individual merit, individual reward. In this way, in Peru, originated the remarkable right of individual ownership under the guise of justice.

This was not all; so that the initial gift became an example, it was necessary to perpetuate the memory of the service rendered by permitting the gift to be passed on by inheritance, and not to an heir chosen by the deceased or designated by custom. It went to the collective descendants, for they appeared equally able to profit from the memory and follow the example. Lands received in this way, as gifts, could not be transferred, and had to be handed on under an indivisible title to the heirs, who would distribute the products amongst themselves.

[1] It is annoying that the chroniclers' narratives disagree on so many points. Garcilaso de la Vega: *Comentarios reales, op. cit.*, book 6, chaps. 16 and 25; B. Cobo: *Historia del Nuevo Mundo, op. cit.*, t. 3, chap. 27; J. de Betanzos: *Suma y Narración de los Incas, op. cit.*, chap. 14; De Diez Canseco: *Pachacutec Inca Yupanqui, op. cit.*, p. 222.

THE STATUS OF WOMEN IN NOBLE FAMILIES

Food, clothing, and dwelling-houses were graded amongst the nobility in accordance with their status, and at a lower level than that of the sovereign. This privileged class could have several wives, but not to an unlimited extent as did the supreme Inca; the regulations fixed variable maxima according to the position of the persons concerned. If the Inca gave a wife to a chief she had priority and could not be repudiated whatever the local custom. Women were considered to be most precious possessions because of the services they were able to render, and they could be transferred by right of inheritance.

In general, a princess of the imperial blood could not be the wife or concubine of a man of lower rank even if he were an Inca by privilege. This is the theme of the drama of *Ollantay* to which we have already referred. The monarch refused to give the hand of a princess to the bravest of his generals, although they loved each other. In fact, at the end of the play, the successor to this obstinate Inca gave permission for the marriage. Apparently this rule was not always observed, for a sister of Huayna Capac refused to marry according to the wishes of the sovereign. As punishment he gave her to an old and ugly *curaca,* but he was so worn out by the weeping and moaning of his wife that he allowed her to enter a 'house of chosen women'—or as we say in Europe, a convent.

In noble families the sons were trained in the Cuzco schools. Until they were old enough to go to school, women of experience and especially widows, were entrusted with their care and with giving them sex instruction.[1]

Young daughters of noble houses, at the age of eight, entered establishments called 'houses of chosen women' directed by experienced matrons who initiated them into the duties of wives. They occupied a position corresponding to the status of their family in the administrative hierarchy of the Empire, from those associated with the direction of government to those who remained the servants of others. They prepared food and drink for the gods and the supreme Inca, and spun and wove and made clothing for the imperial pair. With them

[1] B. Cobo: *Historio del Nuevo Mundo, op. cit.,* t. 3, chap. 34.

were educated young girls of great beauty chosen from different localities by special officials.[1]

These houses were numerous. In the little town of Caxas, the first that the Spaniards found still intact after the conquest—the others, of which Tumbez was the best known, had been devastated during the civil war between the two brothers Huascar and Atahualpa—a recently discovered document mentions three of these houses which totalled about 500 women.[2]

The Spaniards made this subject even more confusing for the girls were divided into several categories which the Spaniards ignored.[3]

At the lowest extremity of the ladder were servants whose work consisted either in caring for other young girls of higher rank, or of making up garments for the Inca, caring for llamas destined for sacrifice, or for the sovereigns' lands.

Above them were the girls of the cloister, obliged to follow various occupations such as spinning, weaving and tilling the soil.

THE 'VIRGINS OF THE SUN'

The true 'Virgins of the Sun,' set in the topmost rank, but living in the cloister, worked neither for themselves nor for others. They prepared food and drink for the Sun to whom they were wedded, and a rigorous chastity was imposed upon them under the threat of dire punishments. If they violated this rule they were buried alive, their guilty partner was hanged, and the agrarian community to which they belonged was destroyed—a brutal application of the solidarity of the members of the *ayllu*.

Not anyone could become a Virgin of the Sun. The young girl who was chosen had to serve her novitiate. At Cuzco the following conditions were laid down.

First the girl presented herself before the imperial council who examined her consanguinity, her physique, and enquired her age and tastes. If she was accepted, an income in kind

[1] Garcilaso de la Vega: *Comentarios reales, op. cit.*, book 4, chaps. 1 and 2.
[2] R. Porras Barrenechea: *Una Relación inédita, op. cit.*, p. 14.
[3] M. de Morua: *Historia, op. cit.*, chap. 35.

and a servant were assigned to her. Then the high priest or one of the ten ecclesiastical high dignitaries conducted an interrogation on the sacrifices made by the family at varying stages of the life of the candidate. Her hair was dressed by cutting part of it away, leaving curls on her forehead and temples. It was covered with a grey or brownish veil, she was clothed in grey robes, and the priest who presided at the ceremony instructed her in her duties towards the gods. The girl then became a novice and joined a group of ten candidates under the direction of an older and more experienced person. The directress of the house was assisted by other experts, especially in medical matters.

These ceremonies took place when a girl reached the age of puberty, that is at about the age of twelve years. The novitiate lasted for three years, during which a complete practical instruction was given. In the practical field they learned to spin and weave, to prepare food and drink, and to organize the house; in the religious field they learned to care for the sacred objects, tend the sanctuary flame, etc. The mother superior and the directresses were members of the nobility and maintained a strict discipline. Although the different categories of girls, living in their own special apartments, were separated by doorways which were closed only by simple hangings, a novice would never dare to enter the rooms of the Virgins of the Sun, or inversely. The division was all the more rigorous in that there were amongst the novices daughters of high-ranking persons who came to perfect their education without any intention of consecrating themselves to the worship of the Sun, and who were withdrawn by their parents at the age of eighteen. But if one of them felt she had a call for a religious vocation, the time she had passed in the 'house of the chosen women' counted towards her novitiate.

After three years had passed, the high priest, accompanied by the sovereign or his representative, went to the temple and ordered the candidates and their directresses to appear before them. They were invited to make a definite choice between marriage and consecration to the service of the Sun. In the latter case the girl was dressed in white, decked with a golden garland, covered with a white veil and shod in new sandals. She proceeded to make sacrifices, say prayers and take the rank of Virgin of the Sun; *accla*. Henceforth she could no longer leave the temple unless she was going to other sanctuaries. Then she would be entrusted with the task of adorning them, and she was obliged to be accompanied by at least one of her companions, by certain aged women employed in the house, by her servants, and by two of the temple guards carrying a lance and bow. She also had the privilege of walking in the garden of the house, where she kept the domestic animals which were her main diversion.

Each year after harvest, at a sumptuous banquet, the chief members of the nobility gathered together under the presidency of the governor, or, at Cuzco, the Emperor, and in the presence of the idols themselves. The Virgins performed sacrifices, paid homage to the sovereign, and renewed their vows of chastity and obedience. Then they served the feast and offered to those present clothes woven from vicuña wool, belts, and ornaments of all kinds. In their turn the guests gave presents of gold, llamas, or precious objects. The high priest was not present at this banquet where people ate and drank to excess.

We shall pass over without comment the details given by the author of an anonymous account which is suspect because of the analogy drawn with Catholic rites, and because of the absence of confirmation by other chroniclers. For instance the writer mentions the distribution of small pieces of maize bread 'as an offering.' [1]

The destruction of idols, pursued with zeal by the conquering Spaniards, did not find an echo in the realm of the spirit. The old conceptions remained hidden behind new altars. Missionaries, without any opportunism on their part, mingled pagan and Christian ideas in the same way that they applied Quechua names to Spanish forms. They themselves took over, in this respect, the consistency of the religions they condemned and thus eased the transition for the Indians. They spoke readily of monks and nuns as existing in Inca times so as to indicate vaguely the women in the houses of

[1] *Relación de las costumbres antiguas de los naturales del Perú*, in *Tres relaciones de antigüedades peruanas, op. cit.*, text reproduced in *Revista del Archivo del Cuzco*, 1953, no. 4, p. 383. This document is attributed to the Jesuit Father Blas Valera, born in 1545 in Peru, where he lived until 1590. He died in Spain in 1596.

which we have spoken. In the same way they designated as *acclas* of Jesus Christ the Virgins of the Sun who received baptism.

Girls of eighteen of Inca lineage who did not choose a religious vocation and who had not received a gift from the monarch were assembled on a specified day in his presence and in that of young men of noble rank aged twenty-three years and over. There was freedom of choice amongst them provided they were of the same rank socially. The ceremony was similar to that of the marriage of the sovereign; the bridegroom placed sandals on the feet of his intended bride and offered her presents, as did his mother. The Emperor or high official who presided joined the hands of husband and wife, and sacrifices, dances and banquets followed.[1]

The funeral ceremonies of the nobility were similar to those of the supreme Inca, but with a shorter period of fasting.

The rules governing the succession to power differed according to the status of the deceased. If he was a *curaca* the regional customs continued to operate, and these differed from one district to another, hence the uncertainties of the commentators.[2] In other cases the Emperor naturally appointed the successor to high office, but this rule only applied to members of the ruling class. Subordinate officers were appointed by their immediate superiors or even chosen by the people under their administration.

There was the same distinction regarding property. Custom, in all its diversity, applied to the inheritance of a *curaca,* otherwise the children inherited. When the widow was part of the inheritance she could only become the wife of the heir if the union was not incestuous.[3]

[1] Ramos Gavilan: *Historia de Copacabana, op. cit.,* pp. 94 and 99; F. de Santillán: *Relación, op. cit.,* para. 35.

[2] C. de Castro and D. de Ortega Morejón: *Relación y declaración del modo que este valle de Chincha y sus comarcanos se gobernaban . . .* etc., in *Colección de documentos inéditos para la historia de España,* t. 1, p. 244; *Relaciones geográficas de Indias,* Madrid, 1881; t. 2, p. 72 and t. 3, p. 217.

[3] B. Cobo: *Historia del Nuevo Mundo, op. cit.,* book 12, chap. 15.

(*photo:* Grace Line)

3. Near Cuzco, Peru, old Inca ruins

Machu Picchu, Peru. Details of ruins in an Inca mountain-top city never discovered by the Spanish conquerors

(*photo:* Grace Line)

4. The 'sun-stone' at Machu Picchu

A gateway in the walls of the fortress of Sacsahuaman, Cuzco

CHAPTER 7

ADMINISTRATION

ALL the work of organization and control in this enormous Empire was secured by picked personnel, of whom the Inca's Council provided the nucleus. Four high officials composed this supreme power, which was at the same time administrative, political and judicial. Each one undertook one section of the Empire, north, south, east, and west. These were the men whom the Spaniards called viceroys, who had carried out the general scheme of rationalization imposed during the reign of Pachacutec.[1]

Since this regimentation was conceived in a temporal outline, the calendar had first of all to be fixed. The year, which was a lunar year, began on December 21 at the solstice; the result of this was an inaccuracy in the solar year which apparently was never corrected in spite of many attempts to obtain accurate observations.[2]

THE TWO SPOKEN LANGUAGES: QUECHUA AND AYMARA

A major difficulty encountered by the rulers was the multiplicity of dialects; according to Father Acosta more than 700 were counted. Some of them are still spoken at the present time by very limited groups, such as Yunga or Mochica at Eten (on the northern coast), and Kauke at Tupe (in Yauyos province south-east of Lima).[3] When the Empire was at its zenith, three languages, described by the Spaniards as being 'general,' were dominant—Quechua, Aymara, and Uru. The

[1] P. de Cieza de León: *Segunda Parte de la Crónica del Perú, op. cit.*, chap. 39; Poma de Ayala: *Nueva Corónica, op. cit.*, p. 365.

[2] An anonymous text gives some indication of these efforts. J. H. Howland Rowe: *Inca culture at the time of Spanish conquest*, in *Handbook of South-American Indians,* Washington, 1946, p. 328; G. V. Calegari considers that the Peruvians calculated the solstices and equinoxes: *Conoscenze astronomiche degli antichi Peruviani,* in *Rivista Abruzzese,* 1914.

[3] J. Matos Mar: *Marco geográfico del area cultural del Kauke en el Perú,* Lima, 1950.

last named was already on the decline and we know that today it has disappeared to the point where specialists are reduced to gathering, rather affectedly, its last traces.[1]

By contrast, the first two were in vigorous use and are today still alive in the Andes. The 1940 census in Peru showed that more than half the schoolchildren speak Quechua or Aymara, and that more than 35 per cent of them do not know any Spanish. Linguists agree in recognizing that these two sister languages, similar both phonetically and in numerous grammatical analogies, are quite remarkable. Their vocabularies are rich and varied, and because of their polysynthetic and close-knit character, they are able to express a whole phrase by a single word. They are a model of construction, since they develop like trees from simple roots. In the Aymara tongue, from the root *ali* which means 'plant,' eighty-two words are derived, from 'germinate,' 'grow,' 'spread' to 'contract,' 'barter,' and 'buy'—including such details as 'growing the plant into a tree,' 'a well-grown plant,' 'covering a place with vegetation,' 'barter piles' and 'buy worthless objects.' Each of these meanings is expressed by one word of never more than five syllables.

Aymara has an odd resemblance to Turkish in the perfection of its structure. Some daring language experts have concluded that this language was the mother of all others; Onffroy de Thoron did not hesitate to call his study of the language 'The Discovery of Paradise and of the First Language,' and Villamil de Rada called his thesis 'The Language of Adam.'[2]

The formation of words in Quechua is both logical and simple. For example, *kay* expresses abstraction, *runa* means man; humanity is called *runakay*. *Siki* means custom, *hillu* means food; greed is translated *hillusiki*.

The plural is formed by adding the suffix *cuna* to the singular, but is not used for inanimate objects. In the latter case, one must indicate the quantity since there is no plural

[1] J. Vellard: *Contribution à l'étude des Indiens Uru, op. cit.*, 1949, p. 145; 1950, p. 51; 1951, p. 3.

[2] J. M. Camarcho: *La Lengua aymará,* in *Boletín de la Sociedad geográfica de La Paz,* December 1945, p. 3; R. Porras Barrenechea: introductions to *Lexicon* and to *Grammática* by Fray Dominingo de S. Tomás, and to *Vocabulario* by Gonçalez Holguin, Lima, 1951–1952; L. J. Cisneros: *La Primera gramática de la lengua del Perú,* in *Boletín del Instituto Riva-Agüero,* 1951–1952, no. 1, p. 197.

indefinite. As in French and Spanish, nouns are not declined. There are four conjugations of verbs and the present-indicative is the basis of all the other tenses. There are also impersonal and defective verbs. Each verb produces derivatives which assume special shades of meaning; imperative (one must love), reciprocal (love one another), intransitive (love oneself), optative (wish to love), self-denying (to act through love for others), etc.—all these derivative verbs are conjugated normally. The imperative has two tenses, present and future (act immediately —act in the future).

The first persons plural, whether of pronouns or verbs, differ according to whether the person addressed is included or not. An Indian talking to a Spaniard and expressing himself on behalf of a group around him would say, 'We were born here in the Andes, but we are also the children of God.' The first 'we' would be translated by *ñaycaco* the second by *ñocanchic.*

The Quechua method of numbering, which is by decimals, does not go beyond 100,000. The Aymaras had a system of counting by sixes.

The purest Quechua was spoken at Cuzco, where it was taught in the schools; there are words which mean 'archaic,' 'well-spoken,' and 'wrongly-spoken.' Without any doubt there was a certain desire for perfection of speech amongst the nobility.[1]

Abstract expressions are rare, but some are worthy of note —*collanan* meaning 'the principal thing,' whatever the object under consideration; *caucasca,* 'the living thing'; *viñapay* meaning 'the thing which continues' like 'truth,' 'existence,' 'eternity.' In his dictionary, D. Gonçalez Holguin translates *cay* as 'spirit,' and derives from this a mass of compounds, most of them adaptations to suit the Spanish conception of religion.

According to European ideas, the drawback to these two Andean tongues is their harshness, for phonetically they are guttural and explosive. It is difficult for us to pronounce certain

[1] Here are the words which, according to R. Porras Barrenechea, reflect the desire to speak pure Quechua. 'He who speaks badly and with hesitation,' 'he who speaks badly,' 'to talk freely and of good things,' 'to speak well and with elegance,' 'he who speaks a language mingled with foreign words.' (Introduction to *Vocabulario* by D. Gonçalez Holguin, p. 41.)

words and still more difficult to write them down. Aymara has 2 *ch,* 4 *k,* 2 *r,* and 2 *t,* and the sounds are distinguished by doubling the letters when writing them, except for the *k* when other means are employed (we find *k, kk, kh* and *q*). Onomatopœia are often used and these give considerable expression or even prettiness to a sentence. In Quechua, 'eternally' is *atchicuni*, 'baby' is *huahua,* and 'suffering' is expressed as a lament, *alau.* In Aymara certain birds have an imitation of their call as their name—*kotchitchi, lékéléke.*

THE KNOTTED STRINGS AND THE METHOD OF NUMBERING

At this period of Inca history there was no writing in Peru. The Indians used *quipus* or knotted cords 'for paper and ink' as M. de Morua explains. Thanks to them officials could record the amount of supply and demand, and the controllers sought to balance one against the other. Without this means of calculation, the administration of a rationalized Empire would have been impossible, since no price mechanism existed. It is no exaggeration to say, with Poma de Ayala, that 'the Empire was governed by the *quipus.*'[1]

The *quipu* was composed of a single cord to which were attached strings of different colours, some running parallel, some springing from a common starting point. By using knots and colours these strings were able to express both numbers and meaning.[2]

At the extreme end of the string the knots represented the units, above them tens, higher still hundreds, then thousands and tens of thousands. We cannot but admire the ingenuity of the Indians who invented a sign for nought—an interval without a knot, an empty space.

The number on the string was arranged in the same way

[1] The chronicler gives us a picture of two secretaries carrying *quipus* with an abundance of knotted strings: *Nueva Corónica, op. cit.,* pp. 358 and 360.

[2] L. Locke: *The ancient quipu,* in *The American Museum of Natural History,* 1923; E. Nordenskiold: *The secret of peruvian quipus,* Goteborg, 1925; P. D. Kreichgaver: *Das Rätsel der Quipus,* in *Anthropos,* 1928, p. 322; J. G. Llosa: *La Estadística en el Imperio de los Incas,* in *Revista Universitaria de Cuzco,* 1950, 1, p. 105. For the *quipu* in the Musée de l'Homme in Paris, see the *Bulletin du Musée d'Ethnologie du Trocadéro,* January 1931, p. 16.

as we write it on paper, and was read in the same way, beginning with the figure corresponding to the highest category. In the same way the string was read by starting with the highest knot. We do not know the meaning of the most complex knots—these were perhaps reserved for multiples.

The colours were used to indicate meanings or qualities. But their number is limited even if the shades are mingled, although the objects they are capable of designating are not, and so the meaning of the colours and their mixtures varied according to the general meaning of the *quipu.* One had to know the general meaning before making a correct interpretation. For example, yellow referred to gold in the list of booty captured, but to maize in the record of production. So these documents remained secret, since only those who knew their object could interpret them.

To facilitate the interpretation of the cords and strings, people and things were arranged in an unchangeable order of precedence. In the population *quipus* men came first, and then women and children; in the listing of weapons the following order was observed—spears, arrows, bows, javelins, clubs, axes and slings.

The absence of a string along the whole length of a cord, or the absence of a colour, both had a meaning, as did the absence of a knot in a string. This was the method of expressing 'none.' It was so certain that everything was recorded that the absence of a *quipu* was considered as a 'negative witness.' If there was no string recording the number of any objects, that was because the objects did not exist.[1]

The interpreters, called *quipucamayucs* which means 'the keepers of the *quipus,*' possessed very well-trained memories, whose accuracy was ensured by a radical process—the least fault or omission was punished by instant death. Each man specialized in the reading of one category of strings; religious, military, economic, etc., and he was obliged to instruct his son so that he could take over later on. So as to remember the records more easily, he made up verses and sang them in recitative.

The centralization of the *quipus* was arranged in the simplest way. Junior officials collected the basic statistics in their

[1] R. Porras Barrenechea: *Quipu y Quilca,* in *Mercurio Peruano, op. cit.,* p. 28.

districts and forwarded them to their superiors, who added them together. Stage by stage the Empire-wide figures reached the capital where they were collated by the central bureau of statistics.

Besides serving as enumerators these *quipus* also recorded historical facts and magic rites. In certain areas they were supplemented by a system of notches cut on pieces of wood, or by hollowed-out slabs of stone or wood in which were placed stones, seeds, or beans, similar to the 'counters' used by the Caras.[1]

There is no doubt that the Indians had a flair and a liking for figures. Everything was recorded. It was impossible, says one chronicler, to hide even a pair of sandals.

ADMINISTRATIVE OFFICERS AND THE TRIUMPH OF ARITHMETIC

A system of counting and classification is not enough for the direction of a whole economy, and an administrative system had to be set up to facilitate the service of collection and distribution. There was in existence an ancient and natural division which corresponded to that of the various tribes: Collas, Cañas, Contisuyus, etc., and which had been created by geographical data and historical facts. This is what was so striking to strangers. The Spaniards called these natural divisions provinces and their chiefs governors.

The capital was recognized by the addition of the epithet *hatun* which means 'great,' to the name of the province—Hatuncolla, Hatuncaña, etc. But these districts were very unequal in size and importance, and such divisions were quite unsuitable for a rational economy. The directors, without destroying the original divisions, devised another logical method, as follows. Heads of families aged from 25 to 50 years were taken as units, and ten of them were placed under the command of one of their number to constitute the basic unit called by the Spaniards a decurion. Above them were groups of fifty families (the upper decurion), of 100 families (the centurion), of 500 families (the upper centurion), of 1,000 and 10,000 families. Arithmetic gave way to geography

[1] For further details, see L. Baudin: *L'Empire socialiste des Inka*, p. 125.

in the largest groupings, where we find governors of provinces and viceroys.

If one computes, as do the commentators, that a family consists of at least five persons, it must be agreed that this classification on a basis of five and ten is very reasonable.

Since the government was inflexible, everything depended on the central power, with the result that the grading was vertical; each official found himself in constant touch with his superiors and inferiors in rank, but never with his equals. His power was great and his responsibilities heavy. His functions, although variable in a certain degree according to rank, were also very extensive, since it was his duty to direct the life of his subordinates down to the smallest details, and in conformity with the regulations, to exercise over them a detailed and constant control, reporting all infringements, and in certain cases enforcing punishments.

Men of 25 to 50 years of age were called tributaries and only formed one category, the most important one, of each group of the population. The division into categories according to ages and according to the occupation imposed on individuals, was as follows:

1. Less than one year old, the baby in its cradle.
2. From 1 to 5 years, the child who plays. Cabeza de Vaca claims that they 'had to thread lice on a hair so that no one was unoccupied.'
3. From 5 to 9 years, the child who walks.
4. From 9 to 12 years, the child who chases birds from the maize fields.
5. From 12 to 18 years, the llama shepherd and the manual apprentice.
6. From 18 to 25 years, the man who aids his parents in all kinds of work.
7. From 25 to 50 years, the adult tributary.
8. From 50 to 60 years, the old man still able to do some work.
9. Over 60 years, the sleepy old man only able to give advice.
10. This last class comprised the invalids, infirm, lunatics, etc.[1]

[1] This classification is inspired by that given by Poma de Ayala, but

As births and deaths modified the official arithmetical divisions by enlarging or reducing the hundreds, and had the same effect on the groups of which these formed part, it was necessary, from time to time, to make a fresh count and a new division into groups. These revisions took place either every two years or every five years, it is impossible to specify exactly because of lack of agreement in the texts. In the intervals between these operations and especially at the end of each of them, the division became very approximate, for the real figures tended to differ more and more from the official figures. Equilibrium was re-established, as it must be under a socialistic régime, by adapting man to the plan and not the plan to man. As a result, the over-large groups of growing populations were absorbed into the deficit groups, or else, when it grew too large, a group was divided. Very often the members of the prolific communities were sent to Cuzco and absorbed into the service of the Incas. Thus aptitudes and tastes were forcibly sacrificed to the needs of uniformity.

Needs indeed, because distribution would have been difficult without these simplifications. If it was necessary to distribute a thousand measures of maize, it was easy to divide them amongst the provinces in proportion to the numbers in their groupings, and the distribution was carried out arithmetically by successive divisions. Each group knew exactly what was their share of the quota, without any possible argument, because the grain itself represented a definite fraction of the population.[1] In this way, explains Fernando de Santillán, the reckoning was easy.[2]

General inspectors arrived from time to time and exercised a detailed control and made adjustments. They appointed cer-

there is some uncertainty relating to the tributaries who may have comprised men from 25 to 60 years of age (and not 50 years). Such is the inference from the manuscript of Chucuito. (M. Helmer: *La Vie économique au 16C sur le haut plateau andin,* in *Travaux de l'Institut français d'Études andines,* Lima, 1951, p. 128. But F. de Santillán maintains that Indians of 50 to 60 years of age tilled the land, but did not pay tribute (in the sense we give to the word). (*Relación, op. cit.,* para. 11.) Cabeza de Vaca gives still another classification in *Relaciones geográficas,* t. 2, p. 71.

[1] Polo de Ondegardo: *De la orden que los Indios tenyan en dividir los tributos . . .,* in *Colección de documenta inéditos del archivo de Indias,* t. 18.

[2] F. de Santillán: *Relación, op. cit.,* p. 52.

tain officials, modified or organized administrative arrangements, and, which appears most peculiar to us, chose the young girls destined to serve the Inca and the Sun. We have already alluded to this kind of tribute when describing the 'houses of the chosen women,' but one must not see in this evidence of over-bearing tyranny. A woman's wishes were considered of little importance; she always took second place compared with men, and this choice was regarded as an honour by families who had adapted themselves to the régime —that is those who had long been subjects of the Incas and worshipped the Sun.

These visitors were not only formidable and awesome personages, they bore the disturbing name of *Tucuiricuc,* which means 'he who sees all.'[1] They had authority to exact penalties, and they could dismiss officials or *curacas* so that none of them was certain of holding his position. The chronicler[2] tells us that every one lived in 'a salutary and painful state of alertness.'[3]

THE INDIAN MUST LIVE AND DIE WHERE HE WAS BORN

The statistical data of the problem having been mastered, it was necessary, in ordering the economy, to be certain that these facts were not being unexpectedly altered all the time. Exactness required a certain immobility, and the Indians were forbidden to move out of their district without permission.

Control was easy, for it was only necessary to observe the head-dresses which differed from one region to another. For example, the Collas, on the shore of Lake Titicaca wore woollen caps, the Huancas north of Cuzco wore a black turban, the Cajamarcas a narrow cord, and the Cañaris (to the south of the present day republic of Ecuador) a thin wooden crown.[4] The head-dresses were traditional, and by them warriors from

[1] L. Valcárcel: *Historia de la cultura antigua del Perú,* t. 1, vol. 2, Lima, 1949, pp. 192 and 197.

[2] Damián de la Bandera: *Relación general de la disposición y calidad de la provincia de Guamanga,* in *Relaciones geográficas de Indias,* Madrid, 1881, p. 100.

[3] C. de Castro y D. de Ortega Morejón: *Relación y declaración, op. cit.,* p. 215.

[4] P. de Cieza de León: *Segunda Parte de la Crónica op. cit.,* chaps. 74 and 100.

the same province recognized each other in the confusion of battle. The Inca, in making clothing uniform, was obliged to leave the head-dresses alone.

The only displacements which took place in the framework of general policy, and gave rise to what we might call transfers in the reckonings of the national statistical service, was that of the *mitmac,* called *mitimaes* in Spanish. These were of several kinds, but always collective, always definite, and so had the appearance of human migrations. We have already seen one example of this when groups from over-populated regions were sent to areas where they could find land to cultivate.

Sometimes technical considerations inspired identical movements; families of proved agricultural skill were sent to settle in backward provinces so as to help in their development. Other communities were ordered to proceed to fertile places so that their original province, where cultivable soil was rare, could be improved.

But above all, it was the military type of *mitmac* which interested the Spanish observers. The central authority chose *ayllus* whose loyalty had been proved, and who resided in the centre of the Empire; these were sent to distant regions which had recently been conquered, where they took the place of tribes considered to be unreliable. These in their turn were settled not far from the capital, where they could be subjected to strict surveillance.

Today there still live in neighbouring regions on the ancient frontiers of the Empire, Indians who are very different from those around them. They are the descendants of the unfortunates who had to leave their birthplace and live in a hostile country. The sovereign generally gave them numerous gifts and marks of appreciation but the sacrifice was so great for these peasants, attached as they were to the lands of their ancestors, that nothing could really compensate them. The individual could only obey, for he did not count when the interest of the Empire was at stake.

A GROUP ON THE FRINGE OF SOCIETY

Amongst the different categories of the population which we

have considered, there is one which we have left on one side, because it remains outside all classification and is by way of being a paradox. These are the Yanacunas. Their position was due to an historical event; several thousands of Indians who had taken part in a rebellion had gathered in the town of Yanacu. They had been condemned to death but had obtained a commutation of their sentence thanks to the intervention of the Empress, and they were ordered to become servants of the conquerors. This was a kind of slavery to which they were condemned for ever, they and their descendants, for they were, so to speak, outcasts from society. They were subject, not to officials whose status has been described, nor to ordinary judges, but solely and directly to their masters. They were even excluded from statistical records, which is a startling proof of their insignificance.

However, their origin quickly became blurred and faded, for some of them became intimates of high officials whom chance had brought their way, and some even became members of the nobility. Mingling with the servants, the greater number were absorbed by them, and the name itself remained only vaguely attached to them by the time of the Spanish conquest.

THE REGULATING FORCE OF THE SYSTEM

The structure of the Inca system has now been outlined sufficiently clearly for us to sum up the whole. The mass of the population was compelled to provide goods, either in the shape of food supplies obtained by cultivating the lands set aside for the Inca and the Sun, as we shall describe, or by articles made from basic materials distributed by officials for that purpose. All these goods were heaped in granaries or public storehouses, a series of small buildings erected alongside the roads or on the outskirts of towns, and guarded by caretakers charged with recording the produce. Enough for several years' living was always in hand; maize, potato flour, dried meat, etc., as well as piles of clothing, hangings, animal skins, arms, sandals and cords, in short, everything that would prove of use. Basic materials also had their place in these reserves—wool, cotton, *cabuya* fibre, etc.

The supreme Inca was the sole owner of all this wealth, he could dispose of it at will, and in as arbitrary a manner as he pleased.[1] But the Inca was the State, the Empire, and the future.

These riches were intended for the upkeep of the court, the nobility and the priests, but they had other numerous and essential uses. They met the requirements of the army, they were allotted as rewards to those who had earned them, they were given to foreigners whom they wished to bribe or corrupt, they were the booty of war, inexhaustible stocks to aid regions decimated by earthquakes, floods, invasions and all the frequent catastrophes of the South American continent.

In fact, the granaries represented, in this socialistic state, the capital which individuals build up by their thrift under a liberal régime—state capital of a state system. It would be entirely false to regard these accumulations of wealth as manifestations of the greed of the ruling classes. By a more or less circuitous route, the greatest part of the goods acquired by collective toil returned to those who had provided them. Here was the regulating force of the system, the gigantic natural treasury, without which it would have been impossible to organize adjustments in time to ensure the equilibrium of production and consumption in an immense Empire.

It is easy to picture the amazement of the Spaniards in face of this logic and foresight, and their delight in finding, at all stages of their long journey, these stores from which they could always draw an inexhaustible supply.

As in all human institutions, this perfectly logical system presented some inconveniences and even omissions, arising from the tyrannical discipline which it implies. At first the cost was very high, for many of the products deteriorated and had to be destroyed from time to time on orders from the chiefs. Excessive foresight engenders waste. At last the Incas thought they had eliminated the unforeseen and subdued entirely the caprices of nature and the vagaries of chance to the dictates of cold reason—a pride which the gods did not fail to punish. No one can boast of preparing for every contingency. The

[1] P. de Ondegardo: *Relación de los fundamentos acerca del notable daño que resulte de no guardar a los Indios sus fueros,* in *Colección de documentos inéditos del Archivo de Indias,* t. 18, p. 69.

powerful 'master of the four quarters of the world' did not foresee that his warehouses, of which he was justly proud, facilitated greatly the invasion of his territory by those who came to seize from him his Empire and his life.

In this way stability was established and maintained. The central statistical service held in its knotted strings the destiny of the Empire's economy. It had only to give its orders and each one knew exactly what he had to provide, what he was to receive, what he would have to hand over, and what he could keep. This province had to help that one; one community devastated by a plague was allowed to take what was necessary from public stores; in another region certain public works had to be undertaken.

This unified whole implied a network of means of communication and processes of immediate and rapid transmission.

THE ROADS

The roads of the Empire have been the object of eulogies so poetical that one hesitates to repeat them, but those who sing their praises are often little given to admiration. We must acknowledge that these roads have become 'as famous as those built by Hannibal across the Alps to reach Italy,' as says Cieza de León, and he adds: 'I think that if the Emperor (the Emperor of the Indies, King of Spain) had given orders for another royal road to be built equal to that stretching from Quito to Cuzco, or from Cuzco to Chile, in spite of his power, he would not have been able to achieve it.'[1]

The difficulties arising in the construction of these roads were considerable, because of the lie of the land, and because they varied according to the area through which they passed. They were built as straight as possible so that travellers and messengers should lose no time, and so they frequently ascended the mountain slopes by long and tiring series of steps. The Spaniards grumbled constantly about these, for their horses grew tired climbing them, lost their shoes through kicking the steps with their feet, and arrived at the top of the slope in such a condition that they were unable to charge the

[1] P. de Cieza de León: *Segunda Parte de la Crónica, op. cit.*, chap. 15.

enemy.[1] However the road sometimes climbed at a gentle angle, following the contours of the mountain.[2]

In cultivated areas, pillars, poles, or little walls defined the road so that armies on the march should not destroy the fields. When sandstorms blown up by the wind threatened to cover the ground, stakes driven into the earth indicated the track and guided the traveller. When the ground was marshy, embankments ensured the firmness of the road. On the coast, in places, trees were planted and canals were dug alongside the way.

These roads varied very much in width, and this explains the divergencies in the conclusions of certain modern historians.[3] In the plains it was wide enough to allow six horsemen to gallop abreast, in the difficult mountain passes it was reduced to only 3 feet in width. These narrow paths were none-the-less remarkable; for example, that which still runs between the ruins of the mysterious towns of Vilcabamba and Machu Picchu, recently discovered in the Corderilla. This path skirts the side of a mountain escarpment, is paved with flat stones, interspersed with numerous flights of steps hollowed out of the rock or built out and supported in several places by walls 12 feet high, and it even passes through a tunnel 15 feet long obtained by enlarging a natural fissure.[4] Along certain important main roads, notably that leading to Collao, boundary stones indicated the distances.[5]

The reason why we can still see traces of these roads is that the *pirca* of which the roads on the plateau were constructed, was a mixture of clay, pebbles, and maize leaves which has magnificently resisted the onslaught of time.

More astonishing still, for us, is the siting of several parallel roads in the plains near big towns, where the armies frequently passed, such as was done near Vilcas, the key position to Cuzco towards the west. This arrangement reminds us that these

[1] Pedro Sancho: *Relación, op. cit.*, pp. 142 and 145.

[2] 'Spiral' as the Spaniards described it.

[3] Général Langlois: *De-ci, de-là, à travers le Pérou précolombien, La Géographie*, 1936, p. 29.

[4] P. Fejos: *Archeological Exploration in the Corderilla Vilcabamba South-Eastern Peru*, New York, 1944.

[5] There is one on the cross-road which leads from the Rimac valley to the plateau, at the entrance to the mountains, near Chosica, in the neighbourhood of Lima.

roads were as much strategic as administrative. Those using them most were troops, inspectors on tour, messengers, officials making reports to their superiors, asking for orders, or paying homage to the high dignitaries, and Indians going on a pilgrimage or visiting the markets near their homes.

The lay-out of the roads was as rational as other elements in the economic structure, especially as the lie of the land favoured this rationalization. Coast and plateau appear on the map as two parallel zones running from north to south and joined by the western Corderilla—consequently it was natural to construct two roads, also parallel, one on the coast the other on the plateau, and named respectively by the Spaniards, the *llanos* road and the *sierra* road. It was only necessary to join these two main arteries by a series of secondary tracks across the Corderilla where the passes made this possible, to obtain a model lay-out of ways of communication.

When Francisco Pizarro disembarked at Tumbez, he at first took the coast road which started from this town and which was followed as far as Pachacamac, just south of Lima by one of his lieutenants. He himself took a cross-road which led him up to the plateau towards the Inca army assembled at Cajamarca.

Thus one of these important roads started on the shores of the Gulf of Guayquil at Tumbez, the principal port of the Empire. Here it was that a fleet of sailing rafts lay mouldering, though some of them had ventured at times along the inhospitable coast of the present Republic of Ecuador in the hope of advantageous barter. This town lay under a blazing sun, amongst palm-trees and mosquitoes, on the banks of the river of the same name.[1]

Next the road crossed the ancient realm of the Chimus, whose capital was already no more than a heap of ruins and a source of legend, and passed near the impressive fortress of Parmunca (or Paramonga) which had held up the Inca army and obliged Pachacutec to resort to diplomacy. The way then crossed the Rimac valley where a modest village marked the site of Lima, and served the temple of Pachacamac whose religious importance we have already stressed.

[1] Today it is several miles from the sea. The port, 13 miles away, is called Puerto-Pizarro, as is appropriate.

After more sandy deserts Ica and Nazca appeared, on the banks of the rivers which were their life-line, both towns being noted for their pottery. Now the towns were farther apart and the coast still more desolate. Quilca, Arica, Tarapaca succeeded one another, long distances apart, and the Atacama desert stopped the traveller and ended the highway. The frontier of the Empire was the river Maule, a little to the south of the present-day capital of Chile.

The road through the *sierra* started from the river Ancasmayo which today is the boundary between the Republics of Colombia and Ecuador, near the town of Ipiales to the south of Pasto,[1] and crossed the battlefields where the armies of the Incas and the Caras fought bitterly, near also to the 'lake of blood' and the stronghold of Otavalo where a brother of Huayna Capac was beaten and killed. The road then reached the capital, Quito, a singularly picturesque town with its dwellings separated by deep ravines (*quebradas*), and framed by the temples of the Sun and Moon built on small eminences, and having for background the great mass of Pichincha, and farther away on the far horizon, north and south, a glistening line of snowy peaks.

From the remaining cities of the Caras, Latacunga, Ambato, Riobamba, the traveller passed to those of the Cañaris, a primitive and war-like race. At Tomebamba, the capital, one could admire the temple of the Sun, barracks and public storehouses, and small stone houses with thatched roofs. Towns succeeded one another, far apart and all similar, with their temples, houses for virgins, storehouses, llama paddocks, and their palace and fortress—Ayabaca (conquered by Tupac Yupanqui), Huancabamba, Cajamarca, one of the most famous for it was here in the triangular market-place that the Inca Atahualpa was treacherously attacked and made prisoner. Then Huamachuco and Huanuco, an oasis in the midst of vast grassy plains, and after the formidable cone of Cerro de Pasco—a cold and windy spot—came Jauja, known then, as now, for its moderate climate, proud of its fortress and its silver workers.

The road ran along the course of the Mantaro, the 'river

[1] According to Cieza de León: *Crónica, Primera Parte, op. cit.,* chap. 37.

of destiny,' on whose banks the Inca Huascar was assassinated, serving Vilcas, which was considered to be the geographical centre of the Empire, and whose central square was adorned with a platform on which the *curaca* sat when he presided at a banquet. Then came the quiet city of Abancay, the name of a flower, and a little while after crossing the great bridge spanning the Apurimac river, Cuzco itself appeared.

If the traveller continued southwards, he would have crossed the cone of Vilcañota and descended to Ayavire in the Colla country. Then, after long marches, he would have skirted Lake Titicaca to reach Tiahuanaco on the southern shore, ruins which, even in those days, were mysterious. Then the road turned towards Cochabamba, where, according to legend, a lake was drained dry by the imperial army so that the Inca could reach the town directly and easily. Next came Chuquisaca ('Sugar'), the famous Potosi silver mines, Tupiza, and finally it ended near Tucuman, on the territory of present-day Argentina.

Thanks to these parallel highways, a two-way link was established between the coastal provinces and those of the *sierra*. When the Inca and his suite travelled on the high plateau, the head officials of the corresponding districts on the coast ascended the slopes to meet him, making use of the cross-tracks, so that they could do homage and make their reports. When the monarch travelled by the coast road, the officials who resided on the tableland descended to the coast by the same roads and for the same purposes.

It has been said with some truth that these roads were more difficult to construct than the Roman highways on account of the nature of the terrain.[1] Imperial economic and strategic reasons explain their excellence and their number in this country of uniform planning and conquest.

RIVER CROSSINGS

Amongst works of skill, bridges were notable, and they were indispensable on account of the great number of waterfalls and ravines caused by earthquakes. The best known of these,

[1] For comparison, and a favourable one, see Général Langlois: *De-ci, de-là, à travers le Pérou précolombien*, in *La Geographie, op. cit.*, p. 26.

the suspension bridges, were made of four cables woven from *cabuya* fibre, and fixed to rocks or stone pylons on each bank. A roadway was made from woven lianas or plaited reeds, covered with branches, with guard-rails also of liana. The whole thing was perfectly solid, for important people were carried over in their litters, and later the Spaniards, with their horses made use of them. However, a certain amount of practice was necessary to avoid being intimidated when venturing across these hammocks balanced above the water at the mercy of the wind, and which sagged in the middle under the weight of the traveller. Special guards with stocks of wood and ropes were responsible for their upkeep. Sometimes a special bridge designed for members of the imperial family or high officials was laid alongside the one used by humbler folk.[1]

At times of invasion the suspension bridges were burned to stop the advance of the enemy. Several times the great bridge across the Apurimac, which commanded the road to Cuzco, was destroyed by fire to save the capital.

Some of these bridges were unusual in that they had no guard-rails, and the Spaniards say that they crossed them on all-fours.

Travellers using the secondary roads sometimes had to make use of sensational methods of crossing, such as the *oroya*. This consisted of a cable, stretched above the torrent, along which slid a piece of curved wood, pulled across from the opposite bank, and from which was suspended a basket in which the passenger sat. Or even more simply, in place of a basket, he was lashed to the piece of wood. An even more primitive method was used when there was no piece of wood and no Indian to lend a hand, for then the traveller crossed like a monkey, helping himself with his hands and feet. The cable which was used for this exploit was called *tarabita*.[2]

In each case the first half of the crossing was relatively easy, for the rope sloped downwards; the critical part began at the maximum point of the curve, when the rope slanted upwards.

[1] López de Gómara lists a number of ways of crossing torrents (*Historia general de las Indias, op. cit.*, chap. 194). There are also good descriptions of bridges in Miguel Estete: *Relación, Biblioteca de cultura peruana,* t. 2, p. 80 (bridge over the river Santa) and in Pedro Sancho: *Relación* in the same volume, p. 138 (bridge over the river Jauja).

[2] We ourselves were present at a crossing made in this way over the upper Pastaza, in the west of Ecuador.

There was a risk that the man in charge could not pull up the basket or the piece of wood, and it might break if subjected to too great a strain. At this moment the long-suffering traveller remained suspended over the river in mid-stream just above the current, or more or less in the water itself. The operator, in this case, usually decided to attach another rope, proceeding himself by sheer strength of his arm to the spot where his victim was waiting. Again there was a risk that the cable would break under the additional weight.

Today the old system has been modernized in the form of the *huaro,* described by a novelist in the following passage: 'You are in a sort of car or animal cage where two people cling together against the cross-bar, dangling at the mercy of the wind. This car slides along a steel cable suspended between two posts on either bank, and by a very ingenious pulley device, two oxen plodding away from the bank on one side, pull the rope attached to your car and bring it across from the other bank of the river. There is one anxious moment, the arc of the cable descends very low just above the foaming water, and when you reach it your face is splashed with spray.'[1]

For crossing wide rivers near the coast, the Indians made use of rafts made from tree trunks, pulled across from the opposite bank by cables, or else gourds were joined together and partly submerged, which the man in charge pulled or pushed as they swam, or when possible, steered them by punting with thin poles.

Where the Desaguadero flowed out of Lake Titicaca, the main highway from the *sierra* passed over a floating bridge whose roadway rested upon rafts made from reeds.

WAYSIDE INNS

All along the roads, and especially on the humps of cold and windy mountains, *tambos* or *tampus* were constructed. These were buildings of varying size to provide shelter for travellers

[1] Ventura García Calderón: *Le sang plus vite,* Paris, 1934, p. 108. This excellent novel writer has obtained most dramatic effects from the stoppage of the cage in the middle of the river-bed because of a breakdown, for the young couple in the cage were forced to spend the night in the water up to their waists, while they waited for daylight so that repairs could be effected.

in low-ceilinged rooms and for llamas in near-by paddocks. A caretaker kept stocks of provisions so that he could feed important travellers. The Spaniards were not slow to abuse this means of support by using these places as dwellings, and it was to put an end to these abuses that the 'tambos ordinances' were enacted in 1543.

It is difficult to distinguish between the *tambos* and the public granaries (*pirua*), especially in the towns. Neither the chroniclers nor the commentators agree on this point.

ENFORCEMENT OF THE LAW

An organization so complex must be perfect so that it does not end in disaster. The small bit of dust in a clockwork mechanism unbalances the mechanism. If an error crept into the statistics, or an *ayllu* moved without authority, a province might wait in vain for its food or basic materials, granaries remain empty, soldiers be without necessities.

Moral regulations were essential, and in cases where these were not enough, a rigorous judicial system.

Some moral rules were recorded by Garcilaso de la Vega in the form of maxims; he attributes them to the Inca Pachacutec, considered to be wise amongst wise men.[1]

1. When subjects, captains, and *curacas* obey the will of the sovereign, the country enjoys peace and complete calm.
2. Envy is a worm which gnaws and consumes the vitals of the envious.
3. He who is envious and is envied suffers a double torture.
4. It is better to be envied for one's goodness than to be envious through wickedness.
5. Who envies others destroys himself.
6. To envy the good is to draw away evil from them, as the spider draws poison from the flower.
7. Drunkenness, anger and folly are road companions, but the first two are voluntary and can be restrained, whilst the third is permanent.
8. He who kills without reason or just cause condemns himself to death.

[1] Garcilaso de la Vega: *Comentarios reales, op. cit.*, book 6, chap. 36.

9. He who kills his fellow must die; that is why the ancient rulers, our ancestors, decreed death for homicides, and we confirm this.
10. We cannot tolerate the existence of robbers who prefer to obtain wealth by violence or theft rather than by work and good-will; this is why it is just that a thief should be hanged.
11. An adulterer damages the reputation and qualities of others, he creates insecurity and anxiety. In this case the guilty man is a thief and must consequently be condemned to death without pardon.
12. A noble and brave man is known by his patience in adversity.
13. Impatience is the sign of a base and vile spirit, badly educated and untrained to tradition.
14. When their subjects obey as best they can, without raising objections, rulers and governors must show liberality and kindness towards them, otherwise strictness and justice must be imposed but always prudently.
15. Governors must note and examine two things with great attention. First they and their subjects must respect and carry out to perfection the sovereign's laws. Secondly they must make minute examination of the communal and private economies of their province. He who cannot rule his house and family will be even less able to rule the community. He must not set himself up above others.
16. The healer who does not know the virtues of herbs, or who, knowing some of them, does not seek to discover those of the rest, knows little or nothing. He must work to acquire a complete knowledge of all plants, both beneficial and harmful, so as to be worthy of the name to which he lays claim.
17. He who does not know how to count by the knots, should be laughed at if he takes it into his head to count the stars.

It is possible that most of these maxims are not genuine. We have omitted to mention one dealing with corruption of judges which is obviously inspired by the Spaniards.

Those which refer to envy are not really in keeping with the psychology of the Indian of pre-columbian times. What must be understood in this context is that it is in no way a code of morality of the times of Pachacutec, but evidence of the opinions, held by the Indians after the Conquest, of the wisdom of that monarch. It is nothing to do with rules imposed in the fifteenth century, but some indication of the ideas held by the descendants of the Inca's subjects about the vanished Empire, during the second half of the sixteenth century. One can see how the Emperor was still haloed with virtue.

EFFECTIVE GUARANTEES OF ENFORCEMENT

We are much better informed about justice than about morality. The basic dualism of Peruvian society is met again in this field. On the one side the law of the Inca was implacable because it was divine, and in consequence its violation would have been sacrilege. A judge could not modify the law. On the other hand, the rules deriving from local customs, and therefore varying from place to place, were applied leniently and could be explained. But the penal laws took into account the reaction of the subject according to the social class to which he belonged. In absolute terms the law was kinder to a member of the nobility, since the smallest penalty would harm his prestige, than to a man of the people totally indifferent to this feeling. Censure was considered a severe punishment for the proud *orejón,* but a matter of complete indifference to the humble retainer.

Subjectively, this was yet another manifestation of rationalism. It bore witness to a great arrogance of outlook; society did not try only to defend itself, it sought to find a punishment equivalent to the fault which had been committed, so as to obtain a balance corresponding exactly to that which we understand by individual commutative justice. Because of this principle the judge took into account the age of the guilty person, and a repetition of offences was severely punished; theft by a starving man was not punished, but involved punishment of his responsible superior.[1]

[1] *Relación anónima,* in *Tres relaciones de antigüedades peruanas,* Madrid, 1879, p. 200, rule 23. In France, at the end of the last century,

Judges were the officials we already know, for there was no specialization in this field. They knew of disputes between communities, and crimes against the Inca law. The *curacas* were responsible in so far as they were themselves officials, and retained their ancient jurisdiction in matters relating to local affairs, except in cases which were of special importance.

The special inspectors whom we have mentioned, were charged with certain investigations and sometimes proceeded with cases of important crimes. Above them sat a tribunal of twelve judges. Finally the Inca himself and his Council, aided by the four 'viceroys,' administered justice to the *orejones* and the high officials, and were informed of particularly serious crimes.[1]

The procedure brooked no delay. The accused and witnesses were summoned to appear, and sentence was passed either immediately or after enquiry. There was no appeal. The judge could swear in the Inca, the Sun, or the *huacas*. A soothsayer was sometimes asked to express an opinion, and torture was resorted to in order to extract confessions from an accused who appeared suspect.

Naturally there were prisons where Indians were detained whilst awaiting verdicts, but accused men of high rank had their servants and could receive visitors. Several authors content themselves with the deluding description of a pen full of wild animals which probably was intended as a form of ordeal; the accused who remained alive for forty-eight hours was considered to be innocent.[2]

Poma de Ayala gives an impressive list of punishments illustrated by suggestive drawings. Those applying to members of the nobility were death by beheading, life imprisonment, destitution, cutting of the hair and public reprimand; for the masses the death penalty was usual, by hanging or stoning, and burning of the corpse in the case of particularly serious

an officer condemned to death and pardoned by the head of State, asked the Council of State to annul the pardon because it called for military degradation—a punishment worse than death. (Conseil d'État, January 30, 1893.)

[1] B. Cobo: *Historia del Nuevo Mundo, op. cit.*, t. 8, book 12, chap. 25; H. Urteaga gives a summary of this organization in *La Organización judicial en el Imperio de los Incas*, Lima, 1928, p. 28.

[2] P. J. de Arriaga: *Extirpación de la idolatría del Perú, op. cit.*, chap. 5.

crimes.[1] Next came whipping, banishment to the *coca* plantations in tropical regions, and the bastinado, which often resulted in death.[2]

Poma de Ayala shows us two traitors falling under a hail of stones from their executioners; an adulterous couple hanged from the branch of a tree; a whole family of wicked sorcerers clubbed to death, and a criminal sealed in a dark cave swarming with snakes, toads and other vile creatures.[3]

The Indian knew what was in store for him if he did not obey the laws and regulations strictly. Not only were crimes against the person and private property punished, but those against state property were even more severely dealt with. Whoever stole maize from a field belonging to the Inca, or cut down a fruit tree by the roadside, or destroyed a bridge, was put to death.

An Indian of the nobility was far from inactive. On him rested the entire system. He had at one and the same time the responsibility and pride of the task entrusted to him. Conscious of his superiority, jealous of his prestige, he knew himself to be the indispensable head of a society whose harmony and stability he himself enjoyed. Monotony and sadness, which later struck the conquerors of Peru so profoundly, was for him evidence of the perfect mechanical functioning of a uniformity which could not allow imagination without repudiating itself. Besides, to satisfy his pride to the full, he had the splendour of ritual in which he played an eminent part. As regards his material desires, these were heaped upon him through the privileges conceded to him over people and property. His daily life appeared to him hard, and heavy with responsibility, but useful, glorious and worthy of being lived.

A SPANISH INTERPRETATION

How much the Spaniards appreciated the results obtained by the Incas is revealed to us in a document dated 1589. This

[1] H. Trimborn: *Straftat und Sühne in Alt-Peru,* in *Zeitschrift für Ethnologie,* 1925.

[2] C. de Castro y D. de Ortega Morejón: *Relación y declaración, op. cit.*

[3] Poma de Ayala: *Nueva Corónica, op. cit.,* p. 302 onwards.

appreciation does not adopt a particular attitude to conform with official doctrine, and is judged from a purely moral point of view, with all egotistical interest removed. This could hardly have been expressed by the first conquerors until their death. This document was the will of Mancio Sierra de Leguizamo, who had received, as his share of the booty captured at Cuzco, a golden plaque which he thought was a disc from the temple of the Sun. The following are the essential extracts[1]:

'Before drafting my will, I declare that I have wanted for several years to make known a certain matter to His Majesty King Philip, our prince, whom I see to be so ardent a Christian and so zealous in the service of God our Father, so as to discharge the burden on my soul. For I have taken a leading part in the discovery and occupation of the countries we have seized from the Incas, who were the rulers, and which we have placed under the authority of the royal crown. His Catholic Majesty must know that we found these countries in such a condition that there were no thieves, no vicious men, no idlers, no adulterous or evil-living women. All these kinds of behaviour were forbidden; immoral people could not find a living, and the Inca's subjects all had honest and profitable occupations. Cultivated land, mountains, mines, pastures, hunting, woods and everything else were organized and shared in such a way that each one knew and owned his heritage; no one else could occupy or seize it, and there was no need to go to law.

'Wars, although numerous, did not hinder trade, tilling of the soil, culture and other activities. Everything, from the most important to the smallest detail, was organized and co-ordinated with great wisdom. The Incas were feared, obeyed, respected, and venerated by their subjects, who considered them to be extremely capable rulers. Their governors and captains had the same qualities, and as they had at their disposal power, authority, and the desire to resist, it was necessary for us to deprive them completely of power and possessions by force of arms. In this way we subdued them and compelled them to serve God our Father, depriving them of their lands and placing them under the Crown, thanks to which, and

[1] *Revista del archivo histórico del Cuzco*, 1953, no. 4, p. 91.

because God our Father has permitted it, we have been able to consolidate our domination of this realm, which was composed of many peoples and quantities of riches; and we have made the rulers who submitted to us into slaves, as the world knows. We were a very small band of Spaniards when we undertook this conquest, and I desire his Catholic Majesty to understand why I draft this account. It is to unburden my conscience and to acknowledge my fault. For we have transformed these natives, who had so much wisdom and committed so few crimes, so few excesses and extravagances, so that the possessor of 10,000 gold and silver pesos could leave his door open, and by fixing a broom to a small piece of wood across the door, show that he was away or absent. This sign, conforming with custom, was enough to prevent any one from entering and taking anything away. Also they despised us when they saw amongst us thieves and men who incited their wives and daughters to sin.'

Was this the real feeling of a Spanish soldier? In reality it was the confessor who drafted this historic text and criticism is essential.

First must be taken into account the tendency towards exaggeration which was one of the characteristics of men of this age, who were accustomed to push their thoughts, like their actions, to the farthest point. No doubt this Catholic who indulged in public confession in this way envisaged exclusively the moral point of view without asking himself if morality did not call for liberty; if what he admired in Peru was not superficial since it was made obligatory by rigorous punishments; in fact, if an imposed morality is not a contradiction in terms. We are tempted to believe that these moral qualities were engendered solely by fear of punishment, for the natives of Chimu, of the Isle of Puna, and of other places, practised the worst vices, and the Indians of the Empire immediately and deliberately abandoned all moral principles as soon as they were free to do so. This same Sierra de Leguizamo tells us in the course of his narrative: 'The realm has fallen into such disorder that it has passed from one extreme to another; there was then no evil thing, but today there is no good, or almost none.' The oldest Quechua vocabularies contain a great number of words to designate the vices such as laziness, lying, and deceit.[1]

The indictment is no less striking, since it demonstrates to what extent the organization of the Empire had impressed one of the most modest of the conquerors.

[1] Vocabularios de Fray Domingo de Santo Tomás and of D. Gonçalez Holguin.

CHAPTER 8

A SOLDIER'S LIFE

THE POWERFUL AND PICTURESQUE IMPERIAL ARMY

THE imperial army must have been an inspiring sight. Along narrow roads, across grey wastes, and through squalid villages, there advanced a long column, like a snake with glistening scales. Under a blazing sun flashed lances, axes, and copper breastplates, and the feathered helmets of the chiefs, with their brilliant colours, scattered points of red, blue, and yellow light. Above their heads swayed the litter of the commanding general, who held in his hand the *suntur paucar,* the commander's insignia, which was a long pole ornamented with precious metal and adorned and surmounted with plumes. Around the leader marched the soldiers from the tribes who had been longest under subjection, as they were considered the most trustworthy.

When the supreme Inca led his troops in person he was surrounded by his special guard of Cañaris, and followed by his standard bearer, as sign of his presence, just as in France, from the twelfth century onwards, was carried the red and unembellished[1] standard of St Denis. This cotton or woollen banner was small and square and attached to the top of a pole, and crowned by a cluster of coloured plumes. On the banner were portrayed the imperial insignia—a rainbow, and each sovereign's personal device, a puma, a condor, etc. On important occasions, or on the eve of decisive battles, an idol was sometimes carried by a guard of honour. It was around these symbols, as around our colours, that the fiercest and final battles were waged.

The soldiers were grouped according to their country of origin, which could be a disadvantage. For instance, when General Capac Yupanqui, brother of Pachacutec, attacked

[1] Leon Gautier: *La Chevalerie,* Paris, p. 753.

the fortress of Urcocollac to the north of Guamanga, he launched an assault with Cuzco troops which twice failed. Then he ordered the Chancas to make a third attempt which was successful. The men of Cuzco were humiliated, and the Emperor, who had remained at Cuzco, was very disturbed when he heard what had occurred. He remembered that the Chancas had constituted a grave threat to the Empire, and had even reached the gates of the capital. Their feeling of superiority might incite them to rebel. Already they had appeared to flout the authority of the Inca chiefs, for orders had been given for a policy of clemency to be pursued towards the enemy, and in fact a great slaughter had taken place. The Emperor was filled with apprehension.

DISCIPLINE

The same historical event will show us the rigorous discipline maintained in the army. The sovereign took a radical step and sent General Capac Yupanqui a message ordering him to destroy all the Chancas in his army by whatever means he thought best.

The general, who had continued his advance northward, was in the Tarma valley when the order reached him. It was night, which was not surprising, for messengers travelled throughout the day and night. He had with him the sister of one of the Chanca chiefs and she learned of the project to exterminate her countrymen. She secretly warned her brother, who awoke his men and they fled during the night, taking with them a number of Cuzco men whom they misled. They pillaged the town of Huaylas, crossed the Corderilla, and no one knows into what country they withdrew. General Capac Yupanqui hurried in pursuit but lost all trace of them.

To this mistake the army chief added a second. He had reached the limit of advance as ordered by the Inca, but learning that a near-by province was very rich, he could not resist the temptation of obtaining possession of this wealth. He succeeded in taking prisoner the *curaca* of this region, by means of an ambush, and returned in triumph towards the capital with considerable booty.

But some miles from Cuzco an *orejón* awaited him with an

order for his execution, and for that of one of his brothers who had been his accomplice. There had been negligence with regard to the 'Chanca exodus,' and what was worse, disobedience followed. Victory made no difference to the gravity of these misdeeds; in an army no lapse from discipline could be tolerated.

According to one chronicler, the guilty general did not wait for execution but hanged himself. Because of the disadvantages brought about by the autonomy of tribes united under the command of their own chief, members of the imperial family replaced these captains at the head of the different detachments.

Why not mingle the soldiers who came from different parts of the Empire? They would certainly have fought with less eagerness, for they would have lacked the powerful feeling of group solidarity, and would have had less confidence in their neighbours. Besides, each unit specialized in the handling of their traditional weapons.

A picturesque addition to the procession was that the soldiers' ranks were broken here and there by groups of carriers and wives or concubines of the chiefs, some of whom travelled in hammocks.

These admirably disciplined troops were provisioned from the *tambos*. Soldiers were forbidden, on pain of the most severe penalties, to molest the inhabitants, or to take anything whatsoever from the villages without authority.[1] To enforce this discipline, it was even prescribed that a small quantity of *añu* should be mixed in the food of campaigning soldiers. This was a vegetable substance which reduced sexual desires.

Men were called to the colours, according to circumstances, for an undetermined period[2] and not for regular military service. But always when a war was long drawn-out or pursued in an unfavourable climate (e.g. on the coast), a rota was established so that they could return to their homes. It has been estimated that the number of soldiers benefiting from this arrangement could be between a fifth and a seventh of the effective force.

[1] H. Urteaga: *El ejercito incáico,* in *El Perú,* Lima, 1928, p. 111.
[2] M. E. de Rivero and J. D. de Tschudi: *Antiquités Péruviennes,* Paris, 1859, p. 217.

THE STAGES OF A CONQUEST

Some historians have represented the Incas as conquerors. This assertion has been made in the sense that the Emperors were all compelled to wage long and devastating struggles, first to free themselves from threats which powerful neighbours brought to bear on them, and finally to defend and consolidate their position. But being above all utilitarian, they only decided to wage war after they had exhausted all pacific means of agreement. Diplomacy took precedence over force, and they seem to have been very skilful at this. Envoys made several offers of peace to an enemy, urging upon him the advantages of submission, so that he could share in all the benefits of Cuzco civilization without even having to give up his authority. The emissaries explained the normal process of integration of chiefs into the imperial hierarchy, and in the last resort, stressed the dangers of a refusal by recalling the unfortunate fate of those nations who had revolted, and had been crushed by the Inca armies.

If this failed, the second phase began, in what may be called the preliminary operations. A spy system seems to have been particularly well organized. Its object was, first of all, to inform the military chiefs of the position and strength of the enemy armies, the chief points of resistance, and the situation of supply centres for weapons and food. They had then to determine the importance and strength of alliances, to disorganize the defence by trying to bribe certain people with gifts from the imperial stores, and to spread both true and false accounts of the efficiency and bravery of the Inca armies so as to create an atmosphere of fear. At the same time efforts were made to isolate the enemy by working on his allies by persuasion and intimidation.

The third phase of these preparations, and not the least important, were of a religious character. Fasts, prayers and sacrifices succeeded one another in the temples, soothsayers were consulted, and the Inca himself took part in extraordinary ceremonies in cases of extreme importance.

Finally came the military campaign, which unfolded in conformity with a strategic plan less simple than the Spaniards had supposed. This consisted of preliminary actions aimed at cutting lines of communication for bringing up reinforcements and supplies, and even of simulating a retreat to induce the enemy to fight far away from his support points and over a terrain which was unfavourable to him.[1]

THE PHASES OF THE BATTLE

The battle itself was sometimes preceded by an address designed to bolster up courage, and it was always accompanied by shouting so as to strike fear into the enemy's heart. Some warriors coloured their faces with various colours, generally red or black, so as to appear more terrifying—the Chancas and Cañaris did this. Forest shrubs provided these dyes, *achiote* (red) or *jagua* (black).[2]

Soldiers with slings led the attack, which is understandable in view of the astonishing skill of the Indians in handling this weapon. All children, from their earliest days, learned to hunt birds in the maize fields with stones flung from slings, and they fashioned these death-dealing weapons with the utmost ease from woollen cords or *cabuya* fibres. One single stone hurled with force and well placed could kill a man. J. Pizarro, the younger brother of the conqueror, fell in this way, having been struck on the head at the siege of the fortress of Sacsahuaman. On their side the enemy protected themselves by stretching some hard material over their heads.

After men with slings came the archers, who were always Indians from the eastern forests, those who even today can bring down a bird in full flight with one of their arrows. But a thrower or *estólica* was more frequently used than a bow. This was a wooden stick about 2 feet long and fitted with a lip at one end and a hook at the other. The point of an arrow made from bone, wood or flint was placed on the lip, its heel was put under the hook, and by making the gesture of throwing the whole apparatus and retaining hold of the support, the arrow flew off at an increased speed. As the opposing armies gradually drew near each other, the *ayllos* came into play. This weapon was made up of a cord held in the hand and divided into three strings, each carrying a metal ball at

[1] P. de Cieza de León: *Segunda Parte de la Crónica del Perú, op. cit.*, chap. 18.

[2] A. B. Gayoso: *Relación*, in *Relaciones geográficas de Indias, op. cit.*, t. 3, p. 159.

the end. The whole thing was hurled at the enemy whose arms and legs were thereby lashed together, the impact of the balls causing serious wounds.[1]

Then the conflict began amid shouts, insults and the sounding of trumpets. Lances and javelins pierced padded doublets or broke against metal breastplates; helmets rang under blows from bronze-studded clubs; axes brandished with two hands, or fixed to the end of short poles rather like a halberd, cleft the copper shields and sometimes remained fixed in them, thus disarming the attacker. Soon the warriors, covered with blood, began to stumble among the corpses and confusion reigned.

Captains, recognizable by their plumed head-dresses, fought with their men. Superior officers struggled to obtain a view of the whole conflict so as to direct their reserves towards points which were threatened. When the Inca was present he even hurled stones with his sling from the top of his litter, and if an idol had been brought to preside over the battle, it contemplated with enigmatic eyes the slaughter which would bring victory.

One would have expected this state of affairs to continue for some time when the Indians, as generally happened, fought with equal courage. Sometimes numbers decided the issue, but a new and extraordinary factor could arise which quickly brought an end to the combat. When, at any moment or for whatever reason, one of the armies seemed to be winning, this one factor was sufficient to assure victory. For, from the beginning of the conflict, if this took place in a populated region, Indians who had gathered from all around stationed themselves on the hills to watch the spectacle laid out before them, and when they judged that one army had carried the day, they joined that army to share in the booty. Under these conditions, a situation once compromised could not be retrieved, and any weakness ended in disaster.

Tactics were primitive on the whole, but Pachacutec owed several of his successes to the use of a method which seems to have been new. Instead of attacking all along the front line of the battle, he sought to discover the centre of command and resistance of the enemy—the nerve centre, whether it was an

[1] The *gauchos* of the river Plate use these *ayllos,* called *bolas,* to capture horses.

idol or a chief. Generally he soon discovered this, and whilst the conflict continued, with a few picked warriors he endeavoured to pierce the opposing lines in the direction of the god or the leader. When he had succeeded in capturing them, he and his companions uttered cries of triumph, and the enemy, warned by this uproar, realized that they had lost one of their trump cards and became completely demoralized. In this way he ensured victory over the Chancas by seizing their idol during the decisive battle fought at the gates of Cuzco. He also took prisoner the chief of the Collas at the battle of Pucara before he captured the capital of that tribe.

It is strange to note that it was by the same method that Francisco Pizarro gained an easy victory at Cajamarca by capturing the Inca at the very beginning of the battle.

The Indians often maintained reserves away from the battlefield so that they could intervene at critical moments, and above all to protect their retreat in case of defeat. Their judicious use at the moment when the opposing forces both began to be exhausted by the conflict ensured the victory of Tupac Yupanqui over the Cañaris.

Once victorious, the Inca avoided useless cruelties. What was the use of exasperating a people whom he had to rule, or in devastating a country from which he proposed to draw supplies? [1]

THE TRIUMPH

On his return to the capital, the victorious Inca organized a triumphal celebration which varied considerably in its arrangement, but which always provided a solemn procession. The troops who had taken part in the campaign led the parade to the sound of drums and trumpets, the soldiers in war array, the captains wearing their fine ornaments; then came the prisoners, their hands tied behind their backs, with their wives and children howling with fear and crying out for mercy, and the enemy leader stretched naked on a litter, surrounded by drums made from the skin of his relations; 'the skin, flayed and filled with air, provided a startling likeness of its original

[1] P. de Cieza de León: *Segunda Parte de la Crónica del Perú, op. cit.*, chap. 46.

owner,' says a chronicler. There followed carriers bearing the booty, soldiers bearing the heads of the enemy chiefs on the points of their lances, men who shouted the crimes of the conquered and the exploits of the victors, the *orejónes* in full panoply, and young girls from the 'houses of the chosen women.' These maidens, carrying tambourines and with bells on their ankles, sang and danced as they preceded the high officials who surrounded the litter where the supreme Inca was enthroned, wearing his state robes, unmoved, set in impassive dignity amongst gold and silver. Behind the monarch came relations, princesses borne in litters, and still more troops who formed the rear of the procession.

After the triumph, according to ancestral tradition, the Inca crossed the great square of Cuzco, stepping on the bodies of the prisoners stretched out on the ground. Dances, singing and banquets followed, and all ended, as was customary, in general intoxication.

The treatment of soldiers taken prisoner seems to have been humane, for they were often sent back to their own country. The chiefs who lost no time in making their act of submission were even accorded privileges, for they remained in office, as we have seen. But in other cases, cruelties were not lacking, and finally the principles of moderation established by Pachacutec were forgotten.

Poma de Ayala tells of a captain who put out the eyes of a kneeling prisoner who was still wearing his battle head-dress and who had his hands tied behind his back. During the civil war between Huascar and Atahualpa, the latter's troops committed atrocities in the Cañaris' and Cachapoyas' countries, killing women and children, and they did the same thing when they invaded Cuzco. But these troops were soldiers from the north who had been only recently brought under Inca rule. This was one of the principal reasons for the ease with which the Spaniards achieved their conquest once Atahualpa had been taken prisoner. The true descendants of the Incas had only hatred for this interloper and welcomed the white men with joy.

On the coast the ancient civilizations seem to have been truly barbaric. A design on a piece of Chimu pottery shows a priest slashing with a knife a naked man with a rope round his neck, and giving the blood in a cup to a sea-eagle with ruffled plumes.[1]

Amongst a succession of victory parades let us describe the one organized at the gates of Cuzco when Tupac Yupanqui returned from the discovery of the mysterious islands of the Pacific. Pachacutec, who was old and had remained in the city during the voyage of his son, permitted a general in his army to organize the defence of the town as if threatened by an invader. The invading army was impersonated by troops under the command of the young prince who was later to become the Inca Huayna Capac, and he hurled an assault on the city. A sham battle was enacted before the eyes of thousands of inhabitants who had come from all parts to witness this inspiring spectacle. There were menacing gestures, attacks, retreats, hurling of imaginary arrows and stones; clubs were raised and beat the empty air; curses and war songs, sounding of trumpets and the roll of drums all built up to a rhythm which beat faster and faster until the defenders pretended to give way, and the young hero crossed Cuzco to the cries of a delirious populace.

This kind of theatrical representation marks the culminating point of the grandeur of the Empire. The three greatest Emperors who sat on the throne of the Incas belonged to three successive generations, and each played his part in various appropriate roles. The old Emperor acted as grand master of all ceremonies; the second Emperor was the real conqueror; and the future Emperor was an actor rehearsing on a grandiose stage his triumphs to come.

FORTIFIED PLACES

Campaigning constituted the essence of military life, but there was also garrison life in the forts situated along the frontiers, along roads, and on the outskirts of large towns. These strongholds, built for defence, with a very sure knowledge of basic requirements, allowed their occupants to endure a prolonged siege. They formed small townships, with houses and cultivated terraces, and they were self-supporting, at least for a certain length of time. They were occupied by the *mitimaes*

[1] E. Yacovleff: *Los Falconidos, op. cit.*, p. 66.

of whom we have already spoken. These soldiers had their families with them and undertook civil as well as military activities, and handled alternately the spade and the sling.

These strongholds exist today in a ruined state and in many areas, the most ancient not far from the capital whose approaches they defended. One of these was Ollantaytambo to the north of Cuzco, and others farther away, such as Incahuasi which barred the way to the Chimus, to the north-west. Always linked to urban centres by good roads, their mission was to break the thrust of invaders and give the imperial armies time to mobilize. An invasion by the war-like Guaranis from the eastern forests had miscarried against such defences shortly before the arrival of the Spaniards.[1]

It must be recognized that the Chimus, although they had been subdued by the Incas, were superior to them in building fortifications. To the south of their capital, they had constructed a veritable 'Great Wall of China,' which blocked the coastal plain from the Corderilla to the sea, and which consisted of a series of small forts, some square and some circular. This gigantic work was discovered by an aerial survey. From high in the air one can follow clearly this line of defence which crossed hills and valleys.[2]

The important fortress of Parmunca, or Paramonga, whose outline can still be seen at the foot of the Andes, was the work of this great people. On a hill which was partly artificial were set out three terraces. On the top were dwellings and perhaps a temple, whose walls were ornamented with friezes alternately coloured red and white. Its height above the surrounding plain was about 60 feet. The intermediate terrace was 15 to 36 feet wide, and on it were two rooms with red and yellow paintings. The whole formed a vast quadrilateral, flanked at each angle with a forward bastion which was on a level with the lower terrace. Ramps through narrow passages joined the platforms. Around the fortress was a wall 9 to 18 feet high

[1] A Portuguese from the coast of Brazil found himself with these Guaranis. This brave and lonely man was the first white man to reach the confines of the Inca Empire, in 1526, to the east of Chuquisaca (present-day Sucre). He was called Alejo Garcia. (E. Nordenskiold: *The Guarani invasion of the Inca Empire in the sixteenth century,* in *The Geographical Review,* 1917, p. 103.)

[2] R. Schippee: *Air Adventures in Peru,* in *National Geographical Magazine,* January 1933.

with a parapet and a pathway around the top. About 60 feet from this main fortification an auxiliary fort was built on a hill, and farther north, on the Pacific shore, a peak acted as an outpost to watch both land and sea.

The fortress of Cañete farther south, where the Chuquimancus resisted the Inca invasion, was conceived on the same pattern as at Parmunca. Three enclosures built on the side of a hill contained dwellings and storehouses. As at Parmunca, the Incas did not destroy this stronghold when they had captured it but put it to use. We have already remarked on the mural paintings in the houses in the Chimu fortress; here the victors erected an altar on top of the edifice. This was a platform of beaten earth, 6 feet high, reached by steps and orientated towards the rising sun.

Some of these fortified places, prepared to undergo a prolonged siege, had warehouses where stocks of easily preserved foodstuffs were accumulated (*chuño, charqui,* etc.), and there were also terraces for cultivation, which increased their overall size to considerable proportions. Other strongholds included a palace or temple.

Some of these places were considered impregnable such as the one on a peak near the river Pampas, where neighbouring tribes took refuge when the Incas invaded their territory. The summit was sufficiently wide and flat for a village to be built there which could house the whole population of the neighbourhood, and a spring provided a trickle of pure water. The general commanding the army from Cuzco was obliged to abandon his objective, and Pachacutec came in person to raise the siege of this island of resistance. Hunger and sickness brought the defenders to their senses.

THE CITADEL OF CUZCO

The Cuzco garrison was stationed in the fortress of Sacsahuaman, which reared its sombre and massive walls on a hill to the north of the city. Three concentric enclosures, each formed by an earth platform 'wide enough for three carriages to drive abreast,'[1] contained a courtyard with the indispensable reservoir of water for the besieged, and which fed a long

[1] Pedro Sancho: *Relación, op. cit.,* p. 178.

subterranean canal whose course and source were kept secret. Near by were a few low houses and three square towers, of which one was more important than the others. Each platform was contained between two walls of cyclopean blocks of stone, with zigzag grooves to allow of their mutual engagement, their centre pierced by a narrow gateway which could be shut when need arose by raising a stone slab embedded in the opening. The principal tower contained rooms with partition walls covered with ornaments of precious metal, where the monarch could stay. The other towers served as barracks for a special guard composed of soldiers from the neighbourhood of Cuzco under the command of a captain-general of the imperial blood. Underground passages linked the towers and made a labyrinth into which it was unwise to venture without a guide, according to the tales the Indians told the chronicler Garcilaso de la Vega, when he, as a child, played with his friends in the ruins of this monument.

This descendant of the Incas, through his mother, had a very full knowledge of everything concerning the capital where he had lived. In his great work he devotes no less than three chapters to a description of the fortress, and on several occasions insists that it is impossible, without visiting the site, to imagine the size of the stones which compose the walls. One may well ask how such rocks, at times more than 12 feet high and weighing more than 10 tons, were put into position without mechanical aids, beasts of burden, or high-grade tools. To explain this marvel, several Spanish writers thought that spirits must have been summoned to assist.[1]

Legend has it that the largest of these blocks of stone was dragged, with the help of ropes, by 20,000 Indians, and that it crushed several thousand of them when it toppled over on the sloping hillside. The most highly qualified contemporary architects, as well as the most unenlightened tourist, cannot contemplate without amazement these great walls which even earthquakes have been unable to shatter.[2]

[1] Garcilaso de la Vega: *Comentarios reales, op. cit.*, book 7, chaps. 17, 18, 19.

[2] H. Velarde: *Arquitectura peruana, op. cit.*, p. 39. None of the Inca walls collapsed at the time of the recent terrible earthquake on May 21, 1950, which destroyed two-thirds of the town. Intensity 7 in the Mercalli grading, duration 10 seconds. (*Cuzco,* Publication of UNESCO, Paris, 1951.)

CHAPTER 9

SPIRITUAL LIFE

IT is logical that the priesthood has a predominant influence on a people with a religious mentality, and apparently this was the case in Peru before the Inca dynasty. A process of evolution whose phases have not been clearly revealed, and which may have taken place during certain apparently revolutionary periods, permitted the civil power to disengage itself and assume control. In the second half of the fifteenth century this social transformation was complete. The ecclesiastical hierarchy remained independent of civil control to a great extent, but both were subordinate to the supreme Inca.[1]

THE HIGH PRIEST

The high priest, usually a brother or uncle of the Inca, was elected by a gathering of high dignitaries and proclaimed to the sound of trumpets. He was invested with his pontifical robes, offered up sacrifices, and received the homage of the imperial family, the *orejones,* and the *curacas*. He made a solemn vow to live in chastity, and indeed he lived an ascetic life, eating herbs and roots, drinking water, and fasting often, though never longer than eight consecutive days, for even in this sphere excess was considered sinful.

He lived in the country, but not far from the city so that he could carry out the duties of his office, and at the same time, at night, he could 'contemplate the stars and meditate upon them.'[2]

The high priest was usually simply dressed in a woollen cassock falling to the ankles, and over it he wore a very wide cloak of grey, brown or black. His magnificent robes were only worn on feast days. Then he was clad in a surplice of white

[1] H. Trimborn: *Die Organisation der öffentlichen Gewalt in Inka-Reich,* Vienna, 1928.

[2] *Tres relaciones de antigüedades peruanas, op. cit.,* p. 157 onwards, text from the *Revista del archivo histórico del Cuzco,* 1953, no. 4, p. 362.

wool with a red fringe, falling to the knees, and trimmed with leaves of gold and with precious stones. A silver crescent hung from his neck, his arms were loaded with bracelets, and on his head was a gold tiara shaped like a hood, ornamented with a golden sun and surmounted by a diadem of parrot feathers. After the Conquest, when the Indians saw the bishops' mitres, they had no difficulty in recognizing them as high priests of the new religion. The priests who assisted the pontiff at official ceremonies were robed in white.

The religious hierarchy was composed of a series of specialized ranks. Ten priests 'played the part of bishops'; their districts were very extensive and comprised territories whose limits are unknown to us, since the chronicler sometimes calls them by the very general name of the part of the Empire to which they belonged—Collasuyu, Contisuyu—or else by the names of the people who lived there—Collas, Chinchas, Cañas—or again by the names of the big towns in their areas —Cajamarca, Quito, Huaylas, Chimu, Ayabaca.

A host of secondary priests was associated with the Sun, lightning, ancestors, *huacas,* etc.[1] They obtained their subsistence from the stocks in the public stores when they belonged to the nobility, but they tilled the soil like the rest when they belonged to the common people.

The high priest appointed all the members of the upper priesthood who, in their turn, chose the lower ranks. He also appointed the inspectors who travelled all over the Empire visiting the temples and the 'houses of the chosen women,' to make sure that everywhere the doctrines and exact practices of worship were being properly carried out. These inspectors were themselves controlled by officials who acted secretly and would not tolerate the least failure or complacency. Authority was exercised in the religious field as rigorously as in the civil administration.

The high priest was judge and arbiter in all conflicts of a religious nature; he interpreted the rules and customs of religion, and regulated the allotment of products harvested from the lands of the Sun, and gathered into store-houses as the divinity's share.

[1] P. J. de Arriaga: *Extirpación de la idolatría del Perú, op. cit.,* chap. 3.

On his death the ceremonies and popular mourning lasted for a whole day. His body was embalmed and buried with great pomp on some high place.

The power of the high priest is demonstrated several times in the drama of *Ollantay*. In spite of certain distortions probably imported into the text by the first Spaniard who undertook to set it down in writing, this dramatic work reveals the spiritual state of the Indians in pre-columbian times. The following dialogue is characteristic.[1]

GENERAL OLLANTAY (*addressing the high priest*): Old man, everyone who sees you is terror-stricken. All around you are bones, funeral flowers, horns, and precious stones. Everything about you inspires fear. But what does it matter? Has the sovereign summoned you as a prophet of evil or as a spirit of goodness? Why have you come before the feast day? Is the Emperor ill? Or have you divined that blood will soon be spilt? The day consecrated to the Sun and Moon has hardly dawned and is still far away from us. We have not yet reached the solemn moment for the sacrifices demanded by this feast.

THE HIGH PRIEST: Why do you question me so reproachfully? Am I your slave? I know all, and I shall prove it presently.

OLLANTAY: My heart faints with fear at seeing you unexpectedly today. Perhaps your coming will be fatal to me.

THE HIGH PRIEST: Fear nothing Ollantay, in spite of my presence here today. It is perhaps love which brings me to your side, as the wind carries a dry leaf. Tell me, does reason conquer your heart when it is the prey of evil spirits? I will allow you this day to choose between happiness and perdition, between life and death.

OLLANTAY: Explain your words so that I can understand them, they are like a tangled skein. You should put the threads in order for me.

THE HIGH PRIEST: Listen to me, Ollantay. Knowledge tells me what is hidden from the common man. I have the power to discover all secrets and to make a great chief of you.

(*The high priest talks of the feelings of love which Ollantay*

[1] *Literatura Inca*, in *Biblioteca de cultura peruana*, Paris, 1938, t. 1, p. 201.

has for one of the Inca's daughters, and tells him of the danger which will result.)

OLLANTAY: How can you know what is hidden in the bottom of my heart? Only the girl's mother knows of it, but I see you have discovered all.

THE HIGH PRIEST: I look at the Moon and the most obscure destiny appears clearly before me.

(*Ollantay explains that he cannot renounce his love, and ends by saying:—*)

OLLANTAY: Thrust the knife you hold in your hand into my throat, and cut out my heart; I throw myself at your feet.

A MIXTURE OF RELIGION AND MAGIC

The limits assigned by modern sociologists to religion and magic did not exist. We consider today that religion interprets an impulse of man towards the divine, that its most usual form of expression is by prayer, and that it implies a communion of the faithful.

Magic we consider to be utilitarian, having recourse to direct action, or even a sort of pressure by means of incantation, and only available to some initiated person such as a sorcerer.

But in Peru, religion and magic were intermingled, the latter appearing as the application of the former, putting it into practice, and as its natural and necessary prolongation into daily life. This confusion was favoured by the eminently utilitarian character of the Indian. But this always exists, more or less; even today there is the Christian who believes in the efficacy of a prayer address to St Anthony so as to find something which is missing.[1]

The frontiers of science were equally undefined. Magic rested, in certain cases, on observations and arguments which were the prelude to psychology, sociology, and medicine. It is a commonplace that astrology was the forerunner of astronomy.

In all classes of Peruvian society, science, religion and magic were interconnected and supreme, for nothing escaped

[1] J. Wilbois: *Prolégomènes,* in M. Brillant and R. Aigrain, *Histoire des Religions,* Paris, 1953, t. 1, p. 31.

them since nothing took place by chance, and everything had a profound though often hidden meaning—illness, accident, the formation of a cloud, or the cry of an animal by night in the *sierra*.

The smallest phenomena carried some sort of meaning, and the most deadly wilderness came alive to those who knew how to penetrate its mysteries.

We shall speak of lower categories of sorcerers in connection with the common people. Soothsayers seem to have received special consideration. They were almost always to be found at the entrances to temples ready to help the faithful. They ate herbs, roots and maize, and only ate meat on certain solemn feast days. Some specialized in oracles, others in sacrifices.

The first category interpreted everything which seemed due to chance; the rainbow, the earthquake, the flight of birds. They sought for signs, and advised on observations of stones, snakes, spiders, and llama dung. For them the whole universe was a gigantic book where the future was set out, but which the common people could not read. They questioned the *huacas,* some of whom were famous for their oracles; they lighted a fire which their assistants kept burning by blowing through copper or silver tubes, and called forth spirits who replied through the crackling and sputtering of the flames. 'They spoke to idols in a language which the profane could not understand,' wrote one of the chroniclers.[1]

The group which specialized in sacrifices did not foretell the future, they sought to remedy the consequences of past events. The evils suffered by men are the just return for their sins, as we have said in connection with the Indian mentality. It is possible to correct their effects by providing an immediate compensation, a substitute, namely, by prayer, repentance, and sacrifice.[2]

Prayer is a means to an end, a creation of a favourable atmosphere. The penitent attracts the attention of the divinity and at once makes an offering of some value, that of a humble

[1] L. de Gómara: *Historia general de las Indias, op. cit.*, p. 232.

[2] These ideas remain very vivid. Is it to compensate for the joys of marriage that, amongst the Collas, the husband leaves his wife after the wedding and travels on foot across America selling simples? Oliveira Cezar: *Leyendas de los Indios Quichuas,* Buenos Aires, 1893.

tribute. The Indian, when praying, stood upright in front of the idol, arms stretched out parallel, with hands open. He kissed the air loudly, and then the tips of his fingers; he then pulled out some of his eyelashes or eyebrows and blew them towards the god. It was his way of giving something of himself, one of his 'belongings,' as modern sociologists express it, and as a result, he made himself a servant.

CONFESSION

Penitence was imposed by the confessor, for, to the great astonishment of Catholic missionaries, confession was found to be the usual practice in Peru. It existed also amongst other American peoples, such as the Huichol of Mexico (confession by women whilst their men were away seeking the sacred plant), and also amongst some Eskimos (in a state of mystical intoxication).[1]

Confessors were appointed by the upper hierarchy after an examination designed to ensure that they were fully instructed in religious matters. The panel who presided at this test was composed of four *amautas* and one of the ten high dignitaries whom the Spaniards compared with bishops. They questioned the candidates about the gods, rites, the rules laid down by the Incas and the high priests, and about sinners and repentance.

The confessor placed himself near running water, took a bundle of dried herbs in his right hand, and in the left a string with one end knotted round a stone, or a stick with a stone embedded in a hole; he then called the penitent to him and asked him to speak. The confession was secret and any infraction of this rule was punished with immediate death. The Indians did not hide their sins for they were sure that the confessor could easily unmask them, being himself a soothsayer.

The sins were not very original, for they were the sins of all ages; murder, adultery, theft, frustration, lying, laziness, neglect of religious observances. Disobedience was the sin which presented the greatest diversity of kind, and was held to be the most culpable, as would be natural in a society built up on

[1] P. Gordon: *Les Religions des Primitifs,* in M. Brillant and R. Aigrain: *Histoire des Religions, op. cit.,* t. 1, p. 240.

constraint; disobedience to parents, ancestors, officials, military chiefs, and the Emperor.

Worship of idols was suppressed by both the Incas and the Spaniards, but their idols were not the same; public authority did not acknowledge divinities.

Alongside these sins of commission were those of intention. Penitents had to confess their unhealthy desires and feelings: hatred, desire for vengeance and to do harm, intention to rebel, love for a married woman, etc.

Serious offences could not be pardoned by ordinary confessors; they were dealt with either by priests of a higher rank (in the case of a debauch with a young girl), or by the high priest (worship of idols, attempt to rebel against the Emperor, act of sacrilege, relations with a Virgin of the Sun).

In Collao, during the reign of Tupac Yupanqui, women were permitted to confess to other women, and certain women began to take the place of soothsayers.[1]

When the penitent had enumerated his sins, the confessor talked seriously to the sinner and imposed a penalty according to the importance of his sins. It was a strict rule that a penitence must not harm the collective efforts of the community. So the 'sojourn in the desert,' the obligation to withdraw to the mountains and stay there living on herbs and roots and drinking water, could not be imposed on people of high rank, for the offices they occupied could not be filled and the community would suffer. Besides, the lesser people would notice their absence and would conclude that their leaders had committed serious offences, which would have compromised the secrecy of the confessional. This same punishment could no longer be imposed on the common people, for the decisive reason that already a great number of Indians lived in the Andes as hermits, and inevitably newcomers would have communication with them. In fact the desert was already inhabited, if one can believe an anonymous writer, thought to be the Jesuit Father, Blas Valera, and to whom several later writers refer.[2]

These hermits had to obtain the permission of their superiors; they lived in chastity and poverty; the faithful came to

[1] *Revista del archivo histórico del Cuzco,* 1953, no. 4, *op. cit.,* p. 373.
[2] *Revista del archivo histórico del Cuzco, loc. cit.,* p. 376.

consult them, to ask advice, and sometimes to learn the future.

Once the punishment had been decided the confessor carried out a symbolic ceremony. He lightly struck the sinner with the stone he held in his hand, then he told him to spit into a small bag, and then spat into it himself. He recited certain prayers and threw the bag full of the penitent's sins into the adjacent stream. At the same time he prayed to the gods to bear away this sad cargo in the waters to the abyss from which nothing returns.

The Inca and the high priest made confession, but each of them made it alone before the divinity. The Inca observed a ritual similar to that we have just described throwing his sins into the stream, but the high priest burned the bag and scattered the ashes on the water after praying in the temple.

The Inca had the power of exorcizing evil spirits—the 'demon' of the Spaniards. He did this by calling upon the spirit to show himself, which was sufficient to prevent him from doing further harm. Yamqui Pachacuti Salcamayhua left us the text of such an exorcism:—[1]

'In the name of heaven and earth, and he who lives in the depths of the seas,
Of the creator, the all-powerful, and he who sees all,
Of the lord of seething hell, whether man or woman,
Who art thou? what is thy nature? what are thy words? I beseech thee to speak.'

SACRIFICES

Sacrifices were graded according to a hierarchy of their own. Indians of all ranks frequently chastened themselves, either through some obscure feeling that expiation was necessary, or with a view to allaying the supposed anger of certain spirits whom they had disturbed by passing through their field of activity. For example, they threw away the piece of *coca* they had begun to chew without sucking out all the juice.

More important were the real offerings or gifts, such as food voluntarily destroyed, drink spilt, feathers of many colours burned. Tradition prescribed that maize should be thrown into

[1] *Poesia, música y danza inca,* in *Colección Mar Dulce,* Buenos Aires, 1943, p. 57.

the sea to appease it, and offerings of shells made to springs whose flow they desired to continue. These shells were native to Central America and were used as money in internal barter in certain regions.

When a member of their family died, some Indians undertook to return at certain times to the place of burial, bringing food and drink, and at the same time praying to the gods on their behalf.

Cristobal de Molina, of Cuzco, recorded a prayer for such an occasion: 'O Father Huacas, ancestors, kinsmen, and parents, O Great Creator, provider for our constant needs, our powerful dead lord, call upon your children and grandchildren to draw near the Creator so that your descendants may be happy with him, as you are yourself.'

A llama was often used as a sacrifice. The priest caused it to make several turns round the idol and then cut its throat, keeping its head turned towards the god. Each morning, at Cuzco, one of these animals was killed in this way, and then burned as an offering to the Sun. A brazier was set aside for this purpose. In addition, on the first day of the month, 100 llamas were thrown into the fire together with maize and *coca,* and prayers were said.

The most considerable and efficacious offering was that of living men. Here we turn a dark page of Inca history, which Garcilaso de la Vega, with loving devotion, tried in vain to erase. It is a fact that on great occasions and as an exceptional favour children or young people were put to death. The most handsome amongst them were chosen, they were fed well, and then were given *chicha* to intoxicate them, or drugged with huge doses of *coca*. Then they were led two or three times round the image, like the llamas, and immediately strangled. These human sacrifices took place when an Inca was ill or when war broke out with a powerful nation. At Pachacamac Virgins of the Sun were sacrificed.

Dr Uhle has found the remains of these young girls who met a violent death, and who were not killed as a punishment for sin, for their corpses were surrounded by familiar objects, as was customary when burying people of repute.[1]

The use of llamas prevented this horrible practice from

[1] M. Uhle: *Pachacamac,* Philadelphia, 1903, p. 86.

becoming frequent, as might have happened because of the supposed efficacy of human sacrifice.[1] The author of the anonymous account attributed to Blas Valera tells how the animal came to be substituted for humans. When the burial of an important personage was due to take place, an appeal was launched to all members of his family and to all friends of the deceased, calling upon them to proceed immediately to the great beyond. Viracocha, they were told, would reward them magnificently, and the particular god of the dead man's family would do the same. Not only would the voluntary victim be rewarded, but his children would be overwhelmed with benefits. The choice of means of death was left to those deciding to answer this tragic appeal.

After having made the offer to end his life to go and serve the dead man in the beyond, the relation or friend felt somewhat afraid and naturally rather hesitant. So a custom was gradually established whereby the voluntary victim explained the reasons why he could not give way to his burning desire to leave this life—and one may well believe that he pleaded his cause with great conviction—so the high ecclesiastical dignitaries allowed a commutation of the sacrifice by accepting llamas in place of the man. They were careful to give these animals the name of the Indian for whom they were the substitute. This human quality which was attributed to them conferred a solemn gravity on the ceremony. In this way the individual who survived satisfied the wishes of the dead man to have someone to serve him, and he himself could continue to work and produce for the good of the Empire.

The Incas have been severely censured for their human sacrifices. In their defence it may be said that these rulers found this institution already established in many places before they came to power, and that in reality they mitigated this custom. As a matter of fact these executions were of very ancient origin. We learn of the killing, not of prisoners as is the case with many primitive peoples, but of individuals chosen from amongst the best. In the region of Canta (not far from Lima) at the beginning of each year, an Indian personifying the terrible god Wa Kon came forth from a grotto in the

[1] J. D. von Tschudi: *Contributiones a la historia, op. cit.*, p. 217; E. J. Payne: *History of the New World*, Oxford, 1892, p. 548.

mountain, pursued the children and chose one of their number to be sacrificed. This dramatic chase was transformed into a ritual dance, and the blood of a llama replaced that of a human being.

An analogous custom which is carried out to this day in the province of Huarochiri, in the Casta district, confirms this evolution. A beautiful maiden was chosen each year to be sacrificed to the great god Wallalo who alone could ensure fertility. On the appointed day the inhabitants donned their robes as for a feast, grouped themselves in their *ayllus,* and made their way, singing and dancing, towards a *quebrada* on the neighbouring mountain where the god was supposed to reside. The victim passed along a track strewn with flowers, and everywhere there had to be open gaiety, even in the family from whom the girl had been chosen, for a gift brought reluctantly would not have borne fruit. The young girl hurled herself into the abyss whilst her kinsfolk shouted for joy.

Quite recently the Indians met together at this tragic place for a feast with dances and songs, and they threw a little white llama into the *quebrada.*

As a further advance, the Indians replaced a living thing with a representation in metal or wood. Figurines of human shape, in silver, gold, or wood were buried, or pieces of wood carved in human shape and clad in fine materials were burned. At Casta today, the inhabitants throw guinea-pigs, *chicha,* and *coca* into the *quebrada.*[1]

Here we may stress the difference which exists between the Incas and the Aztecs. The latter were inspired by a philosophy absolutely foreign to the Incas. They thought that man, created by the gods, became the debtor for his own existence, and could free himself either by offering his own body through suicide, or by the gift of a substitute—the blood of prisoners. The two great Aztec gods demanded blood, one by sacrifice, the other through war. This was why some of the native races allied to the Aztecs joined Cortez' troops in his march on Tenochtitlan in 1521. This is also the reason why we still find today in artistic and folk-lore presentations in Mexico this

[1] B. Cobo: *Historia del Nuevo Mundo, op. cit.,* book 13, chaps. 21–22; M. de Morua: *Historia, op. cit.,* book 13, chap. 13; C. de Molina: *Relación de los fábulas y ritos, op. cit.*; J. C. Tello and P. Miranda: *Wallalo,* in *Inca,* 1913, p. 521.

taste for death which so greatly shocks Europeans. The Inca religion in no way presents this characteristic of cruelty.[1]

Ancestors were objects of veneration almost as much as idols. Their mummified corpses, clad in their finest costumes, were present at the most important feast days. After the Conquest, the Indians continued the habit of having mummies participate in the most important events of their lives. They even brought them along when they had to appear before a judicial tribunal. 'It appears,' writes Father de Arriaga, 'that the living and the dead come to be judged together.'[2]

MANY AND VARIED TEMPLES

Religious ceremonies took place in the temples which the chroniclers called mosques and of which they have given many descriptions. These sacred buildings often presented a curious mixture of ugliness and beauty. The celebrated idol of Pachacamac was roughly carved in wood and enthroned in a dirty and noisome hovel, although the graded terraces of the temple were wonderfully situated between the mountains and the sea.[3]

All these monuments exhibited great sumptuousness. At Tomebamba painted doors were encrusted with precious stones[4]; at Vilcas the doors stood at the head of fine stone staircases with thirty or more steps[5]; at Huanca were silver vases fashioned by the craftsmen of that city who were renowned for their skill.

On the shores of Lake Titicaca, rich in legend, rose the temples of Tiahuanaco and Copacabana, both places of frequent pilgrimage. The former, built on the site of a previous Aymara capital, symbolized the ancient traditions of that

[1] This religious dualism expresses itself in history by the contrast between the two heroes Montezuma and Cuauhtemoc, the one 'feels the fascination of suicide,' the other obeys the god of battles, and, the day after the *noche triste,* offers to the idol the still-beating hearts of the Spanish prisoners. (H. Perez Martinez: *Cuauhtemoc, vie et mort de la culture aztèque,* Paris, 1952.)

[2] P. J. de Arriaga: *Extirpación de la idolatría del Perú,* op. cit., p. 8.

[3] M. Estete: *Relación, op. cit.,* p. 231.

[4] P. de Cieza de León: *Segunda Parte de la Crónica del Perú, op. cit.,* chap. 44.

[5] P. de Cieza de León: *Segunda Parte de la Crónica del Perú, op. cit.,* chap. 89.

country. The latter, built by the Incas on a peninsula inhabited by *mitimaes* made up, for the most part, of members of the imperial family, was replaced at the time of the Conquest by a church which housed a virgin famed for her miracles.[1] The Emperor tried in vain to make *coca* grow in this area, situated at a height of 12,000 feet, so as to pay honour to the gods.

On the island of Titicaca itself there was a *huaca* dating from long before Inca times. It was a crescent-shaped rock and the Indians had covered the convex part with a delicate material, and the concave part with thin sheets of gold. They had erected an altar against this and had placed before it a hollowed-out stone to hold *chicha* at times of sacrifices. Forty paces from this rock a temple was built with a number of idols in niches in the walls. Near-by the inhabitants of the island planted fruit trees and hollowed out baths for the Sun.

The Moon also had a temple on another small island near the first but smaller—the island of Koati. The two sanctuaries enjoyed the happiest relations, and the Indians, so say the chroniclers, 'spent much of their time' sailing from one to the other exchanging gifts.[2]

The worship of the gods of light was often matched by the worship of the god of darkness. Naturally this god was honoured in a dark place underground. Here was placed a sacrificial stone, and here was erected his image, the Lanzon, a tall obelisk set between the ground and the vaulted roof. Its large, stylized feline head was surrounded by snakes, and its body was slender at the base. Its appearance was terrifying. At the Chavin temple of Huantar, which seems to have been a very ancient shrine, the doorway cut at ground-level is so narrow that a normal-sized man slides with difficulty into a passage which leads to corridors in the form of a cross, and edged with blocks of stone. At the intersection of the two arms of this cross stands the Lanzon, whose base is fixed into the ground, and whose head is embedded in the slabs of stone forming the roof. It is over 12 feet high and looks like a dagger embedded in the earth, a symbol of death. The impression of mystery is startling.[3]

[1] A. Ramos Gavilan: *Historia del célebre santuario de Nuestra Señora de Copacabana, op. cit., passim.*

[2] B. Cobo: *Historia del Nuevo Mundo,* book 13, chap. 18.

[3] L. Alayza y Paz Soldan: *Mi País,* Lima, 1944, t. 3, p. 300.

THE TEMPLE OF THE SUN AT CUZCO

Let us at last enter the most sacred place in the Empire, the Temple of the Sun at Cuzco.

The main doorway, ornamented with gold and silver designs, opened into a great sanctuary, whose apse was formed by a curved wall of stones, hewn and joined with great care. The walls and gabled roof were panelled with sheets of precious metal. Above the altar, designs covered the wall which referred to the Indian conception of the cosmos.

In the centre of this kind of frescoe sparkled an oval gold plaque, the original egg, the initial spirit, which apparently became confused with the supreme being worshipped by the nobility, the creator who was neither man nor woman, who in prayers was compared with a banner or a leader, and who was called 'the Sun of the Sun.'

Legend maintains that this central spot had been occupied before by a golden sun, as commanded by Manco Capac, so as to conform with the primitive religion taught by that founder. This sun may have been replaced by the original egg during the time of Mayta Capac following a religious revolution, but this seems very doubtful, since Huascar returned to the old tradition, replacing the egg by the sun which the Spaniards saw at Cuzco. Gutierrez de Santa Clara tells us that it was round and as large as a chariot wheel, with a face surrounded by rays like those which appear on images today. It has also been compared with a disc about the thickness of a finger, flat, and without any carving. It was placed in such a position that the rays of the rising sun caught it and made it shine.

There is no need for complicated hypotheses. It was natural that an Emperor thought of placing the god of the ruling class in the centre of this cosmic apparatus, and it was also natural that another king thought that this substitution was a mistake, since the temple was sacred to the Sun and destined for popular worship, as we know. During the times of the great kings in whom we are interested, the egg had the place of honour. It was flanked by two discs, that of the Sun in gold, and that of the Moon in silver. Thus the Sun indeed appeared among the gods, but in second place. When it was put in the place of the egg it was duplicated, which must have appeared extraordinary.

Above the egg was arranged a constellation of three stars in a line, 'the three llamas,' flanked by their two shepherds whose stellar names today are Rigel and Betelgeuse. Lower down, placed symmetrically, were the five stars of the Southern Cross.

In the centre, below this design, and underneath the Southern Cross, were drawn an Indian and an Indian woman, the typical pair.

Other images, placed each side of this central concept, were symmetrical and complementary. Moving from top to bottom, under each of the discs representing the Sun and Moon, was placed a star which represented the two aspects of Venus, morning and evening. Then, still placed symmetrically, were two constellations corresponding to the two aspects of the Pleiades, one summer, one winter, the latter with a surround of clouds. The lower series of designs included on one side a star called 'the female llama' in Quechua,[1] and on the other a male llama.

Underneath was the last of the horizontal series, stretching rather farther to the sides than the rest. This was a zigzag line of lightning with a representation of the earth in the form of a circle, bearing three curvilinear triangles in the lower section; mountains and an irregular receding line; a river and four parallel lines like a bridge symbolizing a rainbow. Right at the bottom, seven little circles each with a point in the centre, represented 'the eyes of things,' for things could see in the times of the Incas. Or it may be that they were the seven eyes of the supreme God—curiously enough an analogy found in the eyes of the Lord spoken of by the prophet Zachariah in the Old Testament.

On the other side, matching the last design in an irregular line, were a lake, a little circle, a spring, a puma—an animal held responsible for hail and eclipses, when he had a fancy to devour the Sun or Moon—and lastly a tree.[2]

[1] This name is Catachillay.

[2] For a summary of this description, see L. Baudin: *La Vie de François Pizarre,* Paris, 1930, p. 69. A reproduction of this collection of drawings can be found in P. A. Means: *Ancient Civilizations of the Andes, op. cit.,* p. 394.

This picture of knowledge seems primitive but we do not know its exact interpretation. No doubt it had an esoteric significance. The description just given has only recently been drawn up.[1]

Other more impressive objects drew the attention of the visitor in the great hall of the temple of the Sun. A whole series of mute presences filled him with fear. The statues represented the Sun in its different aspects, but along the walls were the mummies of the dead Emperors. This guard of honour did not take the form of upright figures so as to look like living people. The mummies were made of very thick cloth to keep them in a vertical position without any framework to support them. They looked like huge bundles of material, and the head was represented by a skin on which had been carefully depicted a mouth, nose, eyes and ears, and which was crowned with a *lautu*. The corpse, previously embalmed, was inside, curled up on itself, and the whole thing had the appearance of one of those huge dolls, without arms or legs, with a big head, which humble parents buy cheaply in the markets.

We may think that in the temple of the Sun many of these 'mummies' were shams without any corpse in the interior—they recalled the Emperors in the same way as do statues.[2] Their majesty came from the sumptuous materials and rich ornaments, and the magnificent thrones on which they were placed. The glitter of gold, the warm colouring of feathers compensated for the poorness of the shapes, and made these mummies, real or supposed, an escort worthy of their father the Sun, a striking symbol of the survival of human beings and of the continuity of the Empire.[3]

Other shrines of less importance were found in the surroundings of the temple and they opened on to an inner courtyard. The temple of the Moon had its walls covered with

[1] R. Lehmann-Nitsche: *Coricancha, Revista del Museo de la Plata,* 1928, p. 1. This writer has established that the description given by the Indian Santa-Cruz Pachacuti Yanqui Salcamayhua, reproduced in *Tres relaciones de antiguedades peruanas, op. cit.,* refers to the designs on the altar of the temple of the Sun at Cuzco. The descriptions provided by Father B. Cobo complete this account.

[2] B. Cobo: *Historia del Nuevo Mundo, op. cit.,* t. 3, p. 325.

[3] P. A. Means: *Ancient Civilizations of the Andes, op. cit.,* p. 403. It was Pachacutec who had preserved the most ancient of these mummies. (Garcilaso de la Vega: *Comentarios reales, op. cit.,* book 3, chap. 20.)

sheets of silver. The face of this astral body was perhaps made of platinum[1]; it was surrounded by mummies of the sovereigns, richly clad and arranged in order of age.

Venus, the planet 'with long curly hair,' and the Pleiades, 'servants of the Moon,' shared the next building.

The fourth and fifth pavilions were consecrated respectively to the thunderbolt, confused with lightning and thunder under the same name (Illapa), and to the rainbow, a heavenly manifestation considered to be particularly favourable. The last building contained the 'audience hall' of the priests, the sacristy.[2]

Round the outer wall of the temple ran a frieze of gold, and in the walls which surrounded the inner courtyard were carved niches ornamented with golden llamas and encrusted with precious stones. Underground channels brought water for five fountains through pipes tipped with gold.[3]

Below the temple lay terraces which descended to the river Huatanay. Here was the golden garden which so aroused the admiration of the conquerors, and which became, for many writers, an inexhaustible source of poetry. Everything there was in gold; grass, flowers, trees, reptiles, birds, and the shepherd himself—a tribute to the Sun, for gold was his earthly emanation, the concentration of the offerings of subject races, the supreme witness of the power of the god of light. In this garden a reservoir had been dug and filled with *chicha* so that the burning and ever-thirsty Sun could quench his thirst at will.

A perimeter of stone surrounded this assembly of buildings with their flower beds, which constituted the spiritual centre of the Empire, the concrete link between men and gods.[4]

[1] R. Loredo: *El Reparto de los tesoros del Cuzco,* quoted in M. R. de Diez Canseco: *Pachacutec Inca Yupanqui, op. cit.,* p. 132.

[2] C. de Molina: *Fábulas y ritos, op. cit.*; P. J. de Arriaga, *Extirpación de la idolatría del Perú, op. cit.,* chap. 5.

[3] When the booty was shared out by Francisco Pizarro, the golden lid of one of these fountains fell to the share of Mancio Serra de Leguizamo, and not the disc from the Sun in the temple at Cuzco, as was wrongly reported. (R. de Lizárraga: *La descriptión y población de las Indias,* in *Nueva Biblioteca de autores españoles,* Madrid, 1909, book 1, chap. 63.) It was this lid which was lost by the knight whilst gambling. The famous saying, 'He loses the sun before he rises' does not rest on an exact historical fact.

[4] The church of Santo Domingo, built by the Spaniards on the walls of the temple of the Sun, was destroyed by the last earthquake in May

THE FEAST DAY OF THE SUN

To understand the importance of the worship of the Sun one had to be present at the great feast day of which the Sun was the central figure, held each year at the winter solstice. Ceremonies took place in all towns, but at Cuzco it became a national demonstration.[1]

From all parts of the Empire, at this time, there hastened to the capital the *curacas* and high officials who came to give account of affairs in their administrative area, to receive new instructions, and at the same time to do homage to the sovereign and bring him gifts.

The city presented a picture of unusual animation. The narrow alleys skirting the black walls of the palaces resounded for several days to the dull sound of llamas' hooves tapping on the small stones of the streets which could be heard above the sound of trumpets announcing the arrival of some high dignitary. The sumptuous dress which the *curacas* donned in honour of the occasion stood out against the greyness of the crowd. Some of the chiefs were preceded by servants carrying the ancient insignia of their tribe, but the greater number were followed by a veritable procession of servants loaded with pottery and cloth for the temple of the Sun and the imperial family; many of them arrived in litters and all bore their favourite weapon in their hand. There were some who came from the bitter highlands of the north, and had attached to their backs immense wings of black and white condors; others, natives of the western forests in the Caras country, proudly exhibited bare torsos streaked with red to look like rich materials. The Chancas, faithful to their war-like tradition, marched in step, dressed in puma skins, the animal's head resting on their own, and giving the spectators the impression of a procession of wild beasts. The different races were easily recognized by their head-dresses; the Cañaris with their hair

1950. It was of little artistic value. It might have been possible to make use of its disappearance to re-build the ancient temple as it had been in olden times. Unfortunately exact information is lacking amongst the chroniclers and the ruins which remain are very few. (M. Chavez Ballón: *El Templo del Sol o Quoiricancha,* in *Revista del Instituto Americano de Arte,* Cuzco, 1952, vol. 2, p. 18.)

[1] Garcilaso de la Vega: *Comentarios reales, op. cit.,* book 6, chaps. 20–23.

twisted round their heads and wearing their wooden crowns; the Chanchis with wide bands across their brows; the Antis with bird feathers stuck in their hair. A note of fantasy was always provided, traditionally, by the Yuncas from the coast, whose faces were hidden by grotesque masks and who made grand gestures and filled the air with the discordant sound of their flutes and drums, as if they had escaped from a madhouse. So the crowd of those who were not invited to the ceremonies had at least the satisfaction of watching the preparations.

The celebrations started with a rigorous three-day fast, during which time it was forbidden to light a fire or to have intercourse with a woman. Everyone was waiting and everyone withdrew into himself. Only the Indian women in the 'houses of the chosen women' were busy, for they were entrusted with the preparation of maize bread and special drinks which were to be much used during the following days.

On the day fixed by the astronomers the supreme Inca made his way to the central square before dawn. There he found assembled the imperial *ayllus*. In another near-by square were grouped the *curacas*. All, in absolute silence, took off their sandals and turned towards the east, motionless, watching the horizon. At the moment when the first light of dawn gilded the crests of the Corderilla, they crouched down and stretched out their arms in a gesture of supplication, kissing the first ray. Then the monarch took in each hand a cup filled with the sacred drink, and standing upright facing the rising sun, he raised his right arm above his head and offered drink to his father the Sun.

The Emperor next poured the contents of the cup into a small channel which guided the liquid towards the temple. He himself took a mouthful from the other cup which he held in his left hand, and divided the rest amongst the cups held out to him by the members of his court, and invited everyone to drink.

The members of the imperial *ayllus* went into the temple of the Sun. The *curacas* followed as far as the doors and remained outside. The supreme Inca then offered to the Sun the two cups with which he had been served, and the others present gave up theirs. Priests advanced to the threshold of the building to receive the vessels from which the *curacas* had drunk, and at the same time took the presents they had brought.

The sacrifices began with the killing of a black llama, considered to be more perfect than any other, for its whole body was the same colour, whilst a white llama had a black muzzle. The beast was not roped, but two or three Indians held it and turned its head towards the east. The executioner laid open the body with one blow from a knife and cut out the heart and lungs which he handed to a soothsayer. He examined them and pronounced his verdict; if he declared the Sun was satisfied, the ceremony continued, but if not, a second and then a third llama was killed in the same way. But they stopped at this number, and when the god obstinately remained in a contrary temper, a great sadness reigned in the city. The future appeared threatening.

Many other animals were put to death by simply beheading them, and their blood and hearts were offered to the god. When human sacrifices were offered up, we have already described how the priests organized this horrible ceremony. The meat from the llamas was cooked in public in the two squares and distributed to those present.

When the religious ceremonies were ended, the Inca invited everyone to drink, beginning with the captains who had distinguished themselves in battle by brilliant feats of arms, and then he addressed himself to the *curacas* from the neighbourhood of Cuzco. This invitation was given on behalf of the Sun; he held two identical cups in his hands and offered one or other of them; that in his right hand if his guest was of equal or superior rank to the person giving the invitation, otherwise offering the one in his left. In this way the Inca offered the Sun the cup held in his right hand, and the one in his left to everyone else. He who received the sacred beverage raised his eyes to heaven, drank and returned the cup to the giver without saying a word, but embracing the air and making signs of worship with the hands.

Members of the Inca's suite proceeded in the same way as their sovereign in dealing with the partakers of lesser degree. After the invitation to drink had been made by those of high degree to the lesser ranks, they returned the invitation. Thus the ceremony was repeated in reverse, a perfect application of the principle of reciprocity—each one paid honour to the one who had honoured him.

The supreme Inca could never really drink the contents of all the cups presented to him without running the risk of reaching a state of intoxication unbecoming to a monarch, so he contented himself with sometimes tasting the liquid with his lips, or sometimes swallowing a mouthful, according to his desire to display favour towards a high official from whom he had received homage.

The cups from which the Inca had drunk or had touched with his lips were kept by those present as sacred objects. No-one else used them and each family arranged them among their household gods as precious objects.

Finally dances, songs, banquets and drinking parties went on for nine days, and then the high officials returned to their provinces proclaiming the glory of the Inca, the beloved child of the Sun.[1]

[1] The feast of the Sun was legally re-established in Peru in 1930 and took the name of the Indian feast. Everywhere in these countries today there may be found ancient rites in Catholic form. Some writers go as far as to speak of a 'composite religion.'

CHAPTER 10

INTELLECTUAL AND ARTISTIC LIFE

THIS chapter might well have been included in the preceding one because of the close connection between knowledge and religion. It has been detached from it for clarity without trying to hide its nature; all manifestations of the mind are at first orientated towards the divine.

THE COMMONPLACE LEVEL OF THEIR ASTRONOMY

Astronomy, which seems to have been of a lower order than that of the Aztecs or Mayas, did not succeed in freeing itself from myths. We do not know if certain initiates had extensive knowledge in this field, we only know that, in practice, observations made on the height of the sun in the sky permitted them to fix the seasons, and so to organize work in the fields. Pillars were erected for this purpose in several towns. Below the equator, they gave no shadow at midday on the days of the equinox, so Quito, situated on this line, was regarded as a holy city.[1]

It is not even certain that those pillars in existence today were used for this purpose, for several may have been used as pedestals for the idols which the missionaries destroyed after the conquest.[2]

What we need to discover is whether the theories of the Mayas were known, at least on the Pacific coast. The legends we have discussed about men coming from the west, and the existence of Peruvian trade rafts sailing along the American coast north of the Gulf of Guayaquil, allow us to suppose that certain discoveries made about astronomy in Central America may have been known, at least in part, in the great

[1] J. H. Howland Rowe: *Inca Culture at the time of the Spanish conquest, op. cit.*, p. 323. These pillars or pedestals are called *intihuatana.*
[2] L. Alayza y Paz Soldan: *Mi País, op. cit.*, t. 3, p. 301.

river centres on the ocean. On a vase at Pachacamac an expert found a design of the body of a feline, and bars and points which in Yucatan had a numerical significance—the bar was worth five and the point one.

A stone axe in the national museum at Lima bears superficial holes which had formerly been used to hold encrustations of shells or coloured stones. Their number appears to refer to astronomical markings on the basis of the Tzolkin calculus (a period of 260 days according to the Mayas).

A ceramic from Nazca, found in 1908, displays several calendars according to F. Buck. It bears an inscription corresponding to twenty Tzolkin years in the systems of Mercury, the Moon, eclipses, Venus, Saturn, the ritual year, and the so-called tropical year. Other ceramics bearing similar inscriptions have been studied.[1]

MEASURES, PLANS AND MAPS

Measuring units, without which there could be no theory or practice of knowledge, were based, as is natural, on the different parts of the human body. They extended from the *yuka,* the distance between the tips of the thumb and the index finger, to the *rikra,* the average height of a man on the plateau, about 3 feet 8 inches. The chroniclers also speak, for measuring distances, of the Indian league, which according to them was equal to 6,000 paces.[2]

Geographical knowledge was put into practical form by means of maps and models of plans in relief. One of these was set up by Pachacutec before rebuilding Cuzco. It is thought that the Sayhuite stone, near Abancay, represents a geographical map, for it is carved on rock with lines or figures. The former indicate rivers, and it has been possible to make out five parallel watercourses which flow into the Apurimac; the figures show the regional characteristics—monkeys, the zone of the eastern forests; llamas, the plateau;

[1] F. Buck: *Inscripciones calendarias del Perú,* in *Revista del Museo Nacional de Lima,* 1930, no. 1, p. 139.

[2] The figure of just over 3 feet given by H. Rowe is a little higher than that resulting from present-day investigations: G. de Crequi-Montfort and E. Senechal de la Grange: *Anthropologie bolivienne,* Paris, 1907, vol. 2, p. 349; G. Rouma: *Quitchuas et Aymaras,* Brussels, 1933, p. 175. For distances: M. de Morua: *Historia, op. cit.,* book 3, chaps. 24 and 29.

and condors the mountain regions. There are many other representations, such as the discs of the Sun and Moon, Indians on guard, pumas, snakes and toads. Relics of this kind, known to exist in Peru today, are of such rarity that this stone has been classed as unique. Experts perceive in the designs Colla and Chanca influence, and do their utmost to fix the site of these countries amongst those represented on the stone, but except for certain hypothetical rivers and the well-known Lake Titicaca, considered as sacred from prehistoric times, the mystery remains unsolved.[1]

THE DEVELOPMENT OF MEDICINE

The only branches of knowledge which seem to have shown a certain amount of evolution are medicine and surgery.

Medicine consisted of empirical processes and magic practices. The healers belonged to a category of human beings distinguished by some unimpeachable sign, some physical anomaly or infirmity, or unusual fact of their existence—such as a man blind from birth or struck by lightning[2]—or else they belonged to a tribe whose members knew the curative properties of plants and jealously passed on their secrets from father to son.[3] The best known of these tribes was that of the Collahuaynas to the north-east of Lake Titicaca, who were obliged to provide doctors for the Inca's court, and whose descendants today wander throughout South America selling simples in towns and villages.

Certain common illnesses in the old world were unknown in America, such as scarlet fever and measles; on the other hand two maladies in particular ravaged the people—*verruga* and *uta*.

The symptoms of *verruga* are the appearance of warts, fever and sometimes hæmorrhages. It attacks men and animals and is well-known amongst the native inhabitants of villages situated at a medium altitude, between 3000 and 9000 feet,

[1] A. Miro Quesada: *Costa, sierra y montaña, op. cit.*, p. 415.

[2] This is the case today in the region of Urcos: Review *Tradición*, Cuzco, January 1951, p. 156.

[3] For a review of this question as a whole, the reader should consult the three volume work of H. Valizan and A. Maldonado: *La Medicina popular peruana*, Lima, 1922, and R. d'Harcourt: *La Médecine dans l'ancien Pérou*, Paris, 1939.

in the western Corderilla, and especially in the Rimac river valley and along the length of the Oroya railway.

Uta is a kind of leprosy which attacks the face and prevents the washing of the affected parts, especially the nose and lips. These mutilations were reproduced on pottery by realistic Chimu artists, and were often wrongly attributed to the harshness of punishments inflicted by tyrannical chiefs of the riverside states of the Pacific.

The existence of syphilis has been questioned since the chroniclers do not speak of it, but there is really no doubt about it, because bone lesions of syphilitic origin have been revealed by examination of various skulls.

Remedies were of three kinds, more or less related to one another. First, curative treatment which we would ordinarily class as normal, given by the healers; secondly expiation by means of prayers and sacrifices under the direction of the priests; and thirdly the expulsion of spirits with the aid of sorcerers.

There were remedies for all diseases; dieting, purging, massage, plasters and bleeding with a lancet constituted the usual therapeutic treatment. On the coast a clyster was used in the form of a liquid-filled tube, into which the doctor blew.[1]

Treatment by herbal medicines was by far the most important. Of course *coca* came at the head of the list.[2] This shrub, a native of the unhealthy tropical lands, reaches a height of over three feet and lives for about forty years. It gives three harvests of leaves each year and these are dried by careful and progressive exposure to the rays of the sun, in such a way that they do not become powdery and break up. To make it edible, some alkaline material must be added, usually ashes of *quinua*. It is administered in the form of a small pellet which must be chewed. It is a powerful stimulant but liable to be abused. Taken in moderation *coca* enables an Indian to show a surprising resistance to fatigue, but taken in excess it leads to stupidity and laziness.

The Spaniards immediately recognized the virtues of this plant, and Garcilaso describes a conversation between two of

[1] L. R. Velez López: *El Clister en el antiguo Perú,* 23rd session of the International Congress of specialists on America, New York, 1928, p. 296.

[2] W. Golden Mortimer: *Perú, History of coca, the divine plant of the Incas,* New York, 1901.

5. The quipu official

(*left*) Huascar is taken prisoner by his brother's soldiers. From the drawings of the Peruvian native Huaman Poma

6. The Inc
king offers t
sacred drink
the Sun

(*below left*
One of the
three sons o
Yahuar
Huacac

(*below right*
Peruvian
builders

From the
drawings o
Huaman
Poma

his fellow-countrymen, one on horseback and the other on foot. The horseman sees native superstition in the habit of chewing *coca,* but the other replies that, since he is unpaid, there is no incentive for carrying out his work properly.

According to the Indians, *coca* cures sickness and hæmorrhages; when infused it puts a stop to diarrhœa and colic, and its juice dries up ulcers. The frequency of ulcers caused the healers to use a variety of treatments. Usually they applied earth rich in sulphate of iron (*collpa*), or else a mixture of either Peruvian balm and resin, or else of fat and some bituminous substance. For syphilitic ulcers they had recourse to sarsaparilla from the shores of the Gulf of Guayaquil.

Purgatives were numerous and gentle in their action. They used the root of *huachanca,* a concoction made from maize husks, and a solution of *molle,* the pink fruit of the false pepper, taken in an alcoholic drink. The sap of this same tree, *molle,* was unrivalled for healing wounds, for which the sap of the *quinaquina* was equally often used, and also Peruvian balm with its green leaves like maize, and the blue-green of *copaquira.* For fever, yellow-flowered chicory, *chinchona* bark, the sap of the *tuna* (cactus) were recommended, but often the simple remedy of contact with a frog was sufficient.

Even today all sorts of leaves fulfil simple requirements. *Quinua* leaves heal swellings of the throat, *yuca* leaves boiled in salted water and applied to the painful part allay rheumatic pains, *apichu* leaves mixed with grease destroy those horrible little insects known as ticks, so clever at penetrating the skin of the feet and laying their eggs there.

Oca juice allayed inflammation of the kidneys and bladder, a concoction of grated *quinaquina* wood was used to treat congestion of the liver and the spleen, and the seed of the same tree placed in a brazier threw off vapour capable of curing migraine. The herb *chillca* was unequalled for soothing pains in the joints and *matecclu* was used to treat affections of the eyes. Small quantities of tobacco taken each morning, fasting, in very hot water cured retention of urine, the fruits of the *gandur,* powdered and mixed with saltpetre, acted on stone in the liver, and an infusion of *datura* calmed the nerves and induced sleep, although taken in large doses it could be a poison.

The use of minerals in the times of the Incas was less usual than the use of herbs. Certain soils had medicinal properties; edible clay (*pasa* or *chacco*) was used to ease the pains of gout; pulverized jasper stopped hæmorrhages, and *coravari,* also powdered, was good for the eyes. Neither gold nor silver figured amongst their remedies.[1]

Some animals were used in the Indian dispensing of medicines. The flesh of the humming-bird was used for epilepsy, the newly-killed flesh of the vicuña for eye troubles, broth made from a young condor for madness, and *chuquichuqui* insects cooked in gruel for warts.

Man himself made his own contribution, and especially great use was made of urine. Every provident mother of a family kept a supply of this ammoniacal and nauseating liquid. It was used as an embrocation for migraines, as a remedy for dental or throat troubles, and for washing feverish babies. Tiny children with colic were treated by rubbing with the mother's saliva. For pneumonia they had recourse to mother's milk; for bites they used excrement: for poisoning they used burnt hair taken with an alcoholic liquid. A great number of medicines were always close at hand.

THE PLACE OF MAGIC IN MEDICINE

All this medication was not sufficient by itself; it was regarded as a complement to magical formulæ. In the eyes of the Indians the material and spiritual were always confused; sin allowed access to evil spirits who roamed everywhere seeking opportunities of doing harm and spreading disease.

First of all the patient and his family offered themselves per contra, that is to say as an offering or sacrifice, and if this proved ineffective they called in a sorcerer.

The sorcerer had first to identify the illness by divination or by directly questioning such gods as were disposed to listen to him. Then he called forth the friendly spirits and proceeded to transfer the evil either to an inanimate object or to a living being. This delicate operation was carried out in the following manner. The skin in the area where the pain was felt was

[1] B. Cobo: *Historia del Nuevo Mundo, op. cit.*, book 5, chap. 17; C. W. Mead: *Old Civilizations of Inca-Land,* New York, 1932, p. 107.

rubbed with a piece of clothing worn by the sick person, or preferably with a guinea-pig, and immediately the one or the other was destroyed and thrown away, since it was supposed to have caught the disease.[1] Sometimes the healer himself sucked the painful part, as is depicted in the manuscript of Poma de Ayala.[2] Logically he should then fall ill himself, but he had the advantage of being able to use remedies, such as meat and alcoholic drinks, which the patient was incapable of taking, and which were provided in abundance.[3]

The problem became more complex when the Inca became ill. He was the living representation and symbol of his people, and the guilt which was responsible for the illness from which he was suffering took on a collective character. Confessions, fast, offerings, and sacrifices were increased amongst all classes of the population.

THE BATTLE AGAINST DISEASE

Each year a special feast of purification called *Situa* took place at Cuzco.[4] The infirm and sick, and strangers to the city, were told to leave and were not allowed to return until after the end of the ceremonies. All inhabitants who were fit and well observed a rigid fast for one day, taking only a small quantity of raw maize and water.[5] Then they kneaded and baked a special maize bread into which they put a few drops of blood, obtained by pricking the forehead of a child of between five and ten years between the eyebrows above the nose. These

[1] This operation, which still exists today, is described by M. Kuczynski-Godard: *Estudios medico-sociales en minas de Puno,* Lima, 1945.

[2] Poma de Ayala: *Nueva Corónica, op. cit.,* p. 279.

[3] The degenerate descendants of the Collahuayas sometimes descend to crude devices. They fill their mouths with small objects representing snakes, toads, or spiders, and spit them out after sucking them to prove to those present that they have inhaled the illness. In other cases they resort to frenzied movements to indicate the presence in their body of the demon snatched from the patient. (G. A. Otero: *La Piedra mágica,* Mexico, 1951, p. 208.) For an historical example of magic and of healing by the transfer of the evil of which Pascal would have been the object, see the study by Dr Mouezy-Eon in *Revue métapsychique,* November 1953, p. 21.

[4] Garcilaso de la Vega: *Comentarios reales, op. cit.,* book 7, chap. 6; J. de Acosta: *Historia natural y moral de las Indias,* Madrid, 1792, book 5, chap. 28.

[5] There was another form of fasting, less severe, which allowed cooked maize, raw herbs, pepper, salt, and *chicha,* but only once a day.

preparations were made by each family in the house of the eldest brother. The same night, shortly before dawn, every one washed and rubbed themselves with a piece of this bread 'to take away illness,' and the head of the family smeared the threshold of the door with this same bread.

Identical ceremonies took place in the temples of the Sun, in the imperial palaces, and in the 'houses of the chosen women.'

At sunrise, the people of Cuzco, purified but hungry, ate ordinary maize bread which they had also prepared, and said prayers. Then a member of the Emperor's family, richly clad, came forth from the fortress of Sacsahuaman. He held a lance whose upper end was adorned with a strip made of multicoloured feathers, like a ribbon, which streamed down the lance and was fastened to it by golden rings. He was a messenger of war and for that reason set out from a fortified place and not from a palace or a temple. Running down from the fortress, he reached the central square where four members of the imperial *ayllu* awaited him. He struck their four weapons with his own and called on those who held them to hunt out disease. These four men set out, running, each by a different route leading north, south, east, and west, that is to the regions comprising 'the Empire of the Four Directions.' As they passed, the inhabitants came out from their houses, uttering loud cries and shaking out their clothes, 'as one shakes out dust,' and rubbing their heads, limbs, and other parts of their bodies vigorously, as one does in washing. In this way the evil germs they were carrying were taken from them and thrown into the alleys in front of the hunter, who chased them away with his lance.

At a given distance from the city, each of these strange combatants met an Indian who was waiting for him, but who only held office in the Inca hierarchy by privilege. He took the lance and continued this relay race which only came to an end far enough away to make it impossible for disease to return. Then all the inhabitants of Cuzco came out from the capital, singing and dancing. Each *ayllu* advanced in a given direction until they reached a river, into which the last of the germs was thrown.

The following night the people of Cuzco armed themselves

with round torches made of straw and woven like a basket. These brands had the great advantage of burning very slowly. The nocturnal hunting of disease was made with these crackling and smoky weapons whose remains were finally thrown into streams.

There remained nothing further to be done but to offer sacrifices and give oneself up to rejoicings in which *chicha* played a large part, and so celebrate in a fitting manner the triumph of public health.

THE GREAT SKILL OF THE SURGEONS

The branch of surgery which seems to have been most practised in Peru was trepanning. Skulls found in tombs often bear certain marks, which is not surprising, for they were often split by blows from axes during battle.

The practitioners of this operation made use of a cutting knife in the form of a T, with the vertical stroke representing the handle and with the upper horizontal stroke concave. They removed a section of the brain-pan either by cutting four narrow grooves which crossed each other to form a small rectangular surface, or by piercing a series of holes in a curve until the ends met and then cutting the bone between the holes. They were extremely skilful, and some skulls found by archeologists had been trepanned five times at different dates, and the last scar was the only one showing any sign of infection.[1]

Surgeons also conducted amputations, as several ceramics bear witness. Some of their methods were very strange, such as that of living sealings for wounds. To join the edges of a wound the operator applied ants which gripped both sides at once, and then cut off their heads, leaving their jaws locked together.

During operations the patient was drugged with cocaine, which was extracted from *coca* by bringing it into contact with a powerful alkali called *llipta,* prepared from the ashes of *quinua,* or, on the coast, from lime.[2] An ancient piece of pottery shows a warrior holding a ball of *coca* in his mouth.

[1] R. d'Harcourt: *La Médecine dans l'ancien Pérou, op. cit.,* p. 142.
[2] L. N. Saenz: *La Coca,* Lima, 1938, p. 14.

THE PROBLEM OF CRANIAL DEFORMITIES

The head was not only the object of surgical practice. Æsthetics, which occupied a prominent place in the Indians' preoccupations, inspired the idea of deforming the skulls of new-born children by squeezing them between planks of wood so as to make them more beautiful and more adaptable to the traditional coiffure of the region. A sense of beauty and desire for uniformity were thus equally served. This custom was not peculiar to the Indians of the Andean tableland; it was of ancient origin, common in South America, but it agreed well with the standards of a civilization which stopped at nothing in its desire to impose on the individùal, from birth, the ineffaceable mark of collectivity. It is even possible that the *amautas* of higher intelligence wished to proceed farther along this road, and that they attempted, by this process, to compress certain cerebral convolutions so as to create individuals of a specified mentality. An Indian chronicler asserts that the Inca used this procedure to make his subjects obedient.[1] This would be the logical outcome of a policy of rationalization, the manufacture of slaves.

Six different types of deformity have been distinguished; some heads were flattened like those of snakes, others took the shape of a sugar-loaf, several were lengthened or widened. This practice was still prevalent in the sixteenth century in the region of Lake Titicaca.[2]

ARCHITECTURAL BEAUTY

The Indian's sense of beauty was magnificently expressed in architecture, as we have already had occasion to point out in connection with a number of buildings. The perfection of the

[1] Santa Cruz Pachacuti Yanqui Salcamayhua, in *Tres Relaciones de antigüedades peruanas, op. cit.*, p. 253. The Museum de la Plata, in the Republic of Argentina (today Cuidad Eva Peron), contains an impressive collection of deformed skulls. See *Revista del Museo de la Plata,* especially an article by Lehmann-Nitsche, on three skulls, one trepanned, one lesioned, one perforated.

[2] M. Helmer: *La Vie économique au 16e siecle sur le haut plateau andin, op. cit.*, p. 129. On these deformations one may also consult the works of J. Imbelloni in the *Anales del Museo Argentino de Ciencias Naturales,* t. 40, 1942, p. 253, Buenos Aires; also the *Anales del Museo Nacional de Historia Natural,* t. 37, 1933, p. 209, and also the article by R. Latcham in the first of these reviews, t. 39, p. 105.

results offers a startling contrast with the simplicity of the technique. What mastery the Indian showed when he split stone at the desired breaking point by means of alternate applications of boiling and icy water! What skill was required to shape rock with enormous hæmatite hammers, and what patience to split it by turning between the fingers a piece of wood with the point plastered with sand and water! What discipline there must have been amongst the workmen who succeeded in putting cyclopean blocks into place without machinery, draught animals, or even the aid of a wheel, dragging them by means of ropes attached to the roughness of the stone, and then pushing them on rollers up earth ramps so as to raise them one upon another!

The problem still remains as to how porphyry slabs were transported from Ollantaytambo when the quarry was the other side of the river. Some of these rocks were left on the way, abandoned, and in Quechua they bear the pleasant name of 'tired stones.'

Experts also wonder how they were able to true up the stones, whose remarkable precision we have already described, without having prepared at the start a series of working drawings.[1]

It is true that one does not find in these huge edifices the flexibility, variety and imagination which come from the use of wood in stone buildings. Inca architecture was composed of compact surfaces and vigorous carvings; 'it was earth crystallized and put into geometrical form'[2]; it was well suited to the spirit of the nobility, which was rational and uniform, enamoured of power and stability.

Of course there were certain differences between the monuments. Ancient houses at Cuzco were circular, with an oval patio for each group of two or three houses; these disappeared when the Inca Pachacutec rebuilt the city.

In the new city the walls were of several kinds. In the cellular type, blocks of carbonate of lime, irregular in shape, had their front surface bowed, their angles and sides trued

[1] The experts are full of praises in connection with this subject. 'Admirable science,' writes Fergusson, 'a perfection which the Greeks and Romans, the engineers of the Middle Ages never attained.' (*Handbook of Architecture*, London, 1865–1867, t. 2, p. 775.)

[2] H. Velarde: *Arquitectura peruana, op. cit.*, p. 56.

up; in the type called 'rounded,' rectangular stones projected with their front wall alone bowed, the other faces were smooth; a third type showed rectangular shapes of Andean stone with all their faces perfectly flat and polished, as in the temple of the Sun. And there were polygonal stones of diorite which joined at many different angles yet coincided perfectly with each other. These types cannot be classified chronologically; they were used according to the importance of any particular structure, and for this reason the same wall could have 'cellular' foundations and a superstructure of rectangular stones.[1]

Certain characteristics could be seen everywhere. Trapezoid doorways with a monolith as lintel, a regular series of niches sometimes slightly leaning inwards, walls which were larger at the base than at the top so as to be more solid in a land often subject to earthquakes.

In describing Cuzco, we have given an idea of what one may rather pretentiously call the urbanism of the Incas. But their technicians adapted themselves to the situations which presented themselves on the different sites. They avoided building on land that could be cultivated because they knew it to be valuable. They canalized water-courses as they had done in the case of the capital city. A few miles from Cajamarca they installed a bathing pool fed by two channels, one bringing cold water, the other bringing natural hot water. The Emperor bathed here when he was in the district, and it was in this building, erected near some thermal springs, that the companions of Francisco Pizarro found Atahualpa.[2]

Provincial towns were not so regular in their features, for those which had been built or rebuilt during the reign of Pachacutec and his successors, and which had been built spontaneously, had escaped uniformity. But all had temples, public store-houses and often palaces and fortresses. Some succeeded in imitating the capital to some degree. An example of this was Coyor, a curious conglomeration entirely perched on a round granite base whose centre was marked by a mauso-

[1] O. Nuñez del Prado: *Diferencias de paramentos inca en el Cuzco,* in *Tradición,* September 1951, p. 4.

[2] Baths still exist in this historic place, with its ancient thermal springs. (A. Miro Quesada: *Costa, sierra y montaña, op. cit.,* p. 173.)

leum, and Chuquilin, its neighbour—both were divided into four quarters.[1]

THE WONDERS OF INDIAN ART

The perfect taste of the Indians was demonstrated even more in their artistic expression than in their monuments. This came about because of the custom of making gifts to the Inca on festive occasions, and also because the Emperor, in his turn, distributed rewards to those whom he wished to recompense. Whole books set out in detail the fine treasures found in tombs and now shown in museums.

What a wonderful arrangement of form, design and colour the people who received these gifts from the different provinces of the Empire were able to enjoy! We can have no idea of this, since the pieces which appear in museums are, of necessity, grouped according to their origin and not arranged so as to form a whole.

CHIMU POTTERY

Chimu produced high-warp tapestries with geometric patterns, and pottery in two colours, white and red-ochre, with tubular necks in the shape of an arch and a short, straight pipe in the middle, through which the liquid was poured either in or out. The prodigious imagination of the inhabitants of this mysterious realm was given free rein in their clay modelling; sometimes a face with regular features and haughty expression recalled that of a Roman Emperor with a braid across his brow; or it might be a negroid face with a broken nose and thick lips, disturbing, hostile; or the face of an Indian, smiling and enigmatic. A series of vessels shaped like human busts shows blind men with a startling realism which hides none of their blemishes—a growth on the nose, a sore on the lips. Artists provide abundant information on the scars left by illness, or perhaps sometimes on the punishments inflicted on their subjects by ruthless chiefs—all kinds of mutilations are faithfully reproduced.

Often animals were used as models. The neck of an

[1] C. Wiener: *Pérou et Bolivie,* Paris, 1880, p. 132.

ingenious receptacle was fashioned in such a way that the snake which it represents whistles when the contents are poured out, and another piece of pottery shaped like a gazelle bubbles as the liquid pours forth. Whole scenes are carved with precision; a healer is in the act of palpating a woman's stomach as she lies stretched flat; a chief with an enormous head dispenses justice to a tiny subject. Small houses have their inhabitants standing at the doorway; two women with deformed skulls carry a third person in a litter; round the inner surface of a dish a path winds its way amid pumas, ending at a miniature temple. Besides these there is an endless series of pots shaped like fruits, or animals with human shapes.

These potteries, fabrics and sculptures are precious evidence. Ideas, facts, beliefs, and details of daily life—the artist is inspired by all that he felt, thought, saw and did. Sometimes realistic, sometimes idealistic, sometimes with a crudity of expression bordering on cynicism, sometimes so exotic that we cannot understand it, their art is shocking, inspiring of enthusiasm, but never of indifference.

Plainly one cannot enquire of the Peruvian artist to what civilization he belonged, nor expect a knowledge of perspective, nor a sense of proportion. He filled the space at his disposal by modifying when necessary the shapes of the objects he reproduced; one might say he had a horror of empty spaces. He loved and understood decoration.

According to the region he worked in he took pleasure in realism, reminding us of modern works of art, and bringing a genuine document to the student of the past. He either remains primitive and simple, recalling infant efforts in the kindergarten, or he becomes geometric through stylization and is engulfed by symbolism.

All the flora and fauna, all the outlines, straight or curved, pass before our eyes. The admirations and fears of the Indians are inscribed on fabric or on clay; in the forest the jaguar and snake reign supreme, on the coast the millipede, grampus and shark, and in the intermediate zone, the condor, the falcon and the puma.

In Chimu art the finest scenes are not carved, they are drawn. They recall the annals of the court, the fortunes of war, work in the fields, trade, fishing, hunting. Messengers run, their heads curiously ornamented with top-hats, discs or plumes, with birds symbolizing speed. Warriors in full array battle with wild animals of colossal proportions who seem to be bearing them away. A chief seated under a canopy receives guests; four rows of dishes are placed between them, loaded with food, and these advance on their own small limbs. Farther away wine-vessels, also provided with limbs, bend over the cups to pour out their precious liquid, just like birds leaning over to drink.[1]

We have described the pottery because it was most universally used for these designs, but gourds were also prettily ornamented by craftsmen. These experts continued to exercise their art under Inca domination and did not allow themselves to be influenced by the geometric rule of the Empire.[2]

THE STRANGE FABRICS OF PARACAS

On the Peruvian coast, but farther to the south, Paracas was for textiles what Chimu was for pottery, an inexhaustible source of beauty, but full of mystery for us today.

On cotton fabrics, in bright and varied colours, men with many-sided heads are symmetrically arranged, pumas with human heads and with snakes for paws, stylized birds, and innumerable mythical beings, flowing and over-elaborate. Everywhere eyes are watching and hands are ready to grip.

Generally the same design is reproduced, identical in itself but following a certain rhythm of distribution. Sometimes the human or feline faces look alternately to right and left, or else the alternation is composed of two vertical lines turned right and then left. In the same lines it sometimes happens that the heads are alternately facing frontwards and backwards. Different colours are used for each pattern and they also change according to a sometimes complicated plan. For example, the design of the first horizontal line is woven in colours corresponding to four combinations, that of the second line is placed zigzag and takes up the same colour combinations, starting from the one which came at the end of the

[1] R. Larco Hoyle: *Los Mochicas, op. cit.*, t. 2, p. 147; J. Tello: *Arte antiguo peruano*, in *Inca*, vol. 2, 1938.

[2] F. Romero: *Papiros circulares del Perú*, in *Revista nacional de cultura*, Caracas, January 1954, p. 40.

preceding line, in this way obtaining the distribution set out below.

1 2 3 4 1 2 3 4 1 2 3 4 1
2 3 4 1 2 3 4 1 2 3 4 1 2 3
4 1 2 3 4 1 2 3 4 1 2 3 4
1 2 3 4 1 2 3 4 1 2 3 4 1 2
3 4 1 2 3 4 1 2 3 4 1 2 3

The artist chose complementary colours so as to produce a harmonious impression, especially for the background and the fringe; when one is red-ochre the other is mineral green; when the first is golden ochre, the second is violet.[1]

THE CRAFTSMEN OF ICA AND NAZCA

In valleys not far from Paracas, the inhabitants of the towns of Ica and Nazca produced fabrics and pottery of especially high quality. At Ica they were content with three colours and liked to draw simple, restful geometrical designs. At Nazca, on the contrary, they used eleven different colours, and although able to paint very ornamental Greek patterns on their double-necked bottles or their wide-necked vases, they preferred mythological designs often meaningless to us. Each of their figures poses a problem, becomes a pleasant guessing-game, and leaves us finally in the dark. The puma with its ferocious expression and bristling moustaches, and its huge, hanging tongue, holding seed in its paws or brandishing severed paws, certainly inspires fear, but what can we make of this being with several interlaced heads, this human head on a fish's body which has a tail divided into snakes, of this quadruped with a cat's head, a bird's body and fish's tail, holding between its paws a mutilated head which stares fixedly at us with wide-open eyes?

The eye—this is what strikes us most. It is the symbol of an all-seeing god and that is why the artist, like Picasso, but doubtless not for the same reason, places it not always where nature has placed it, but on the most significant part of the body, in particular on the abdomen, the seat of fertility. This eye, stylized in the extreme, ends by being alone, or almost

[1] R. Carrión Cachot: *La Indumentaria en la antigua cultura de Paracas,* in the review *Wira-Cocha,* t. 1, 1931, no. 1.

so, surrounded sometimes by lines radiating outwards, and it follows us around on all the native objects of the Nazca people, as the eye of God pursued Cain.[1]

POTTERY AND FABRICS FROM OTHER REGIONS

Many other centres of manufacture had their own originality. Recuay sent to Cuzco its typical pottery of white clay ornamented with scenes in high-relief; Chancay sent its crocks with the neck fashioned like a human or animal face, or adorned with irregular black paintings. Far to the north, the Caras of the realm of Quito, subdued and submissive, specialized in working gold objects such as pins with large heads, breastplates, and ornaments for their *estólicas*.[2]

In the region of Lake Titicaca they modelled simple receptacles in the style called Tiahuanaco today—cylindrical, with a wide neck often adorned with a ribbon carved in relief; above all they used geometrical designs, coloured orange-yellow, reddish-orange, maroon, greyish-maroon, and white; sometimes they inscribed representations of anthropomorphic or zoomorphic divinities, but not scenic reproductions.

Much more beautiful were the Calchaqui urns from the north-west of the present-day Republic of Argentina, charmingly decorated. On their inner surface, as in certain bas-reliefs, there sometimes appeared faces of gods called weeping gods, because tiny lines drawn under the eyes gave the impression of tears—a strange and improbable interpretation.[3] The Cuzco artists also had their own style. They excelled in modelling *aryballas*, vases with a high neck, rounded body and conical base, which could be lifted up by two handles placed on the lower part. Restraint in decoration and discretion in the use of colours enhanced the elegance of the shape. A few designs of fern leaves or spiders, a few geometrical lines, the use of black, white, and red-ochre—this was all the imagination the makers

[1] H. Urteaga: *El Perú, op. cit., passim*; E. Yacovleff: *La Deidad primitiva de los Nasca,* in *Revista del Museo Nacional,* Lima, 1932, no. 2, p. 103.

[2] P. A. Means: *Ancient Civilizations of the Andes, op. cit.,* p. 162.

[3] *Ceramografía peruana,* in *Revista del Museo Nacional,* Lima, 1938, p. 17; N. Silvetti: *Los Lagrimones de la cerámica andina y particularmente del Nordeste argentino,* in *Runa,* Buenos Aires, 1952, vol. 5, p. 72; M. Uhle and A. Stubel: *Die Ruinestätte von Tiahuanaco im Hochland des alten Perus,* Breslau, 1892, p. 23.

of this beautiful pottery, worthy of a place in our own museums, allowed themselves. From all over the plateau there came to the capital materials woven from soft vicuña wool, shawls with fringes, and other carefully fashioned garments. From the eastern forests came necklaces made from the wing sheaths of scarab beetles, from monkeys' teeth, from red and yellow seeds, and cloaks of bird feathers in delicate colourings.

THE UTILITARIAN MEANING OF ARTISTIC OBJECTS

The Indians were so appreciative of form that they seem to have tried of their own accord to give it a rational backing. Art for art's sake found little support amongst them. The designs on their fabrics and pottery are both beautiful and lively; they were meant to be read and understood, not merely for looking at. Of course one must not exaggerate and seek a meaning in every line and every colour. Imagination is not an empty word, but it takes a secondary place, and the utilitarian characteristic dominates in all fields.

THE RITUAL DANCES OF THE NOBILITY

To this static æsthetic sense must be added another that was dynamic. The dance was held in great honour by the Peruvians. In the religious field, as in all other aspects of life, it kept its ritual meaning for the nobility and was a secular manifestation for the common people, an occasion for rejoicing and excess.[1]

The family of the supreme Inca danced the *way-yaya* on the great square at Cuzco by forming two lines, one of men and one of women, holding hands, or else a single line. The dancers advanced slowly and rhythmically towards the Emperor, making two steps forward and one back, to the beating of an enormous drum.

The snake dance was a picturesque variant of the *way-yaya*. The Indians, men on one side women on the other, grasped

[1] We pass over in silence the curious ritual race spoken of by one of the most serious writers, the Archbishop of Lima, P. de Villagomez, in *Exortationes e instrucción acerca de las idolatrías*, in *Colección de libros y documentos referentes a la historia del Perú*, vol. 12, Lima, 1919, p. 173: 'The men ran after the women who strove to reach a certain goal, and they wed those whom they succeeded in catching.'

with both hands a many-coloured rope with a snake's head at the end. The reptile undulated amongst the brightly-coloured costumes of the dancers under the dead gaze of the mummies lined up along one side of the square, and in front of the Emperor, as dignified and impassive as they were.[1]

The nobility danced in groups of three, the man holding a woman by each hand and making them turn and twist without letting go.

MUSIC AND MUSICAL INSTRUMENTS

The musical instruments which provided rhythm for the dances were numerous. The vertical flute (*quena*), made of bone or reed, pierced with holes and with perfect pitch, was the most popular. Then came the Pan's flute, made from tubes of reed, wood, metal, feathers or clay, placed side by side and of varying lengths, drums, tambourines made from llama skin, ocarinas, bells of copper or silver, giant bean shells mounted like necklaces and worn on the ankles, trumpets of baked earth, of wood, gourds or conch shells. The Indians have always been noted flautists. The resonance of this instrument harmonizes well with the gentle and melancholy character of the musicians, and their songs are even more nostalgic because they are composed on a pentatonic scale and usually in a minor key.[2] The flute, in the setting of the Andes, remains the exact evocation of lives of resignation and fallen hopes.

Songs, and rhythmic compositions which were not rhymed, which the Indians used at their feasts were simple, primitive, sometimes poetic, sometimes war-like, often religious. And so they have remained. No coarseness spoils their beauty.

POETRY

Here is the translation of two poems. The first is taken from the *Comentarios reales* of Garcilaso de la Vega, who gives it in Quechua, Latin and Spanish.[3]

[1] A suggestive picture is found in an article by P. A. Means in the *National Geographic Magazine,* February 1938, p. 336.

[2] R. and M. d'Harcourt: *La Musique des Incas et ses Survivances,* Paris, 1925. This music is monodic without modulation. 'One is astonished at the imagination of the Indian, who knows, by rudimentary methods, how to express with such diversity and with such force, the great movements of the spirit.'

[3] Garcilaso de la Vega: *Comentarios reales, op. cit.,* book 2, chap. 27.

Beautiful princess,
your brother
has broken
your vase
and that is why
the thunder rumbles, the lightning glares
and the thunderbolt falls.
However it is you, princess,
who must give us water
by making rain
and sometimes even
hail
and snow.
The creator of the world,
Pachacamac
Viracocha,
created you
and charged you
with this task.

The second poem, quoted by P. A. Means, is of quite another character.[1]

We shall drink from his skull,
his teeth will adorn us,
with his bones we shall fashion flutes
and we shall dance to the beat of a drum made
from his skin.

DRAMA

Poetry, songs and stories were principally the work of the *amautas*. But these 'scholars' went farther. They made use of the pantomime element which the native dances tended to assume. These recalled scenes from mythology, or even popular feasts, historical facts or events of daily life, such as battles or agricultural undertakings. Inspired by these pantomimes, the *amautas* conceived the idea of combining stories and dances to make plays.

Historical tales which were mimed were used to commemor-

[1] P. A. Means: *Ancient Civilizations of the Andes, op. cit.*, p. 436.

7. Inca pottery
(*photos:*
G. H. S. Bushnell)

8. Inca figurines, male and female

(*photo:* G. H. S. Bushnell)

Ruins of an ancient Inca palace near Cuzco

(*photo:* Grace Line)

ate glorious events. When grand feast-days took place on the occasion of an Emperor's triumph, plays of this kind were given in the streets of Cuzco. The subjects of these plays were the battles in which the sovereign had taken part, and were destined to make known, much better than a simple story, the exploits of the Peruvians. Scenes were even played at the funeral ceremonies of an Inca, and these reproduced the principal events in the life of the dead king—history lessons which were living though not impartial.

Amongst the plays only one has survived for us, and its form has certainly been modified by the Spanish scholar who collected and wrote it down. It is thought today that this writer, an expert in the Quechua language, was an Indian with a Spanish name, Espinoza Medrano, precentor and high priest of Cuzco Cathedral, a famous orator, philosopher and theologian, who lived from 1632 to 1688.[1] The basis of the drama is undoubtedly of ancient origin, and all experts on the Americas agree in placing it in Inca times.

OLLANTAY, AN INCA DRAMA

The plot of this Inca drama is as follows: We are at Cuzco in the reign of Pachacutec. On the great square the brave general, Ollantay, one of the most renowned army chiefs of the Empire, is talking to his page, Lightfoot, of his love for a daughter of the supreme Inca called Star of Happiness. All this allows the two speakers to make comparisons, both poetic and humorous, with the stars of night. Lightfoot sees that his master has launched himself on a perilous undertaking and becomes anxious. The high priest arrives and endeavours to distract the general from his amorous projects, and then, acknowledging that his efforts are in vain, makes him promise to confide in the sovereign. Then we are transported to the palace, where Star of Happiness is talking to her mother about her love for Ollantay and complains that she cannot see him. The monarch

[1] J. G. Cosio: *El drama quechua 'Ollantay,'* in *Revista Universitaria de Cuzco,* 1941, t. 2, p. 3. A manuscript of the play was found quite recently at the church of Santo Domingo (the ancient temple of the Sun) at Cuzco. The French translation by Pacheco Zegarra (Paris, 1878) has been criticized. The play was published in Spanish in the *Biblioteca de cultura peruana, op. cit.,* t. 1.

then arrives, declares his affection for his daughter, and is astonished to see her so sad and tearful. At this point songs and dances take place, then Star of Happiness asks to be left alone and begins to weep again.

In another room of the palace, the Emperor is discussing a plan of campaign with the generals Ollantay and Peter's Eye, for stopping the advance of an enemy army from the Chayanta region, in the southern part of the Empire. He wants first of all to try to obtain a pacific surrender, but the two warriors are anxious to give battle. Ollantay takes advantage of the meeting to ask the king to receive him alone, and once he has realized his wish, after recalling his past prowess, he throws himself on his knees and proclaims his love for Star of Happiness. The angry sovereign answers him with a brutal refusal: 'Remember you are a simple vassal,' and orders him to withdraw.

In an unspecified place, Ollantay cools his rage and meditates on vengeance. Lightfoot comes to tell him that Star of Happiness and her mother have disappeared from the palace and that armed men are searching for them. At this point another song intervenes. In the palace, Pachacutec falls into a terrible rage because he gave orders for Ollantay to be arrested and he is nowhere to be found. A messenger arrives from the Urubamba valley bringing a *quipu*. Peter's Eye interprets the knotted cords; Ollantay has seized power and the messenger confirms that this disloyal general has been proclaimed Emperor by the inhabitants of the valley. Peter's Eye is given the order to put himself at the head of 50,000 men and to seize the rebel.

By a change of scene we are now at Tambo, in the fortress amongst Ollantay's supporters, who acclaim him and prepare to repel the men of Cuzco. A detailed plan of defence is drawn up, the location of the troops is set out, with the names of the places they are to occupy. They are to allow the enemy to enter a defile, and then soldiers hidden on the peaks along the slopes will roll rocks on the enemy and cut off his retreat.

The next scene takes place after the battle. Peter's Eye bemoans the fact that he did not even encounter the enemy and that his soldiers were crushed under an avalanche of stones and that he had been obliged to flee.

The conversation which comes next in the play takes place in the 'house of the chosen women.' We meet a young girl called Bella, whom one of her companions, and later one of the matrons, tries to persuade to enter this convent. We learn late that she is the daughter of Ollantay and Star of Happiness, and then we know that the general had already been intimate with his loved one; this we have already deduced from certain phrases in the conversation between the girl and her mother. The whole drama turns on this very strange point.

A meeting between the high priest and Lightfoot in a Cuzco street is clearly designed to inform us that Pachacutec is dead and that Tupac Yupanqui has succeeded to the throne. The author allows us to be present at the short reception given by the new monarch in the throne-room—a few words from the Emperor, a favourable prophecy from the high priest, a reprimand for Peter's Eye, and that is all. We now understand from the reply of the conquered general that he is preparing his revenge, and from the intervention of the high priest that this will be overwhelming.

Peter's Eye employs a ruse. He appears, covered with wounds, before the fortress held by the rebels, and having obtained an audience with Ollantay, he explains that Tupac Yupanqui, the heir to the throne, is a ferocious tyrant, and that to punish him for his defeat at Tambo he handed him over to the executioner who was responsible for his pitiable state. Ollantay welcomes the fugitive and has him cared for.

Now a quick change of scene takes place. Bella learns from her companion that her mother has been shut up in a cave. She manages to see her and to exchange words of tender filial love.

We now return to the imperial palace. The high priest tells the Emperor that Tambo is in flames. A messenger brings a *quipu* confirming the victory and setting out the facts. The Inca's soldiers had hidden in caves in the mountains near the fortress, and at the moment agreed with Peter's Eye, when Ollantay and his troops were celebrating the feast of the Sun and were generally intoxicated, the Inca's soldiers, during the night, made their way noiselessly into the city's perimeter. The rebels, taken by surprise, were captured and Peter's Eye himself had bound Ollantay hand and foot. 'Ten thousand prisoners will arrive at Cuzco,' concluded the message. Soon Peter's Eye appears and receives the Emperor's congratulations. Ollantay appears, bound, and all he says is: 'Ask nothing from us, O Father, we are stifled by our crimes.' Tupac Yupanqui asks Peter's Eye and the high priest: 'What punishment shall be meted out to these rebels?' The general calls for the death penalty, but the high priest is more inclined towards clemency. Then the monarch orders the bonds to be taken off the captives, and addressing Ollantay, he returns him his command. The guilty general bursts into sobs whilst expressing his gratitude. The Emperor wishes to give him a wife, but the general replies that he is already married. The sovereign expresses his astonishment that he knows nothing of this. Whilst this is going on Bella appears, throws herself at the Emperor's feet and begs that her mother shall be freed from the cave or she will die. More and more surprised, Tupac Yupanqui orders Ollantay to go to this place, and then, at the instance of the girl, goes there himself. At the entrance to the cave we find them all; Ollantay frees his wife and the play ends in general happiness.

There is no doubt that the composition of this drama is often disconcerting. There is delay in explaining certain situations, some scenes give an impression of being unbalanced and disconnected. There are essential passages which are passed over in a few lines; others, unimportant, are developed at length. Ten years elapse between the beginning and the end although one is not always aware of their passing. At times there seem to be scenes inserted or left out, which is quite possible.

But, having said this, the characters are well drawn, the dramatic tension is happily broken at times, thanks to the intervention of the clown, Lightfoot, the soldiers have dignity, and the women charm. Many of the ideas expressed are, of course, in conformity with Indian mentality.[1] Pachacutec is harsh and stubborn, as befits a monarch whose power rests on a tyrannical regimentation of which nothing can be modified. But the other characters could have lived anywhere. Peter's Eye is a cruel and brutal soldier, Lightfoot is timid and astute, Star of Happiness plays the part of a great lover without

[1] V. Fidel López: *Les Races aryennes du Pérou*, Paris, 1871, p. 327.

flinching, and Ollantay gives rein to violent and unbridled passions.[1] The whole play leaves a profound impression. The surprised reader wonders how a people ignorant of the wheel and of writing succeeded in reaching such a high peak of culture.[2]

A STORY AND A FABLE

If the theatre is only revealed to us by a single play, rich Peruvian folk-lore has preserved several stories whose pre-columbian character is admitted by experts. Here is one of them which stages both man and nature, following the custom of Indians of olden times. It is called *The Greedy Brother.*[3]

'Two brothers were members of the same community, with their wives and children. One was rich and the other was poor. One day when the rich brother, with a number of guests, was feasting "the hair cutting," the other brother, the poor one, appeared.

'Seeing him, a friend asked, "Isn't this your brother? Why don't you ask him to come in?" "This man is a servant," replied the rich man. The poor brother heard this. Filled with sorrow at his brother's contempt, he decided to abandon him and left, as was his custom, to seek the plants his family needed for food.

'He stopped to rest on a hill-side in the *puna* and was lamenting his misfortune. He heard the *puna* speaking to him, consoling him and showing him a path which led to a cave. He followed the directions and found a venerable old man who gave him a stone and told him to return home with it and not to be turned aside under any pretext.

'The poor man began to walk fast but nightfall compelled him to stop. He took refuge in a grotto, with the stone on his

[1] We have replaced 'the astrologer' of the Spanish translation by Pacheco Zegarra by the 'high priest.' This personage was treated with respect by Ollantay and by the Emperor himself, who on several occasions calls him 'high priest.'

[2] For the different arguments put forward in favour of the antiquity of this drama, see the introduction by Pacheco Zegarra in t. I of the *Biblioteca de cultura peruana, op. cit.,* p. 163.

[3] This account and the following one are taken from t. I of the *Biblioteca de cultura peruana, op. cit.,* p. 163. The distinction between *puna* and *pampa* is vague, one is somewhat rocky, the other grassy. The former is rougher and more wild than the latter.

shoulder. He was not able to sleep for he was hungry and miserable, but as he dozed, he heard a conversation between the hill, the *puna,* and the *pampa.*

'The *puna* asked the hill why this man was weeping. "He is a poor man who weeps because his brother, who is rich, despises him."

'The *pampa* then asked, "Why does this unhappy man complain?" "His brother is rich and leaves him to die of hunger," replied the hill.

'"In that case I will give him a gruel of white maize."

'"And I of brown maize," cried the grotto.

'"And I of yellow maize," declared the hill.

'The sleeper awoke with a start; three little pots were set before him. He ate ravenously, but kept a small quantity of the contents of each pot for his family. Then he slept soundly.

'At daybreak, he prepared to resume his journey, but found that he could not lift his burden, it had become so heavy. He looked and found to his surprise that the gruel of yellow maize had been transformed into gold, the white into silver, and the brown into copper.

'He buried some of these riches, and quickly made his way home and told his family what had happened to him.

'The wealthy brother, seeing that his poor brother had suddenly become rich, treated him as a thief. To prove his innocence, the newly rich brother told of his adventure. His brother's avarice was aroused, and the following night he set out for the cave where he found the old man who gave him a stone. He slept in his turn, but the hill gave him horns, the *pampa* long hair, and the *puna* a tail. He awoke completely transformed.

'When he reached home, his wife refused to recognize him and set the dogs on him. And from that time, changed into an animal, he wanders always across the *pampas* and the *punas.*'

Now follows an example of a fable which, like the greater number of similar tales of Indian origin, suggests a moral without stating it. It is called *The Night Butterfly.*

'Once upon a time a family with one child lived happily together. The husband had to undertake journeys, leaving his wife bathed in tears, and passing the nights in watching and spinning. One night, the child, who could not sleep, asked his mother what it was that flew around and spoke to her. The mother replied, "It is my lover, my true friend, who comes to keep me company."

'The husband returned whilst his wife was away and began to talk to his son and to ask him what his mother did whilst he himself was absent. The child replied that his mother's lover came every night, and that they sat up very late and talked to each other. Scarcely had he heard these words, when the husband went to meet his wife, struck her down and killed her.

'One night, his thoughts far away, plunged in melancholy remembrance, he was looking at the dim light of the room, and the child suddenly exclaimed, "Here is my mother's lover, her companion," and pointed to a butterfly which had been in the habit of coming whilst his mother kept watch. The husband realized his mistake, and in despair he died of grief.'

PART THREE

THE LIFE OF THE COMMON PEOPLE

CHAPTER 11

RELIGIOUS LIFE

THE CROWD OF WATCHFUL SPIRITS

WE know that the common people did not have the same religious conceptions as did the nobility, but the practices of worship were analogous, though more formal and on a smaller scale. The whole of existence was encompassed with a network of rites which demanded constant attention. Those we call spirits, that is inanimate objects, natural forces or entities, presumed presences as distinct from things, and all formed an exacting throng which would tolerate neither indifference nor abstraction of mind. It is remarkable that even today the Indian does not swear or blaspheme because he would inevitably be heard and promptly punished.

Under these conditions, every circumstance, even those which appeared completely insignificant, were given some meaning. The entry of a bat into the house, the presence of a double ear of maize in the harvest, a whistling of unknown origin. Immediately a system of defence had to be put into operation; they must dance all night to counteract the evil omen, being careful to sing certain appropriate airs; they had to brandish their weapons to avoid hail, uttering wild cries, and a thousand other requirements had to be satisfied according to tradition.[1]

It goes without saying that a dream, however unintelligible, was considered as a premonition. If a pregnant woman dreamed of snakes, her child would be a boy; if she dreamed of toads, it would be a girl. The danger was great if animals were seen distinctly in dreams, for the new-born child would be sure to resemble them.[2]

[1] L. Valcárcel: *La Religión de los antiguos Peruanos,* in *Revista del Museo Nacional,* Lima, 1939, p. 75.

[2] Dreams had even more importance in California and Mexico.

What precautions had to be taken so as not to offend any of the beings surrounding them! What care had to be taken to establish reciprocities! Before any work in the fields, it was cunning to spread *coca* and *chicha* on the earth, for that would invite the earth to give a good harvest in return. Before crossing a river, courtesy required one to drink a little water, asking politely that the river would favour the crossing. It was wise to make a prayer to the unknown spirit who might be occupying the grotto one proposed to enter, so as not to provoke his displeasure; one should always place a stone, in homage, at the summit of a mountain pass when one reached it. Even today we can see these piles of stones (*achachila*) at the highest points of the roads, which continue to increase in size.[1]

In cases of trouble, appeal to the tutelar deities was normal, but it was best to choose the most suitable divinity, just as today some Latins in Europe choose the saints who specialize in the recovery of lost objects, or in the healing of certain diseases. At Ayacucho, today, in a case of theft, the victim repairs to a certain hill-top, whose spirit is evidently the great protector of individual property, and makes offerings to him.

The humble Indian felt himself nearer to his family deities than to powerful idols enthroned in temples. His household gods, the *conopas,* were his personal affair; he displayed them in a niche in his house, or kept them carefully wrapped in cloths, and took them out when he wished to pray to them. Sometimes he gave them presents. The spirits of things were not neglected either. A model of a small llama of baked earth, hollow inside, as we have described, was set in a niche and received grains of maize. All entities had definite tastes. In this field, too, ancestral knowledge was passed from parents to children. For example, it was well known that *chicha* was appreciated in the spirit world, when *espingo,* a forest plant with a very strong taste, was added to it.[2]

Quantities of talismans were and are kept by the Indians as being very precious; these were black and red beans from the tropical valleys, statuettes of men, animals, maize, potatoes, and especially 'bezoard' stones—these were stones formed in

[1] B. Cobo: *Historia del Nuevo Mundo, op. cit.*, book 13, chap. 11; A. Bandelier: *The Islands of Titicaca and Coati, op. cit.*, p. 99.
[2] G. A. Otero: *La Piedra mágica, op. cit.*, p. 212.

a llama's stomach and having a considerable magic potential. Amongst the most efficient objects prized by the Aymaras were the *svastica.*

THE MANY SHRINES

Outside the home, where the *conopas* reigned supreme, the worship of the *huacas* absorbed a large part of the time when the Indians were not actually working. One is surprised by the length of the lists of *huacas* which appear in the voluminous work of Father B. Cobo. In this everything is listed; mountain peaks, rocks, springs, rivers, even Lake Titicaca and the Inca's house at Tampumachay! Sacred stones were especially numerous. At Machu Picchu each quarter had a stone and a religious centre; the ninth *huaca* on the road to Chinchaysuyu had no less than five stones.[1] It is true also that a number of legends speak of men being turned into stones.

One can see, by reading the chronicles, that the meaning of the word *huaca* was very vague. The Peruvians gave this name to everything which was capable of being incarnated in any object whatever, and by extension to the object itself.[2] It is difficult to know if the term reached the generality of the Indonesian Mana, which is impersonal and undetermined, an emission which is outside all manifestations of the Cosmos, which acts at a distance, is transmissible, a vital force, 'which charges human accumulators,' and contact with which can be dangerous—hence *tabus.*[3] The *huaca* had already become degenerate in pre-columbian times. There was the case of a *Chanca Huaca,* which consisted of a vase dressed in female clothing held in place by gold pins. The word ended up by designating a grave or even an ordinary topographical feature.[4]

The principal offering made to a *huaca* was *chicha.* We know how the Indian prayed, but often he contented himself with

[1] B. Cobo: *Historia del Nuevo Mundo, op. cit.,* book 13, chap. 13 onwards; Jijón y Caamaño, *La Religión del Imperio de los Incas,* t. 1, Quito, 1919, p. 381.

[2] Gonçalez Holguin: *Gramática y arte nueva de la lengua general de todo el Perú,* Lima, 1607.

[3] M. Brillant and R. Aigrain: *Histoire des Religions, op. cit.,* p. 275; Jijón y Caamaño: *La Religión del Imperio de los Incas, op. cit.,* pp. 32 and 74.

[4] J. de Arona: *Diccionario de peruanismos, op. cit.,* p. 233.

a prayer followed by a raising of his open hand towards the sacred place. He never knelt.[1] Offerings were so frequent and became so costly for a poor country that a further evolution took place. The rites remained unchanged, but the objects offered narrowed to the point where they were transformed into tiny models, unsuitable for other use. These reproductions in miniature have been found in tombs where custom decreed the deposit of objects necessary for life in the great beyond. Economy gradually prevailed over religion, and reality gave way to the symbol.

THE SORCERERS' EXTRAORDINARY POWERS

It is not surprising that, in a world where the natural and the supernatural were so closely intermixed, sorcerers enjoyed great prestige. Poma de Ayala, in his picturesquely illustrated manuscript, gives a summing up. Thanks to him, we are able to witness the apparition of a fire demon with horns and huge claws; then an act of magic in three stages; a dream, its interpretation by the demon, and the inhalation of an illness by suction, with the help of the demon, who later plays the part of an angel; finally, the sorcerer is shown to us surrounded by a whole menagerie—birds, snakes, butterflies, etc.[2]

There were several categories of sorcerers, and some of them were specialists. For example, the healer, the weaver of spells, the expert in affairs of the heart who sold herbs designed to arouse amorous feelings, and fruit whose presence alone set the too pressing suitor at a distance.[3]

Today, missionaries and engineers are frequently compared with these magicians and become objects of fear and distrust in the remote villages of the Andean plateau.

The most extensive powers were attributed to these magicians, who were thought able to transform themselves into animals or to disembody themselves. The different parts of the body could each live independently in accordance with the wish of the individual, and even sometimes without him suspect-

[1] P. J. de Arriaga: *Extirpación de la idolatría del Perú, op. cit.*, p. 20. This writer quotes the case of a beautiful young girl from the district of Conchucos married to a stone *huaca* idol and condemned by this to virginity.

[2] Poma de Ayala: *Nueva Corónica, op. cit.*, pp. 274–82.

[3] L. Alayza y Paz Soldan: *Mi País, op. cit.*, t. 3, p. 395.

ing it; this curious phenomenon always took place during sleep. The sorcerer profited by this to send his own head wherever he wished. Where a woman was concerned, the head progressed by using the hair as a bird uses its wings, making a whistling sound which produced a shiver of anguish; if a man was involved, the head proceeded by leaps, making a dry, rhythmic sound called *tactac*—an onomatopœia.

One still hears of the case of an Indian who went to a neighbour's house seeking a remedy and found only the man's trunk lying on the ground without even a drop of blood which might point to a beheading. A little later he heard the characteristic *tactac* of the runaway head.

More startling still is the story of the Indian who, unawares, had married a female sorcerer. One night he noticed that only her trunk was lying beside him. Very angry, he covered it with a piece of cloth. When the head returned, not knowing where to go, it took vengeance by fixing itself to the shoulder of the husband, who thus became two-headed.[1]

When a healer could not cure a disease with the aid of simples and incantations, the sorcerer tried hypnotism. He placed himself in front of the sick man, stared into his eyes, recited prayers, swore at the evil disease, then passed his hands gently over the whole body as though gathering up fluids, then shook his hands so as to throw away what he had been able to capture.[2]

SPELLS

The most formidable of magical operations was the weaving of spells. It began with the identification of the victim with an object which represented him, or more exactly his spirit. This might be a large doll, or an animal, but usually a toad. The doll was made of rags and had to contain things belonging to the victim, such as hair, nail parings or excrement. The toad was wrapped up in the same way. After prayers and incantations, the sorcerer seized thorns and pricked the object in the place where it was desired the pain should be felt by the victim. He had to be very intent on provoking the evil spirit, that is he had to desire deeply the end he sought. This con-

[1] H. Castro Pozo: *Nuestra Comunidad indígena,* Lima, 1924, p. 218.
[2] H. Castro Pozo: *Nuestra Comunidad indígena, op. cit.,* p. 287.

dition was especially remarkable, for thus a spiritual force entered the game and contributed to the success of the transfer.

Once all these operations were completed, the sorcerer took the object away and left the house without looking behind him. He went and hid the object, if he could, in the victim's home. If not, he put it in a place where the victim often passed, or threw it on to the roof. When the victim realized that he was the object of a spell, he too called in a sorcerer who indulged in incantations and prayers, running round the house until he discovered the doll or the toad, which he threw into running water.

It was cunning to let the victim know he was under a spell, for he was at once plunged into terror, which by auto-suggestion made him 'the executioner's collaborator.'[1]

On the coast, the weaving of spells by imprisonment consisted of shutting up the spirit of the victim in a receptacle and making it pass into the body of an animal, so making a martyr of it.

KNOWLEDGE OF THE HEAVENS

It appears that the astrologer occupied a high rank in the hierarchy of magicians, being a scholar. There was, however, a popular astrology about which we know practically nothing.

Poma de Ayala recounts that the gods formerly lived on the earth, where they changed their nature, becoming absorbed in the 'ideological protoplasm' where everything intermingled. But they finally returned to heaven, so to speak, where they became identified with the stars. From this stems the importance of the study of the stars.

These divinities, of their own accord, transformed themselves into idealized animals endowed with supernatural powers, and sometimes, but rarely, into human heroes. And did not the stars assume animal forms? The Pleiades represent a supreme deity who showed himself in the thunderbolt and was able to devour the sun or moon (eclipse). The snake was the exact linear representation of lightning; the condor symbol-

[1] G. A. Otero: *La Piedra mágica, op. cit.,* p. 203; H. Valdizan y A. Maldonaldo: *La Medicina popular peruana, op. cit.,* t. I, p. 131.

ized the sun, for the Indians had observed that these birds kept watch over the sun; the fish, more discreet, was the symbol of the moon. Orion became the llama who crosses the firmament each night to drink from the sea and in this way prevents the waters of the Pacific from overflowing and flooding the earth.

One of the most celebrated legends of the forest, that of the twins, transposed to certain districts of the plateau, explains the formation of the sun and moon. An Indian woman, symbolizing mother earth, nature and fertility, gave birth to twins of different sexes. She was the wife, either of the god Pacha Camac or of a feline god (the jaguar). In the first version her husband was drowned in the sea and changed into an island, and the widow, wandering in the darkness which surrounded the earth, entered the cavern of an evil spirit named Wa Kon, who tried to seduce her, but not being able to do so, devoured her. In the second version, it was the jaguar who feasted on the unfortunate woman. The twins were saved, either by the family of the fox, who, crafty as ever, pushed the evil spirit into an abyss, where he died, or by the mother of the jaguar who hid them in a gourd, a wad of cotton wool, or somewhere, until they grew up, when a bird told them of the crime, and they killed the monster. In all these versions, the twins ended up in heaven, sometimes, poetically, by the use of a liana, and were transformed into the sun and moon, benevolent heavenly bodies, protectors of humanity.[1]

The Indians prayed to the Moon rather than to the Sun. The Moon seemed to them more familiar, more accessible, and less uniform and rigid than the Sun, which was the official god. He was the more imposing, endowed with a greater number of temples, he was immovable and always the same. The Moon, on the contrary, was gentler and more feminine and frequently changed her appearance, each of her phases carrying its own meaning. He who sowed his corn when the Moon was full was imprudent; but wise he who hurried to pray as soon as her face was surrounded by an orange-tinted halo, a sign of misfortune.

[1] J. C. Tello: *Wira-Kocha,* review *Inca,* 1923, p. 203; R. Lehmann-Nitsche: *Studien zur südamerikanischen Mythologie. Die actiologischen Motive,* Hamburg, 1939; H. Trimborn: *Francisco de Avila, Dämonen und Zauber in Inkareich,* Leipzig, 1939.

MOTHER EARTH

The earth was respected even more than the stars by these agricultural people; Mama Pacha, mother earth, the great foster-mother. Certain stones were buried in the fields to make them fertile, and on some of these dangerous animals were carved so as to make them harmless. On the Yalla stone, in the Ayabaca region, are carved snakes, which are numerous in that neighbourhood.[1]

TWO PRAYERS

Folk-lore has handed down two popular prayers.[2] The first:

'O Creator! thou who art at the ends of the earth, thou who givest life and soul to men, and sayest to each man, "Be thou such a kind of man," and to each woman, "Be thou such a kind of woman," thou who, speaking thus, didst create and fashion them and didst give them life. Protect these men whom thou hast made, that they may live safe and sound, sheltered from danger, and in peace. Where art thou? In the highest heaven or in the depth of the thunder and the storm clouds? Hear thou, answer me, be kindly disposed towards me. Give us life eternal, hold us in thy hand, and receive this offering wherever thou mayest be, O Creator!'

The one which follows mentions the sovereign:

'O Creator! May the subjects of the Inca, the peoples in subjection to him, and his servants, rest in safety and peace in the reign of thy son, the Inca, whom thou hast given us as king. Whilst his reign lasts, may thy people multiply and be kept safe, may it be for them an age of prosperity, may everything increase, fields, men, and beasts, and guide always with thy hand the monarch to whom thou hast given birth, O Creator!'

In most of the prayers which have survived to our times—their origin is unknown—one finds the same ideas and words arranged in a different order. In this field the vocabulary seems limited, and certain terms constantly repeated seem to have a value which is suitable and magical, a power which lends itself to the object of the prayer.

[1] H. Castro Pozo: *Nuestra Comunidad indígena, op. cit.*, p. 185.
[2] *Biblioteca de cultura peruana, op. cit.*, t. 2, pp. 78 and 82.

CHAPTER 12

FAMILY LIFE

NATURE on the Andean plateau compelled man to be extremely ingenious. The Indians had a remarkable knowledge of plants; they domesticated six kinds of grain, seven species of fruit, four roots or tubers, and two condiments.[1] In our day, for a long time past, domestication has come to an end. 'No country in the world,' writes a contemporary historian, 'has cultivated more vegetable species of such high nutritive value as Peru.'[2]

WHAT THE INDIANS ATE

We have already listed the chief animals and vegetables found on the Andean plateau. Edible substances prepared from them were treated with a view to their conservation. It was a matter of the highest importance, so as to avoid being taken by surprise, to build up family stocks in anticipation of seasonal variations. With this end in view, maize and *quinua* grain were made into flour, tubers were reduced to *chuño,* and a quantity of herbs, under the generic name of *yoyo,* were cooked in two or three waters and then dried in the sun. These various commodities were preserved in earthenware jars, in bins made from maize stalks, or, for want of anything better, buried in deep holes.

To grind corn, the Indians crushed it on a flat slab with the aid of a semi-circular stone which they held on its edge by the two ends, rocking it alternately from right to left.

Chuño, the preparation of which has already been described, could contain potato, *yuca,* and *oca.*

As a rule, llamas could not be killed for meat and they were exclusively used to provide wool and a means of transport. There remained the domestic guinea-pig, only edible twelve

[1] F. Herrera: *Ethobotánica,* in *Revista del Museo Nacional,* Lima, 1942, no. 1.

[2] L. E. Valcárcel: *Historia de la cultura antigua del Perú, op. cit.,* t. 1, vol. 2, p. 62.

hours after being killed, and game killed under official orders. All meat was cut into strips, salted, dried and kept under the name of *charqui*.[1]

Birds, frogs, edible worms, insects similar to a horse-fly, and mushrooms, were used to flavour soups.

Add to this list a few fruits, especially that of the cactus, *tuna,* dried snails and, in sea or lake-side areas, fish, which abounded on the coast and were bartered by the fishermen for products from the tableland. They were almost the exclusive means of barter amongst the Urus of Lake Titicaca.

Were the Indians sufficiently well nourished?[2] Their many contrivances and their strenuous work assured them a minimum living in this country with its growing population, where, according to Polo de Ondegardo, land had sometimes to lie fallow for six or seven years, and where three out of five harvests were lost on account of frost.

If the Incas' subjects had been lazy and weak, it has been said, they would not have been able to carry out so many colossal tasks. But perfection of organization, severity of discipline, and above all the absence of all considerations of cost in terms of human life and effort are sufficient to explain the results.

Most recent calculations lead to the conclusion that in terms of calories their food was insufficient. Today they are estimated at 3,400 daily in favourable periods, but they could not have reached these figures in Inca times. Technicians exaggerate when they put the total at only 2,000 calories and attribute to this cause the inferiority of the dark-skinned men in comparison with their white enemies at the time of the Conquest.[3]

[1] *Chuño* and *charqui* are very common today in the Andes.

[2] M. Kuczynski-Godard and C. E. Paz Soldan consider the Indian as always having been undernourished: *Disección del indigenismo peruano,* Lima, 1948, p. 105; L. E. Valcárcel considers, on the contrary, that sustenance in Peru, both now and in olden times, is rational: *Historia de la cultura antigua del Perú, op. cit.,* t. 1, vol. 2, p. 75 onwards. The present-day estimates of M. Cépède and M. Lengellé are inaccurate. (*Économie alimentaire du globe,* Paris, 1953, p. 192.)

[3] M. Druesne: *Les Problèmes économiques de la Technocratie,* Paris, 1933, p. 16. These estimates have no foundation on fact. J. Kuon Cabello gives the present-day ration of the Indian as 2,500 to 3,000 calories. (*Alimentación del Indio peruano,* in *Revista Universitaria de Cuzco,* 1948, t. 3, p. 130.) According to Dr Kuczynski-Godard this figure rises, at certain times, to 3,400.

Food balances were not certain either. *Chuño* contains 76.5 per cent of sugars against 8.5 per cent of protein and 0.5 per cent of fats,[1] and as a result the carbo-hydrates are too high. Proteins were rare; they are found in *quinua, cañihua,* and *mañi* (26.5 per cent), and the Indians sadly lacked the milk, eggs and meat of European diet. Fortunately vitamins were found in several commodities: A is abundant in *apichu*; A, B and C exist in maize; A, B, B2 and C are found in the potato. Calcium and iron were provided by *quinua* and by the edible clay used as a condiment (*chacco*); the Indians' fine teeth bear witness to the abundance of these vitamins.[2]

The technique of preservation was as follows: in damp valleys the food was placed in small open-work wooden cases with a large quantity of *muña,* a plant related to mint, with insecticidal properties. In dry areas the products were placed in a covering of dry straw and *muña,* which enveloped them completely. Potatoes kept in this way were still good after eight or nine months.[3]

DRINK

The famous drink, *chicha*, coveted by everyone, was prepared from maize by the old men, and above all by the old women, who were less busy than adults. They chewed it so that the action of the saliva facilitated fermentation. They then put it in water in an earthenware jar which they kept warm by burying it. Strong alcoholic drinks were forbidden, and *coca* was also forbidden to the common people.

SIMPLICITY AND UNIFORMITY OF CLOTHING

On the plateau to be clothed was an absolute necessity, while on the coast and in the eastern forest clothing was necessary only as a protection. It covered only certain sensitive parts of the body and for that reason was a mark of social distinction;

[1] For basic theories, see P. and L. Baudin: *La consommation dirigée en France en matière d'Alimentation,* Paris, 1942.

[2] A. Posnansky: *Nuevos Datos refernetes a la quina,* in *Boletín de la Sociedad de Geográfica de La Paz,* December 1945, p. 132.

[3] C. Vargas: *El Solanum Tuberosum a través del desenvovimiento de las actividades humanas,* in *Revista del Museo Nacional de Lima,* t. 5, no. 2, 1936.

morality did not enter into question. Nakedness was not degrading and in no way caused offence. We have seen that a captured enemy was carried entirely nude on a litter in the conqueror's triumphal procession.

Amongst the common people rules about clothing were strict. On the day of his marriage an Indian received two garments of llama wool taken from the public store, one for working days and one for feast days and holidays, and he kept them until they were completely worn out, patching them with great skill if they were torn, in the manner of modern experts.[1] The cut and colour was uniform for both sexes. The different garments which we have described in connection with the Inca were used in a simplified form by his subjects. For men, trousers (*huara*), a white sleeveless shirt like a sack with three holes, one for the head and two for the arms (*cushma* or *uncu*), a brown woollen cape thrown round the shoulders and knotted across the chest (*yacolla*), and the arrangement of the hair, as we have learned, varied according to the province. For women, a long belted tunic, open up the sides and showing the leg for ease in walking (*anacu*), and a grey cloak fastened across the breast by a large-headed pin (*lliclla*). Both sexes usually went barefoot, but sometimes they wore sandals (*usuta*) of a very practical design. The sole was made of llama leather chosen from the neck, where the skin is thickest, and it was shorter than the sole of the foot so that on the slopes the overhanging toes could cling to the irregularities of the surface. A brightly-coloured woollen cord was attached to the vamp which covered the greater part of the foot, and was gracefully wound round the ankle.[2]

The whole was simple and uniform. To modify it in any way was strictly forbidden without special authorization from the higher officials. Notice that the arms and legs remained bare—a proof of the Indians' hardiness, for the air of the high tableland is very sharp and at times icy.[3]

[1] P. A. Means: *Ancient Civilizations of the Andes, op. cit.*, p. 312.
[2] B. Cobo: *Historia del Nuevo Mundo, op. cit.*, book 14, chap. 2.
[3] J. de Acosta: *Historia Natural y Moral, op. cit.*, chap. 5; L. de Atienza: *Compendio historial, op. cit.*, chap. 5; J. de Betanzos: *Suma y Narración de los Incas, op. cit.*, chap. 13; P. de Cieza de Léon: *Segunda Parte de la Crónica del Perú, op. cit.*, chap. 41; A. de Zárate: *Historia del descubrimiento y conquista de la provincia del Perú*, in *Biblioteca de autores españoles*, t. 26, Madrid, 1853, book 1, chap. 8.

THE INDIAN DWELLING

The dwellings of the common people were very primitive. The community built the little house allotted to a young couple at the time of their marriage. The walls were of beaten earth, or, on the coast, of brick; only exceptionally were they of stone, for those Indians occupying a higher station than that of the ordinary tiller of the soil, and the roof was of thatch. There was no window, for, having no glass, to make an opening was to let in cold and wind as well as light; the door was low 'like an oven door' and was covered by a hanging.

In this dark and smelly hovel, sometimes divided into two by a light partition, children and guinea-pigs were crowded around a little clay hearth, amongst the dishes, jars and mortars required for cooking. Llama skins thrown on the ground and folded double served as beds, one half serving as mattress and the other half as a covering. In a chief's house a couch of straw or dried grass was spread under the animal skin. Clothes hung from projecting pieces of wood or were folded into earthenware pots. A box of plaited reeds held the Indian woman's belongings—wool, spindle, and needles made from thorns. Niches cut in the walls held knives, spoons, pins, ornaments and idols.

The family hardly ever gathered in this den until after nightfall or on wet days; either they were scattered to their various occupations, or else they were crouched on the threshold in their usual position, limbs folded, feet crossed, with their knees up to their chins.

This modest dwelling was subjected to inspection by officials twice a year, and the hanging over the doorway had to be opened at a meal-time so that the inspectors could be assured that all the rules were being observed. Everything that might have adorned or beautified the hut was forbidden, for nothing could be allowed to divert the Indian from the economic and utilitarian end assigned to him by the State.

FROM BIRTH TO DEATH

Birth

Now we know the background of family life, we can follow the Inca's subject throughout the whole course of his existence.

As soon as the Indian woman was pregnant she prayed to the *conopas* and increased her offerings, but in no way altered her working life. When the confinement was near the cradle was prepared: it was a plank with two side pieces and raised on four very short legs. The two legs at the head end were slightly longer than the others so that the new-born baby should not be absolutely horizontal, and they were prolonged above the cradle, meeting in a circle, so that the mother could throw a covering over the cradle to protect the baby without stifling it. A blanket was laid on the plank for the reception of the baby. The whole thing was as light as possible, for the mother often had to carry the cradle, as we shall see.

The woman, without changing her daily routine, was delivered of her child wherever she happened to be, and usually with great ease. She cut the umbilical cord with a potsherd or with her nail, and when necessary hastened the healing by the application of plasters. She bathed the new-born child in the nearest stream and washed herself too. These ablutions had to be done in cold water so as to accustom the child to hardship from the moment it saw light. The mother showed her affection by refraining from plunging the child into the water; she took the liquid in her mouth and sponged the delicate body of her infant.

Deformation of the skull

The mother bound the baby to the plank of the cradle, after having wrapped it in the blanket, and applied to its head the small pieces of wood needed to deform the skull, as custom required. There were several ways of achieving this end. The small planks were placed on the forehead and the back of the head and tied together with cord made of wool or vegetable fibre. Or else the child was kept flat on its back with its head fixed to the wooden end of the cradle. Sometimes circular bands tied round at the desired spot were sufficient to induce a modification of the cranium. To avoid immediate difficulties, the mother tightened these barbarous instruments a little more each day until she had obtained the desired shape, generally at about three or four years of age.[1]

[1] L. de Atienza: *Compendio historial, op. cit.*, p. 105; Garcilaso de la Vega: *Comentarios reales, op. cit.*, book 9, chap. 8; J. Imbelloni: *Deformaciones intencionales del cráneo en Sud-América*, in *Revista del Museo de la Plata*, 1924, p. 329.

The intervention of the sorcerer

Since the child was looked upon as the family's main wealth a miscarriage was always considered a misfortune. As soon as it was feared that a miscarriage might occur, the sorcerer was called in and a rather complicated ceremonial was enacted. He took the *conopa,* unwound the wrappings and placed them on the woman's stomach. Then he chose two or three stones about the size of his hand and rubbed them with a piece of silver which he took from a leather purse, together with a small amount of *coca,* some ground cinnabar or crushed sea-shells. He placed these powders on the stones and beside them placed guinea-pigs, bowls of *chicha* and a little *tejti* (*chicha* mixed with *mañi*). The maize from which this *chicha* was prepared had to be chewed by young virgins, or by women who, during the preparation, had remained chaste and had eaten neither salt nor pepper. After this the sorcerer put the *conopa* on a clean straw couch and prayed for a long time. Next he played a game of heads or tails by throwing some object into the air. First he asked if the Sun was displeased; if the reply was negative he again threw the object into the air asking if this or that *huaca* was displeased, and so the game went on until an affirmative answer was received. At this stage the cause of the evil was established. There remained appeasement by prayers, offerings and sacrifices. The ground cinnabar or powdered shells were dispersed by blowing on them. A guinea-pig was killed and its lungs examined to know if the sacrifice was accepted; if not, other guinea-pigs had to be killed until the examination produced favourable results. Then *chicha* was thrown on the ground and the last guinea-pigs sacrificed.[1]

The father of the family contributed to the success of these operations by fasting. He had to stay near his wife during the first days after her confinement, or find some member of the family to replace him, so as to drive off the evil spirits.[2] A few days after the birth a provisional name was given to the baby, a name suggested by some physical characteristic or particular circumstance, for example, 'big head,' or in an allusion to the

[1] Jijón y Caamaño: *La Religión del Imperio de los Incas, op. cit.,* vol. I, p. 107.

[2] R. A. de Matos: *L'Organisation sociale dans l'île Taquile,* in *Travaux de l'Institut français des études andines,* 1951, p. 82.

spot where the event took place, 'fine sand.' This name, since it was only temporary, was not chosen with any special care. If the infant seemed weakly, it was recommended that it should suck the umbilical cord, which its mother, with great foresight, had preserved.

Severe discipline from birth

Up to the age of three months the child's arms were bound in swaddling clothes so as to harden them. The rules absolutely forbade anyone under any pretext to pick up the newborn child in their arms, for this would infallibly make it tearful and cross. To move the child, the whole cradle was lifted and carried along—hence its lightness. After the Conquest, the Indian woman went to mass with the cradle in which her baby lay.

To give suck, the mother leaned over the child, and she was only allowed to do this three times a day, morning, midday, and evening. She had the entire care of the child, even if she was of a noble family, unless she was ill.[1] The child was weaned at about two years of age.

The wish of the rulers was that from birth the subject of the Empire should be bound hand and foot by a detailed set of rules from which he would never escape, and to which he would become accustomed.

So that the baby should not be taken into its parents' arms, when the time came for it to leave the cradle, they placed it in a hole in the ground lined with rags. When the child could crawl he knelt on the ground to suck from his mother as she bent over him.

The first solemn ceremony

When the child reached a certain age, which varied in different regions, but was between five and twelve years, a solemn ceremony took place. The family gathered together and chose the godfather, who then proceeded to carry out the first cutting of the nails and hair. Armed with a flint, he began the operation and then passed this instrument to other members of the family who continued it. Hair and nails were care-

[1] Garcilaso de la Vega: *Comentarios reales, op. cit.*, book 4, chap. 11; J. de Arriaga: *Extirpación de la idolatría del Peru, op. cit.*, chap. 2.

fully preserved so that no third party could acquire an influence over the child by getting possession of them. Then gifts were offered and the final name chosen.

This name was composed of two parts, one designed to indicate the child's integration into the community which corresponded more or less to the *ayllu,* the other specifically belonging to the individual, and recalling some particular circumstance. Father Arriaga quotes the name of Paucar Libiac. The first word designated the *huaca,* and the second was linked with a thunderbolt because the child was found one day near a place struck by a thunderbolt but was unharmed.[1] This chronicler adds: 'There is no child, however small, who does not know the name of the *huaca* and of his *ayllu.*'[2] In certain regions the cut hair was carried off to the *huaca* and hung up there.[3]

This ceremony was of very ancient origin and deeply significant. From the time of its celebration the child was conscious of his integration in the group; he felt personally all wrongs committed against the *ayllu,* and at his death he was buried in the same spot as his ancestors. He was not, however, freed from his filial duties. He owed the same absolute obedience to his father as his father owed to the State. According to custom, the feast ended with dancing, singing and drinking.

If the child was a boy his chief responsibility was now to guard the maize fields from birds. This allowed him to practise handling a sling. Then he herded llamas, which were his best friends and usually the objects of his great affection. If the child was a girl she helped with domestic affairs and learned to spin and weave.

Second solemn ceremony

Another great occasion brought the family together again. This was when the child reached the age of 12, 13 or 14 years, according to local custom. After integration in the *ayllu* there came, at the age of puberty, incorporation into the nation. The old men whipped the legs of the young man

[1] J. Mejia Valera: *Organización de la sociedad en el Perú precolombino, op. cit.,* p. 34.
[2] J. de Arriaga: *Extirpación de la idolatría del Perú, op. cit.,* chap. 7.
[3] P. de Villagomez: *Carta pastoral de exhortación contra les idolatrías de los Indios del Arzobispado de Lima, op. cit.,* p. 168.

and reminded him of his duty towards his parents and his superiors, and then they presented him with a sort of loin-cloth (*huara*).[1]

A young girl was the object of a ceremony at the time of her first menstruation, but her future could be completely changed if she was sought out by the Inca's envoys and cloistered in one of the 'houses of the chosen women,' as we have already learned.[2]

To prepare herself for this ceremony, the girl observed an absolute fast for 48 hours; on the third day she ate a little raw maize, and on the fourth day she bathed herself and received new clothes and plaited her hair. Now the definite rank of woman was accorded to her.

The utilitarian marriage

We come now to marriage customs. Monogamy was not imposed, but it existed in actual fact because each Indian only received enough of the earth's surface to enable two people to subsist; consequently he could only afford a second wife if he was in receipt of a supplementary grant of land. There was a parallel between the wife and the other goods which made up part of the patrimony. There was a common minimum for all the subjects of the Empire, and that was a bare necessity. Above this minimum there could only be luxuries assigned occasionally to those who had earned them.

Would not polygamy in one part of the population risk a shortage of available women, especially as the Virgins of the Sun seem to have been numerous? On the contrary it is probable that this was a way of establishing the balance between the sexes, for there was an insufficient number of men compared with women. This was due to continual wars, some of which, like those waged in Ecuador against the Caras, were long and bloody.

Marriage in pre-columbian times very much resembled marriage in the Andes today—an economic institution, or in more precise terms, a utilitarian mating.[3] A modern jurist has

[1] L. de Atienza: *Compendio historial, op. cit.*, p. 108; P. Sarmiento de Gamboa: *Segunda parte de la historia general llamada indica, op. cit.*, chap. 13.

[2] M. de Morua: *Historia, op. cit.*, book 3, chap. 35.

[3] P. M. Oliviera: *Memorandum sobre matrimonio civil y divorcio*, in *Actos de la Comisión reformadora del Código Civil*, t. 2, p. 123.

given the following definition of it—a contract for procreation and mutual aid, the duration of which equals the will and affection of the parties.[1]

Trial marriage

Custom, mistress of this field, imposed from earliest times, on the Andean plateau, a period of test or trial marriage (*servinacuy*); the affianced pair lived their life in common, the time varying according to the district from a few days to several years. The parents made an agreement to this effect. This apprenticeship enabled the young man to try out the capabilities of his future and eventual wife, who had to be able to cook, make his clothes, and help him in his agricultural labours. Besides, though of secondary importance, it gave the girl the opportunity to appreciate the character of her suitor and so avoid being tied for life to a drunkard or a brute.[2]

If the interested parties did not suit each other, the girl returned to her parents and suffered no moral prejudice. If a child was born of this brief union it remained with the mother, and the father suffered a considerable penalty in that he had lost a precious helper.

It must be understood that *servinacuy* was in no sense concubinage and could only exist under a system of 'economic marriage.' To have been invited to undergo a trial marriage was and is something of an honour for the girl.[3] Virginity was never prized by the Indians of the Pacific states and is not today. The girl who had relations with men simply proved her attractions thereby and her prestige was increased.[4] Father Cobo explains that 'virginity was regarded as a drawback for the woman, for the Indians held that only those remained virgins who had not learned to make themselves loved by someone.'

[1] V. J. Guevara: *Derecho consuetudinario de los Indios del Perú y su adaptación al Derecho moderno,* in *Revista Universitaria de Cuzco,* 1924, p. 120.

[2] L. Baudin: *L'Indien dans l'économie des États andines,* in *Zeitschrift für die gesamte Staatswissenschaft,* 1949, Band 105, Heft 2, p. 347.

[3] J. de Arriaga: *Extirpación de la idolatría del Perú, op. cit.,* chap. 5; E. Romero: *El Departamento de Puno,* Lima, 1928, p. 221; P. de Villagomez: *Carta pastorale, op. cit.,* chap. 44; L. Alayza y Paz Soldan; *Mi País, op. cit.,* t. 3, p. 427.

[4] B. Cobo: *Historia del Nuevo Mundo, op. cit.,* book 11, chap. 7.

The chroniclers cite many typical examples from the period of the Conquest. An Indian was opposed to the marriage of his sister with an honourable suitor, arguing that the young people had not had sexual relations with each other. A husband, quarrelling with his wife, reproached her for not having had lovers before her marriage.[1]

In Inca times, when a man married, he left the shelter of his parents' home and was given a plot of ground and a cottage.

Obligatory marriage

The ceremony of marriage did not take the form it acquired under the Spanish occupation; it was purely administrative and had no religious formality. An inspector, representing the supreme Inca, came to the locality at a fixed date and ordered the young men and girls into two ranks, face to face. He asked which of them had agreed to marry, and whether or not they had undergone the trial marriage. Generally the affair was already concluded, the parents had arranged the marriage beforehand, or else the girl had told them of the relations she had had with young men and what decisions had been made between them.

There remained the young men who were not betrothed. The inspector invited each of them to choose a girl, beginning with the one holding the highest post in the administrative hierarchy. If they remained hesitant, the inspector, by right of office, assigned a girl to them.[2]

It can be seen that in a relative sense marriage was obligatory.

Celibacy was not recognized. Population was the factor of economic wealth and military strength. No one could escape from his duty as a provider of workmen and soldiers. The Empire was a factory of men.

When the official ceremony was over the young man went to the house of the girl's parents to inform them of the result. All then depended on local customs. Often the husband

[1] J. de Arriaga: *Extirpación de la idolatría del Perú, op. cit.*, chap. 6.

[2] P. de Mercado de Peñalosa: *Relación de la provincia de Pacajes,* in *Relaciones geográficas de Indias, op. cit.*, t. 2, p. 60; M. de Morua, *Historia del origen y genealogía real, op. cit.*, book 3, chap. 33; F. de Santillán: *Relación,* in *Tres relaciones, op. cit.*, p. 24.

solemnly put a sandal on his wife's right foot as the Inca did; then he offered gifts to his parents-in-law, a survival of former marriage by purchase.[1]

The diversity of the other ceremonies was unlimited. Some of them can be found today, though somewhat altered. Amongst the Pacasmayos a fire was lighted and on it was placed a vessel full of maize and grease, and the godfather spoke in these terms, 'You are married, you must work together as you have cooked together, and you will be lovers since it is impossible for one to remain cold whilst the other is passionate.'[2] Usually the old men reminded the couple of their duties, and the families exchanged presents. Of course there was plenty of *chicha* and drunkenness.

The girl wedded in this way was considered to be the legitimate wife and the marriage was held to be binding. Repudiation only existed for concubines. Adultery and rape were punished by death, but in the latter case the penalty was less if the victim found a husband. The general interest was no longer in question from an economic point of view, which was most important, since it did not result in a state of celibacy, which would have been against the general interest.

An Indian cottage home

Let us now make our way into an Indian dwelling, 'which must be called a cottage or hut, and not a house,' Father Cobo tells us.[3] It was necessary to bend down to get under the lintel of the door, or even sometimes to crawl on all fours, which greatly displeased the missionaries.

At first it was impossible to distinguish anything because of the darkness, for the entrance by which we crept in was the only way by which light and air could enter. A sharp and nauseating smell of dung, urine and smoke seized one by the throat. The walls were covered with layers of dirt caused by dust and sweat. When the Spaniards wished to make some deaf Indians come out of their home they tapped on the

[1] C. de Castro y D. de Ortega Morejón: *Relación y declaración, op. cit.*, p. 241; M. de Morua: *Historia del origen y genealogía real, op. cit.*, book 3, chap. 30; J. Basadre, *Historia del derecho peruano,* Lima, 1937, t. 1, p. 160.

[2] L. Alayza y Paz Soldan: *Mi País, op. cit.*, t. 3, p. 69.

[3] B. Cobo: *Historia del Nuevo Mundo, op. cit.*, book 11, chap. 6.

thatched roof with a stick, and there fell into the room so many dirty things that no one could stay inside.[1]

When sleeping the Indian removed only the *yacolla,* and the Indian woman her *lliclla,* and both stretched themselves on the ground on an animal skin as we have described. 'In this way they avoided having to dress in the morning,' says Father Cobo humorously, but he adds that the clothing was always stained and that there were no napkins nor handkerchiefs.

There were two meals a day, in the early morning and at sunset. They were prepared in the family clay oven, the upper part of which was pierced with holes where earthenware dishes were set. By rubbing two sticks together they set fire to the wood, or more often to the dried llama dung which they used as fuel. The dishes were placed on the ground, and each person crouched down, taking in his hand a spoon and a half gourd which served as a plate. The wife sat behind her husband, back to back. The food was often badly cooked and unappetizing, but they flavoured it strongly with salt and pepper. A man was very offended if his wife ate from the same bowl as himself, but guinea-pigs and dogs thrust their noses into the food at will.

No one drank from his wooden goblet before he had finished eating. The most refined Indians, in some provinces, used a *pakcha* for drinking. This was 'a wooden article with two feet, and composed of a cup with a handle on one side and a long spout on the other, hollowed out into a little winding channel, so that the liquid flowed gently into the mouth through a little hole pierced in the bottom of the cup at the end of this channel.' [2] *Chicha* taken in this way, by tiny doses, became a divine drink!

Indians ate little when at home, but when they partook of banquets, like all undernourished people they ate far too much. The Catholic missionaries came to the conclusion that their customary sobriety was due to poverty and not to abstinence. One of them acknowledged with some indignation that on these occasions his parishioners 'filled their bellies

[1] B. Cobo: *loc. cit.*; J. Delgardo: *Folklores y apuntes para la sociología indígena, op. cit.*, p. 18.

[2] M. Frezier: *Relation du voyage de la Mer du Sud,* 1732.

like wolves and drank until they fell to the ground.'[1]

The second room in the hut, when there was one, opened out of the first and contained earthenware jars and pots for preserving food. There too were crowded the Indian pigs whose dung carpeted the floor, giving off an incredible stench; the animals were alive with fleas and ticks, which spread throughout the dwelling and infested all clothing. These insects, added to the lice, obliged the inhabitants to scratch themselves constantly.[2]

We must not forget two important members of the family who introduced a note of elegance and nobility into this unattractive assembly—a pair of llamas kept in the communal yard. 'The only animal,' says Father Cobo rather charmingly, 'which domestication has not degraded, for it only agrees to be made use of when asked, and not when ordered.'[3]

No doubt the picture we have painted is sombre, and it has to be modified immediately one begins to ascend the social scale. The chiefs, even subordinate ones, had large and much cleaner houses. Besides, our picture is only valid for Inca times and the beginning of the colonial period. The progress of hygiene does not allow this description to hold good today, except perhaps in certain remote places; but the Indian dwelling still appears wretched and the Indian enjoys no comforts, although this is because he does not really bother about them.

The distressing position of women

In the Indian home of pre-columbian times woman was considered inferior to man. 'She was a thing,' wrote a chronicler, 'and could be treated as such.' This was an accurate observation, for she formed part of the patrimony and was transferred by inheritance. Absolutely enslaved by her husband, she was overwhelmed with work; collecting fuel, gathering herbs and fruits, preparing food, looking after children and animals, keeping the orchard, spinning and weaving material for clothes, observing ritual practices, helping in the fields and, from time to time, bartering in neighbouring markets.

[1] B. Cobo: *loc. cit.*
[2] L. de Atienza: *Compendio historial, op. cit.*, p. 43.
[3] Flore Tristan: *Peregrinaciones de una paria,* Lima, 1946.

When she went out and the child had left the cradle, but was still unable to walk, she carried it on her back in a fold of her cloak, as she still does today—a charming sight when the little head, with open eyes, curiously scrutinizes the stranger whilst taking cover behind the mother's hair. But, if the journey lasted more than half a day, she took with her food for the family, a jar of *chicha,* gourds, and small dry sticks for lighting a fire. If she still had her hands free, she spun as she walked, or chewed maize, so as not to waste time. And when she crouched, exhausted, on the threshold of her hut, she deloused her children, either by crushing the tiny insects between her teeth, or by rubbing the children's heads with a concoction of *cebadilla.*[1]

Under these conditions, a woman had scarcely any leisure to care for herself. As a young girl, and for a time after marriage, she still retained some fastidiousness; she washed her clothes and cleaned them by rubbing them with the pungent leaves of the *cabuya,* which rather inconveniently turned them red; to fasten her cloak she chose a straight, polished pin with a large head; she arranged her hair, using cactus spines for combs and an obsidian mirror; she removed grease from her hair with urine and depilated herself by applying ashes mixed with warm urine.

But, older and bowed under the weight of her family duties, she neglected herself, washed seldom, made hasty repairs to her garments with great reinforcements of pins, some of which she always kept stuck in her bosom so as to mend any tears which might appear. She was generally 'so dirty and dishevelled that she inspired pity,' and so worn out by her life that at thirty years of age she looked fifty.[2]

The men hardly ever washed either, but painted their hair, which they wore long or short, according to local custom: short in Cuzco, long amongst the Collas and the Rucanas. They never wore beards. The Indians and the Emperor Atahualpa himself designated the Spaniards by the scornful term of 'bearded'—the chroniclers protested about this, alleging that the beard was a sign of 'boldness, constancy and wisdom.'[3]

[1] B. Cobo: *Historia del Nuevo Mundo, op. cit.,* book 14, chap. 7.
[2] L. de Atienza: *Compendio historial, op. cit.,* pp. 40 and 67.
[3] L. de Atienza: *Compendio historial, op. cit.,* p. 59.

We know that the Indians had naturally good teeth. They used a process, especially the women, to make the gums healthy. Cooked herbs were applied, still hot, to the mucuous membrane. The pain thus set up was so great that only liquid nourishment was possible for several days. But after this the dead skin came off, and the gums appeared a good red colour.

Multiplicity of feast days

If leisure time was scarce on working days, by way of compensation feast days were many. There were always three each month, but many more were added and they sometimes lasted a very long time. One writer has estimated that they totalled 158 during the year.[1] Always certain feast days were reserved for the nobility. We have already described some, and there were a number of others of interest to the whole population.

During the second month of the year (which began at the winter solstice), approximately at the end of January and during the greater part of February, on a predetermined day, the *orejónes* went to the reservoirs high above Cuzco, poured into the water the ashes of sacrifices made during the past year, and then opened the flood-gates, so that the two little rivers that flowed through the capital, the Huatanay and the Tulumayu, and finally the Urubamba into which are fed all the waters from the valley, could carry away these unattractive offerings. Some Indians were then despatched along the winding course of the Urubamba as far as Ollantaytambo so as to make quite sure that the ashes flowed with the current.

In the fifth month, the maize feasts were celebrated. The Indians sang, and for three nights running they watched over a small quantity of maize placed in a cloak, whilst a sorcerer chanted invocations.

During the sixth month the feast of the Sun unfolded in all its glory.

The seventh month was especially revered by women, for it was the feast of the Empress. The feast of Situa, already described, took place at this time.

All these ceremonies were followed by banquets; the invited guests brought their own food and, placing it on the ground, crouched in two parallel lines. The *hurin* and *hanan* usually placed themselves facing each other.

[1] J. D. von Tschudi: *Contribuciones a la historia, op. cit.*, p. 34.

The governor of the province, the *curaca,* or some other high official, presided at the feast, seated on a throne at one end of the two files. There followed songs and dances, and the recital of stories. Table-companions invited each other to drink as we have seen the Inca do at the feast of the Sun.

It must not be thought that because the Indians were generally taciturn, they remained so in each other's society and were sparing of gestures or words. On the contrary, they liked emphasis in their conversation; they were not afraid of hyperbole, and they accompanied their remarks with appropriate mime. If we are to believe Brother Domingo de Santo Tomás, eyes and hands were used to express feeling more than words. Interjections were much used, notably '*gua!*,' which the people of Lima have preserved and repeat today.[1]

Popular dances

Popular dances often required special costumes, and sometimes the dancers painted their faces or wore masks. On the coast they embellished their dance movements with a feather fan. Some dances were just leaps into the air and were reserved for men. A few kept a religious flavour, but the greater part were inspired quite simply by the deeds of everyday life. This is logical, for they were the fulfilment of past toil and a stimulus for work to come. As we have seen in connection with the nobility, the dances acquired more and more the appearance of diagrams or mimed parodies, with shades of historical background, of regret, mockery or hope.

The dances we are about to describe are still practised in our own time.[2] The slow and solemn dance of the llama shepherds was executed to the sound of soft music from flutes, and it went on around their animals who were adorned with bells and rings, covered with fabrics woven from their own wool, and who were as impassive as gods.

The *pulis-pulis* dance recalled the hunting and capture of the birds of that name, and those taking part were decorated

[1] R. Porras Barrenechea: Introduction to *Grammática* by Fray Domingo de Santo Tomás, *op. cit.*, p. 27.

[2] J. Uriel Garcia: *Pueblos y paisajes sudperuanos, op. cit.*, chap. 6. The most unusual of these 'historic' dances today is that in which the Indians, dressed in the costumes of the conquerors and the Incas, mime a ceremony in which the victors pay homage to the Incas—a sort of delayed rectification of history, and an artless revenge by the vanquished.

with feathers. In the same way, the participants in the dance of the *parianes,* a kind of heron, used a covering of the red feathers of this bird as a disguise. In olden times this dance accompanied one of the most important ceremonies of the year, the opening of the irrigation canals by the chief of the *ayllu.* It had, as had many others, a mythological meaning, being consecrated to the divinity of the waters.

To dance the *chaco,* the couples made a circle round the musicians, as they would do round wild beasts at the imperial hunt, the men armed with slings and the women with sticks.

During the tilling dance each one carried a spade, and during the warriors' dance they staged a mock battle. The meaning of the potato dance was clear, for the women held their cloaks with both hands, shaking them as if they were scattering seed on the ground.

Finally the *huaïlla* was the most celebrated of the country dances; the steps were light and fast to the point of frenzy, giving the impression that the feet were beating the soil to smooth it after seed sowing.

Games

Besides dances, the Indians also indulged in games on feast days. These may be divided into two categories.

Children's games, few in number, for children had to carry out their allotted tasks, as we have described, and they had very little time to get together and give themselves up to the pleasures of their age. There remained only feast days, when their parents ate and drank. Added to which, the chroniclers are very cautious on this subject. Poma de Ayala calls the top ancient; we do not know if the ball or the balloon existed; we do not even know if the little girls made dolls as they do in other parts of the world. We hope they did, but perhaps the parents did not like to see in their children's hands those human representations in rags which they used as charms, as is proved by those found in tombs. Besides, these might also remind them of the practices of casting spells.

Sporting games for adults—running, jumping, wrestling, mock-combat and throwing the *ayllo.*

Games of chance: dice existed, in bone or wood, and each of its sides was worth 1, 2, 3, 4, 5 and 20 respectively.

In the *wayru* each player marked the points obtained by advancing stones or beans in holes hollowed out of a flat stone. This was a ritual game, Father P. J. de Arriaga explains, but it might well have not been so. Even its name comes from that of a concubine of the Inca Tupac Yupanqui, who was present one day in his country house at Yucay at a game in which the Emperor was taking part. He won brilliantly and, attributing his good fortune to this gracious presence, he gave the young girl the jewel which had been the stake and decreed that the game itself should bear the name of her who had so ably presided.

In the *chuncara* there were five holes whose value went on increasing by tens from 10 to 50. The one who first reached this last figure won the game, but we do not know the details of this dice game, for which they used different coloured beans, no doubt giving them different values.

It is said that *apaytalla* was invented by the wife of the Inca Pachacutec. The player stood up and made round bean seeds leap from their pods. Whoever made his seed go farthest and made the most noise in falling was proclaimed the winner. It is probable that this game was of Chimu origin, for it is undoubtedly represented on certain vases. It would be difficult to imagine that these drawings referred to scriptural signs, as some people think.

Ritual games consisted of flailing oneself on the legs with cords. 'The native Peruvians,' said an expert on these questions, 'have a strong tendency to beat themselves.'[1] We shall have more to say of a typical ritual game in connection with funeral ceremonies.

An Indian burial

We have reached the end of life. The funeral rites obey custom. In the central regions of the Empire, the corpse was dressed and watched over by his family and friends during the first night. The women cut their hair and threw their cloaks over their heads, weeping and groaning and singing the praises of the deceased. Food and drink were offered to the guests, then sad songs were sung and dances followed, evidently religious dances which soon degenerated into ordinary dances.

[1] E. Romero: *Juegos del antiguo Perú,* Mexico, 1943, p. 25.

This often happens today in many Indian locations, when sometimes their macabre dance ends only at the cemetery or the place where the dead person has just been buried.[1]

Meanwhile they proceeded with the distribution of some personal belongings of the dead person which could not follow him into the grave. The game of dice to which they had recourse took on a magic meaning: it was the dead man himself who chose the beneficiaries by making them obtain the highest score.

The corpse was generally positioned as if it were in the womb—the cycle of life was complete and man ended as he began. He was wrapped in his own clothes. On the coast he was enclosed in an urn. At Jauja he disappeared in a llama skin which took his shape and on the outside of which was modelled a face.[2] The whole thing looked like a parcel, as did the mummies.

Tombs differed greatly according to the regions. Frequently, on the plateau, they were hollowed out of rock, and several corpses often shared one of them. At Collao they built mausoleums with the door opening towards the rising sun. These ruins look like towers, square as at Acora, or rounded as at Sillustani.[3] At Paracas, on the coast, the tomb had a peculiar shape, like a wide bottle with a vertical neck made flush with the ground, with an opening surrounded by a small circular wall.

With the dead man were buried his fetishes, lucky charms, talismans, his working tools, some maize and a bowl of *chicha*. When the burial was completed, the members of the family bathed after taking a communal meal. Some days later they gathered together again to pray and to offer food to the dead.

The variations of these ceremonies were numerous, but there were always tears, songs, feasts and drinking.

Hereditary transmission of property

An informed sociologist has written that the Inca succession was by public law, that of the common people by

[1] H. Castro Pozo: *Nuestra Comunidad indígena, op. cit.*, p. 162.
[2] P. de Cieza de León: *Primera Parte de la Crónica del Perú, op. cit.*, chap. 63.
[3] C. W. Mead: *Old civilizations of Inca Land, op. cit.*, p. 90.

private right.[1] In the latter case, tradition imposed the same rule as the law. The only property free from this was that received from the Inca, which was subject to a special rule of devolution as we have already seen.

The inheritance usually only concerned a very modest patrimony, since the right of individual property was very limited. A degree of freedom to make a will existed in certain areas, such as amongst the Chinchas, where the father chose his heir from amongst his sons or, if he had no sons, from amongst his relatives or friends.[2] The survival of matriarchy made itself felt where the brother or the son of a sister inherited on the maternal side, or again, more rarely, there was a tradition of female inheritance.[3]

The will, which had to be oral, was made by means of a declaration in front of witnesses.

Amongst family duties there were included the guardianship of children and the maintenance of near relatives.

After death

Death did not end the Indians' existence. The survival of the dead in the invisible world was an accepted truth. A sort of 'double' continued to live in the earth's atmosphere, with his ideas and wishes. For this reason ancestor worship was of great importance.

'After the *huacas,* the objects of greatest veneration were the *malquis,*' writes P. de Villagomez.[4] This was the name given to the tombs of ancestors. Food was taken to them, their tombs were adorned with fabrics and feathers, so that they could carry on with their second lives under the best possible conditions.

It must be understood that the 'double' remained closely allied to the earthly body from which it had come. The corpse, as has been said, remained living. But to carry this out the body had to be kept in a perfect state; this was the basic

[1] H. Trimborn: *Familien und Erbrecht in präkolumbischen Peru,* in *Zeitschrift für vergleichende Rechtswissenschaft,* 42, 1937.

[2] C. de Castro y D. de Ortega Morejón: *Relación y declaración, op. cit.,* p. 244.

[3] B. Cobo: *Historia del Nuevo Mundo, op. cit.,* book 12, chap. 15.

[4] P. de Villagomez: *Carta pastoral, op. cit.,* chap. 42; J. Mejia Valera: *Organización de la Sociedad en el Perú precolombino, op. cit.,* p. 38.

reason for embalming, and also the reason above all others why the Indians feared being burned. Atahualpa agreed to become a convert to Catholicism (which horrified him) because he had been promised that he would not be burned alive. He thus escaped annihilation and assured his survival.

CHAPTER 13

ECONOMIC LIFE
AGRICULTURE AND FISHING

THE CULTIVATION CALENDAR

THE Indians were above all tillers of the soil; the calendar of production and harvest was established in the following way, in terms of cultivation.[1]

The first month of the year was always reckoned from December 21, with reference to the moon, of whose importance we have already spoken. Even the name of the month was 'moon'—*quilla* in Quechua. The Indians earthed up the potatoes, maize and *oca,* and cleaned the fields. They went fishing and with slings in their hands helped the children to drive the beasts away from the fields; the women helped too by beating on a drum. As it rains frequently at this time of the year, the family was obliged to remain indoors for long periods, where they busied themselves with caring for their clothes and sanctifying themselves by prayer, penitence and sacrifices.[2] It was a time of contemplation and preparation. Food consisted of preserved provisions taken from the store jars, maize and early potatoes, herbs and fruits, and fish if possible.

The second month of the year, approximately February, was the month of hope, for the harvest was near. Breaking new ground was easy in soil moistened by the rains. Everyone tried to increase the area of cultivation with the help of his neighbours, and roads and canals were repaired.

The third month was that of ripening. The maize came up and the children were hard put to it to defend the crop against the birds. On the coast fish was particularly plentiful, and

[1] The calendar we have described is for the most part borrowed from Poma de Ayala: *Nueva Corónica, op. cit.,* pp. 1131 to 1157.

[2] This month is 'the beginning of showers' (*aguaceros*), writes Poma de Ayala.

dried fish arrived along the trade routes to the heart of the *sierra*.

April, the fourth month, brought an abundance of flowers and fruits, and homage to the sovereign, whose feast this was.

May, the fifth month, was justly regarded as the most important month of the year. The family harvested maize, pulled off the leaves, shelled the ears, sorted the corn, and providently set aside the seed-corn. This tender maize was good to eat, but no good for the preparation of *chicha*. Then they had to gather herbs and dry them, and also prepare *charqui*, for May was the hunting season.

In June it was the turn of the potatoes and *oca* to be dug from the ground and turned into *chuño*.[1] In between whiles they gathered *quinua*, repaired their dwellings, roads and canals. Inspectors came round to see that each family was building up the necessary reserves of food, and prepared statistics of the population and of stocks of all kinds.

The harvesting of plants took place in July, and then the Indians worked on the lands of the Inca and the Sun. They spread manure and began to plough their own strips of ground and to sow maize in them. The redivision of communal lands took place at this time.[2]

In August potatoes as well as maize had to be planted. Prayers and sacrifices took place to ensure the favour of the gods for future harvests. Quantities of vegetables were gathered, also salt and pepper.

The sowing of seed went on in September, and during this month the Empress' feast was celebrated. When there was a drought they had recourse to religious ceremonies to bring it to an end.

October was a month of preparation. Seeds were watered, wood collected, ropes woven and thatch repaired. If rain was still delayed, prayers became more pressing and offerings more numerous.

In November and December, months dedicated respectively to the dead and the Sun, they had to live on their food reserves.

[1] Poma de Ayala names the month of June *Chuño Mocaya Zaroy Quilla*, that is to say the month during which they peel the frozen potatoes and crush them underfoot to make *chuño*.

[2] The transport of the products belonging to the Inca and the Sun took place at this time.

But during December there was plenty of fruit. Before the end of the year potatoes, *ocas* and vegetables were again sown.

The land which was the scene of the agricultural activities we have just described belonged to the agrarian community. But its area was little by little extended so as to match the increase in the population, at first spontaneously by individual initiative, and then in the time of the Incas by State intervention. In both cases the procedure was the same. Work was communally carried out, and fertilizers were used.

EXTENDING CULTIVATION: TERRACES AND CANALS

This work of extension consisted of the construction of terraces and the digging of canals.

Terraces, such as exist in all parts of the world, make sloping areas of land into horizontal strips, so that the soil can be cultivated. In this way certain Andean valleys have been transformed into staircases. The banks were held up by walls of stone the height of which varied with the steepness of the incline; and they leaned slightly in the direction of the slope the better to resist the pressure of the enclosed earth. Conduits arranged on the hill-side allowed the flow of rain water.

The canals were no less remarkable. Sometimes as long as nine miles, they crossed mountains and valleys, making a system of irrigation of which one chronicler wrote: 'There are no better at Murcie or Milan.'[1]

The question of water always preoccupied the Peruvians. Its great value explains the care brought to the fashioning of receptacles to hold it. Several legends of pre-columbian times show the lengths to which they went to obtain it. It is said that at Ica, Pachacutec made advances to a young girl who repulsed him because she already loved a young man. Instead of being angry, the monarch was struck with admiration and asked the girl what she would like. She replied that she herself had no particular desires, but she would be happy if her village could have water at its disposal. So, by order of the sovereign, the 40,000 soldiers of his army laid aside their

[1] J. de Acosta: *Historia Natural y Moral, op. cit.*, book 3, chap. 18; B. Cobo: *Historia del Nuevo Mundo, op. cit.*, book 14, chap. 8.

weapons, took spades and dug the canal which waters the valley.

Another legend much resembles this one but is less charming. It is set in the district of Chachapoyas. When the ruler of Cuzco conquered this province, he fell in love with the daughter of the chief, the *curaca,* who also asked that water should be provided. Unfortunately for this village, the Emperor perceived that the princess was entangled in a love idyll with the son of a neighbouring chief, and he was less generous that Pachacutec, for he stopped the work, flew into a rage, and struck the ground with such force that a crack appeared. The Indians show this fissure to this day, and say that this is how the town suffered from lack of water on account of a jilted lover.[1]

The work of making terraces and canals was carried out by the members of the community divided into teams (*mincas*). As a general rule, whoever took part in an enterprise which was not his own had to be fed by the recipient of his labours during the time he was working. If the works were considered to be for the benefit of the public, the workers received their subsistence from officials, who took them from the public storehouses.

INTENSIVE CULTIVATION: MANURES

Intensive cultivation went on and was also extended through fertilization of the soil. Formerly human and animal excrement was used for this purpose on the plateau; on the coast the tribes used the heads of the fish they had eaten, and also bird dung, *guano*. The Incas organized the methodical exploitation of this by dividing the Chincha islands, where there were mountains of this excrement, between the provinces of the Empire, and they specified the period at which they were allowed to send Indians to lay in a stock. Whoever killed any of the birds or disturbed them at the nesting period was punished by death.

PRINCIPLES OF LAND DIVISION

Once the yield was increased in this way by the application of intensive and extensive cultivation, the area was shared

[1] A. Miro Quesada: *Costa, sierra y montaña, op. cit.*, p. 186.

amongst the Emperor's subjects under the direction of officials and in conformity with a rationalized plan drawn up at Cuzco. The Indian community, in principle, could only rely on itself, but as the unforeseen was the responsibility of the State, the latter took what quantity exceeded the minimum in order to face up to this charge.

To apply this principle strictly, the products of the community had to be stored communally and shared out to each according to his needs, the rest returning to the State. This system, which could have been communistic, would have destroyed local customs. Very wisely the directors of the State waived the exigencies of integral rationalism and shared out the land and not its produce. They found it of immense advantage to leave the Indians a certain amount of initiative and responsibility. The ownership of their land was taken from them, but the fruits of their soil remained. In this way one of the most formidable consequences of the communist system was avoided, the rupture of all connection of the individual with production and fulfilment, a rupture which would have obliged those in authority to make a choice between two alternatives. Either all stimulus to work would have disappeared, since each man would have been sure, whether he worked or not, of obtaining the vital minimum, and consequently the almost inevitable appearance of famine; or else the instigation of a system of forced labour, both dictatorial and totalitarian.[1]

At the time of the Incas, thanks to the laws adopted, the lazy were punished, since they could not obtain from the land allotted to them the products necessary for their existence, and they ran the risk of being hungry. The workers were recompensed, for not only did they have enough to sustain life, but they could dispose of a surplus harvest in the most suitable manner, especially by bartering for other products. Plainly the co-operation of nature could be favourable for the production of this surplus, just as contrariness could make it disappear—hail and frost could not be controlled by imperial regulations. In any case, if the punishment threatened to be

[1] For explanations relative to the economic systems of the Empire, the reader is referred to L. Baudin, *Manuel d'Économie politique,* 7th ed. Paris, 1953, p. 288 onwards.

severe, the recompense remained modest. This was the motive power in the national economy.

It can now be seen why each family received, on marriage, a plot of ground which should be sufficient for sustaining life, and which was called *tupu*.[1] This plot varied according to the quality of the soil, which is logical. With the birth of each son a supplementary plot was allocated to the parent, and with the birth of each daughter a half plot. The family was thus assured of a minimum of existence. Once all the families in a community were provided for, the surplus land was allotted to the Inca and the Sun, that is to say to the State and to Religion. And so a surplus was guaranteed, thanks to the work the sovereign at Cuzco had arranged to be done under the direction of his officers.

Nothing was changed with regard to the ancient tri-partite division of the agrarian community. Woods and pastures remained at the disposition of the members without being shared out amongst them; houses and enclosures belonged to families; all cultivable land was redivided amongst them each year, having regard to fallow fields. Each head of family had the right to a pair of llamas whose wool and dung he took, and which he used for transport, but which he could not slaughter, with the exception of large herds in certain districts (amongst the Collas). Sometimes the community grazed llamas on its pastures and these provided wool for distribution amongst its members.

Besides working on their own lands, the Indians in a community had to cultivate those belonging to old men, invalids, widows or orphans—what we would call a natural service of public assistance—those of the *curacas* in conformity with local traditions, and also those of the Inca and the Sun.

THE LANDS OF THE SUN AND THE INCA

The lands appropriated to the Sun varied in extent according to the importance of the temples and the *huacas* which had to be provisioned—their size varied with the number of priests and the number of sacrifices.

[1] Polo de Ondegardo: *De la orden que los Indios tenyan en dividir los tributos é distribuyrlos entre si,* in *Colección de documentos inéditos del Archivo de Indias,* t. 17.

The Inca's lands were the only ones whose dimensions were not fixed according to conditions already existing, they made up 'the rest.' Under these arrangements it is easy to understand the interest shown by public officials in all measures capable of producing an increase in these holdings. The minimum was assured to both visible and invisible beings, the economic and religious basis was firmly established, the surplus came to the State. The Inca's lands were watched over by special guards who lived on them, and did not necessarily belong to the community.

A complication arose when, through an increase of population or an increase in the aridity of the soil, a community was not able to ensure even the minimum for existence. We know that in this case a certain number of families could be displaced by public authority, but another solution was sometimes adopted, especially when only certain products were lacking. The central administration assigned to the community plots of land in the coastal valleys, impressing upon them the necessity of taking every precaution to sow and reap these areas.[1]

The public storehouses not only received the produce from the lands of the Inca and the Sun, but also the wool provided by the herds of llamas which belonged to these two divine beings and which existed only in high altitude areas. The wool from animals captured during imperial hunting parties and especially that of vicuñas was also brought to the same stores.

DAILY LABOUR

Let us imagine ourselves in the days of the Incas and follow the Indian as he sets out to work one fine morning in July. An immutable order provided that the lands of the Inca and the Sun came before all others. Nothing could be more just. That day, at dawn, a trumpeter climbed the slopes of the hill overlooking the village and blew into his conch shell to call the inhabitants together. They all came, with their wives,

[1] Polo de Ondegardo: *Relación de los fundamentos acerca del notable daño que resulte de no guardar a los Indios sus fueros* 1571, in *Colección de documentos inéditos del Archivo de Indias,* t. 17, p. 46. The Marquis of Cañete, Viceroy of Peru in 1555, after enquiries, returned to the province of Chucuito the lands they held on the coast in Inca times so that they could be assured of a livelihood.

gathered in their family groups, spade on shoulder and wearing holiday clothes. To serve the god of light or his representative on earth was not work, it was a pleasure. Everyone knew, moreover, that the Emperor himself each year at this time went to the field of Kolkampata, sacred to the worship of the Sun, and ploughed the soil in homage to his creator.

Once the little party had arrived, officials divided the tasks amongst the group leaders, and they amongst their individual members, assigning to each of them a long and narrow strip of land so that the leader had only to move backwards in a straight line and all the other men in the group followed parallel to him. This system, like that of sharing portions between the members of the community, had the advantage of fixing responsibility. He who finished first did not help the others, 'otherwise,' explains a legal expert, 'they would have done nothing.' In fact, no one finished before or after the others, for the Indians placed themselves in line, each on his strip of land, with his wife in front of him. They began to sing in chorus and worked back evenly in line, matching the rhythm of their actions to the song. The refrain which regulated the general speed was 'victory'—*haylli*—victory over nature, over evil spirits, over famine and death.

The instrument of toil was a very simple tool which was used to turn the earth, the *taklla,* a piece of hard wood slightly more than 3 feet long, having, in Ecuador, a groove towards the centre so that the left hand could more easily hold it. In Peru a second piece of hard wood, bent round, was bound near the centre. This was held by the right hand whilst the left held the first piece of wood upright. In both models, just above the tapering end, were fixed two small crossed sticks on which the worker placed the right foot to drive the stake into the ground like a spade. However this was considered to be inferior to the *taklla,* for it dug out large lumps of soil, whilst the *taklla* crumbled it.[1] Poma de Ayala shows a delicious drawing of Adam digging with a *taklla.*[2]

To till the soil, the Indian lifted this tool and drove it with all his strength into the ground, then he leaned on it with his

[1] P. Rodriguez de Aguayo: *Descripción de la cuidad de Quito,* in *Relaciones geográficas de Indias,* t. 3, p. 95.
[2] Poma de Ayala: *Nueva Corónica, op. cit.,* p. 22.

foot and added the pressure of his arms backwards and forwards so as to break up the soil. His wife picked up the stones and broke up the sods with a large stone. The tilling took the form of a series of holes into which the seed was thrown, and there was no continuous furrow. After making a series of these broken parallel lines, the group of workers dug another series of identical lines at right angles to the first.

Instead of two people, there were sometimes three, two men and a woman, so as to break the soil up more deeply. The presence of the women had not only an economic but a magical significance. The earth was considered to be feminine, she was the foster-mother, and Indian women were supposed to be in closer contact with her than their fathers or husbands.

Tools varied according to the country. The Araucans used a *taklla,* shaped like a trident, and a perforated stone attached to the handle gave it extra weight. In the Chiloe islands, two Indians operated a tool, one drove it into the ground, the other raised the embedded point with a stake, thus levering up a huge sod.[1]

For earthing up potatoes, the farmer used a bronze adze with a curved wooden handle.

After working on the lands of the Inca and the Sun, the Indians prepared the land of those who were unable to work on their own, of whom we have already spoken. For this they wore their working clothes and were supervised by their officials. But when they finally came to their own plots, they worked as they pleased. They always began by carefully marking out their domain, placing stones or planting cactus; then they decided the order they would follow in carrying out the work.[2]

To watch over their fields, they had a very practical arrangement: they put certain stones in charge. Since everything on earth was living, especially beneficent rocks fulfilled this mission best. They were called *huancas,* and they survive to this day in a few places. At Piruro, in the province of Huanuco,

[1] R. Latcham: *La Organización agraria de los antiguos indígenas de Chile,* in *La Información,* December 1926.

[2] We have not mentioned the lands belonging to the *curacas,* for the information about them is contradictory. The account relative to the province of Chucuito does not tally with the information given by Fernando de Santillán and Falcón.

a block of stone has been from time immemorial the guardian of the fields, and also of the animals which it protects from the thunderbolt. To win favour, the Indians adorn the rock with wild flowers and water it with *chicha*. The existence of these silent sentinels, unexacting and alleged to be efficient, was recorded by the Spanish missionaries in their search for idols.[1]

FISHING

On the shores of Lake Titicaca and on the Pacific coast, fish was the staple food of the family. The Indians used hooks, nets, traps, and at night lanterns which enabled them to exercise their skill in shooting with arrows the fish attracted by the light.

The fishing boat of Lake Titicaca was identical with the one that today's tourists regard with amusement from the steam-boat which maintains a service between Puno in Peru and Guaqui in Bolivia. It is constructed of bundles of *totora* reed, closely tied together, five or six feet long and about two feet wide, a yellow spindle on which are raised two small masts supporting a sail also of *totora*. It glides like an eel through the jungle of reeds which covers the mouth of the Desaguadero. Its builders, as of old, are the famous Urus whose antiquity we have described, and whose decline we have deplored.[2]

The skiff used by the fishermen on the Pacific coast was also a reed spindle, but more primitive, in the shape of a cigar the centre of which was like the back of a charger and the rear raised—hence the name given to them by the Spaniards, 'the little reed horse.' The rider had his legs hanging in the water and guided his mount with a paddle.

For more ambitious fishing the coast-dweller used the ocean-going raft. This vessel, sometimes very large, was made of balsa trunks, a hard and light wood very common in the forests bordering the Pacific to the north of Tumbez. These trunks, laid side by side and strongly bound together, were all of the same size, but of different lengths; the middle one was the longest and the others to the right and left were shorter,

[1] A. Jimenez Borja: *Imagen del mundo aborigen,* in *Tradición, Cuzco,* January 1951, p. 9.

[2] For a charming description, see the opening of *Balseros del Titicaca,* by E. Romero, Lima, 1934.

like the fingers of the hand. A deck was constructed on these and a reed shelter. A cotton sail fixed to a mast enabled them to make use of the winds and a huge stone attached to a rope served as an anchor.[1] Very ingeniously, boards fixed between the pieces of wood acted as a keel and replaced the rudder. As a result, when the rear boards offered more resistance than the front ones, the force of the wind on the sail turned the prow; and in the opposite way the stern direction was changed. Thus it was sufficient to raise or lower these boards and by combining their effects to obtain the exact result required.[2]

The Changos in the Tarapaca region replaced balsa, which they did not possess, by skins inflated like water-skins and bound together.

On all the rivers of the Amazon basin in the eastern forests, on the undefined outskirts of the Empire, the classical Indian pirogues glided on the current.

[1] Pedro Pizarro: *Relación del descubrimiento y conquista del Perú*, *op. cit.*, p. 276.

[2] Thor Heyerdahl: *The Kon-Tiki Expedition.*

CHAPTER 14

ECONOMIC LIFE

THE CRAFTSMEN AND THE PROVISION OF SERVICES

THE subjects of the Empire were providers of both goods and services. The greatest number of them, unless they had some particular service to fulfil, were craftsmen. Officials distributed to them their basic materials taken from the public storehouses, in conformity with the orders of the government, who in their turn were guided by the statistical returns. The finished articles were then returned to the keepers of the stores, and that is why the Spaniards found so much wealth in them.

DEFICIENCY OF EQUIPMENT

That any articles should be manufactured at all was remarkable in view of the deficiency of the equipment. A bronze chisel and a copper axe were commonly used. A heavy stone held in the hand was used as a hammer, and a polished flint served as a knife. A level was made from a ruler of hollowed out wood, the cavity being filled with little round stones like marbles. They did not use nails, they bound things together. Cords made of plaited aloe were extremely strong.

Ignorance of the wheel seems extraordinary amongst a people who knew the circle and whose directors practised a super-rationalism with effects which we have already summarized. It proves that, in spite of their efforts, the Peruvians still remained narrowly submissive to the influences of nature, as indicated in the first chapter of this book. In other words, the wheel is rational and not natural. Our own physical or biological background provides many examples of this. We must acknowledge once again that the principal factors of production, today much blurred, were discipline and the weather.

Let us examine the most usual techniques in the main branches of economic activity.

POTTERY TECHNIQUE

We have on several occasions alluded to the perfection and variety of the pottery of Peru. Here again the craftsman gave proof of great skill, for he did not know of the lathe. He moulded the different parts, joined them together and added the neck and handles when he had completed the main object. The clay he used was often mixed with chopped maize straw to prevent breaking during firing or drying. It has been found that certain Nazca potters used wooden envelopes to prevent oven dust from harming the painting during firing.[1]

TEXTILE TECHNIQUE

Textile technique was complicated. Cotton and wool were the basic materials, but although the cotton is still considered today to be of excellent quality,[2] it only grows in the hot regions of the west (on the coast), or in the east (Tucuman in Argentina, Santa Cruz of the Sierra in Bolivia). Cotton clothing for the imperial family was provided by loans from the public stores in these provinces, or by gifts brought by the chiefs who lived in these countries so far away from the capital. On the plateau the Indians made their clothes from llama wool.

Women spun cotton and wool, using a wooden spindle, sometimes carved. They busied themselves with this work whenever they had a free moment, especially when going from place to place, and so long as they were not obliged to use their hands for carrying the cradle, a jar, or other objects for which room could not be found on their backs.

The threads were wound round small sticks or reeds in skeins or balls. Most of the cloth found in tombs was woven with a double thread. The weaving loom was small and of the vertical type. Two parallel sticks of wood stretched the warp thread, both fixed in the ground, or one suspended from the branch of a tree or a post, the other attached by a belt to a crouching or kneeling worker, who varied the tension of the threads by bending her body one way or the other. Two other wooden rods were placed between these sticks and parallel to

[1] L. Capitan and H. Lorin: *Le Travail en Amérique avant et après Colomb,* Paris, p. 141.

[2] *Gossypium peruvianum* with long fibres.

them. The warp threads of the odd rows were passed under the first stick and over the second, those of the even rows followed the reverse of this. The worker then slipped a wooden needle between the warp threads thus separated, making a shuttle on to which was wound the weft.[1]

The workers used the natural shadings of the cotton and wool with much taste. When they had recourse to dyes, they applied them to the thread and not to the cloth. Vegetable colours were usually used, but in this case it was necessary to make the threads hard and porous by using an aluminium mordant, either silicate of aluminium, silicate of lime, or iron oxide.

Many kinds of textiles have survived to our times, bearing witness to the great skill of the workers. Sometimes the warp is of a different quality and shade from that of the weft; sometimes the weft is composed of various colours; sometimes very fine gold or silver threads mingle charmingly with the others. Sometimes it happened that regular perforations gave the whole the appearance of drawn-thread embroidery.[2]

One writer, after studying Peruvian textiles, believes it impossible to draw up a list of techniques, so great is their diversity.[3]

Their knotted threads deserve a special mention. Knots were made quite simply with the fingers and were very closely packed together, rather like our 'macramé,' and this implies working for a very long time. The designs were often complicated and their main characteristic was the multiplicity of oblique lines, accentuated by the choice of bright colours. From these spring the beautiful conventions which we admire.

Gauze fabrics were woven in classical manner by stretching the warp round other adjacent warp threads. This work took a very long time.

In embroidery a great many stitches were used, stem stitch, cross stitch, back stitch for horizontal lines, overcast for vertical lines

A pre-arranged pattern was necessary to make a rayed cloth

[1] P. A. Means: *Ancient Civilizations of the Andes, op. cit.,* chap. 11.

[2] L. Capitan and H. Lorin: *Le Travail en Amérique avant et après Colomb,* op. cit., p. 150.

[3] L. M. O'Neale: *Tejidos del periodo primitivo de Paracas,* in *Revista del Museo Nacional de Lima,* 1932, no. 2, p. 61.

which usually produced a complicated and harmonious blend of colours. For example, the prettiest effects were obtained by combining red and black on a white background.

For outer garments wool was better than cotton, and it was easier and more suitable for dyeing. A pretty grey was obtained at Paracas by mingling woollen fibres of cream and brown and spinning them together. The Indians in the Chincha valley were renowned for their skill in weaving fine cotton materials.

The manufacture of materials had become so important in the days of the last Incas, and the clothing of the common people was worn for so long, that the public stores were bursting with lengths of cloth and the required quantities were wisely reduced.[1]

Amongst plaited articles, slings came first. There was no child who did not own one. They were made from aloe fibre covered with woollen threads, often many coloured.[2]

FEATHER TECHNIQUE

Lastly the method of making fabrics from feathers deserves to be mentioned. The basic material consisted of feathers of all sizes and all colours. The smallest came from the humming-birds of the *sierra*, the larger ones from the parakeets of the forest. They figured amongst the items exacted as tribute.

The Indians of the eastern forests were so wild, explains a chronicler, that they did not have a known domicile, and their lands were so lacking in resources that the only contribution the officials had been able to extract from them was bird feathers. They owned a large number of parakeets which they had domesticated and which they used as watch-dogs, for these volatile chatterers uttered strident cries when they saw a newcomer, so that it was impossible to pass by unseen. The stores contained quantities of feathers. Pedro Sancho states that in some of them one could count more than 100,000 dried birds.

The craftsman worked in this way. The point of the horny

[1] F. de Santillán: *Relación, op. cit.*, para. 73; C. de Castro y D. de Ortega Morejón: *Relación y declaración, op. cit.*, p. 218.

[2] R. d'Harcourt: *Le Tressage des Frondes au Pérou et en Bolivie*, in *Journal des Américanistes de Paris*, 1940, p. 103.

tube of the shaft was folded back on itself so as to form a loop which was held in position by a cotton thread bound tightly round the neck. The same thread passed through the middle of the loop, and the stem was thus suspended. The feathers were aligned horizontally close together, and the rows overlapped one another vertically so that there was no gap between them.

One writer describes a ceremonial stick covered with feathers of three colours—warm orange, purplish-black and chrome yellow—and another stick of the same kind was covered with red and blue. This, as he explains, was a real piece of jewellery, for the smallest feathers measured 11 mm long and 6 mm wide and were placed 1 mm apart. It is incredible that a craftsman could achieve such work without tweezers or magnifying lenses.[1] The reason for using feathers seems to have been for decoration, and they were not reserved for the Incas, for they could become personal property and could remain in the individual inheritance.

Feathers were above all used as crests or plumes for the head-dresses of chiefs, in the same manner as for the *mascapaicha*. It is remarkable that the Inca preferred feathers of modest colourings from the birds of the plateau for this ornament, rather than those of the parakeets with their brilliant shades. On the coast there were feather fans with handles made from a bundle of *totora* stems; these were used in ritualistic ceremonies.

All these articles aroused the admiration of the Spaniards. The Indian craftsmen obtained delicate and graded combinations of colour such as European painters had never succeeded in producing. The shimmer of materials, the brilliance of plumes, provided for the festivities we have described a splendour the memory of which still has not faded.

OTHER TECHNIQUES

The work required of the Empire's subjects could also consist of making objects in stone, leather, wood, bone, rope or metal.

[1] E. Yacovleff: *Arte plumaria entre los antiguos Peruanos,* in *Revista del Museo Nacional de Lima,* 1933, no. 2, p. 146; J. de Acosta: *Historia natural, op. cit.,* t. 1, book 4, chap. 37.

The museums of Europe and America show mortars, dishes for sacrifices, hammers, and all sorts of axes and clubs of polished stone. The skin of the llama provided very supple leather. All Indians knew how to dry it and preserve it in containers filled with urine; then they beat it to make it supple and made water-skins, or, after cutting it, soles for sandals.

Wood was used in making certain weapons, such as clubs and *estólicas,* looms for weaving, spindles, litters and framework for roofs. Pretty wooden goblets were decorated with ornamental designs in bright colours. From bones were made flutes, shuttles, spoons and jewellery. To make cord, the Indians carried *cabuya* fibres to the river, as they still do today in some places, set themselves in line, and either singing or chatting, soaked and beat the fibres, finally drying them in the sun and plaiting them. Nets and hammocks were made from this cord.

METALS

Amongst the metals known in the pre-columbian era were gold, silver, copper, lead, platinum, and tin. Iron was unknown. This fact has been contested, but a recent and strange discovery has brought proof. The high officials in the suite of the Inca Atahualpa envisaged, shortly before the capture of their Emperor, the possibility of seizing the white invaders and putting them to death. One of their number asked that the smith of the Spanish army should be spared so that he could tell the Indians the secrets of his trade.[1]

Platinum was found in small quantities on the coast of Ecuador, to the north of the Gulf of Guayaquil. We know today that it was used as an alloy with gold and silver. The Indians in the district of Esmeraldas took about 7 per cent of gold, 18 per cent of platinum and 12 per cent of silver to produce the white gold which appeared in the record of the division of booty after the capture of Cuzco, under the heading 'a sheet of white gold heavier than anything else.' They wondered what this white gold could be, why it was so heavy, and why the rulers of Cuzco had adulterated gold which was their most

[1] R. Porras Barrenechea: *Una Relación inédita, op. cit.*

precious and almost divine metal, thus diminishing its value. Again the religious aspect must be considered. The sheet of gold in question had been placed in the temple of the Moon, and, to contrast with the Sun, had to be of a precious metal of the same colour as the moon. As to the weight, the amount set down in the record of which we are speaking corresponds to more than 500 lbs. of gold, which is not surprising when one learns that this sheet of metal measured about 9 feet long. Also there was no scale on which it could be weighed; this could only be done at the time of melting.[1] The use of platinum and resort to an alloy proves to what extremes the far-distant peoples had been driven by the Incas to make up their supplies of basic materials, for the countries where platinum was found had not come under the domination of Cuzco to any permanent degree.

Tin was only used to obtain bronze, which was known to the Aymaras before Inca times.

Copper, which became sharp when it was thinned down and polished, appears in our museums in the form of large needles, breast-plates, axes and knives. These knives were usually semi-circular in shape and the handle was fixed to the middle of the rectilinear part. They thus correspond to certain modern tools rather than to actual knives. The axes follow their natural evolution which little by little rendered them unsuitable for their original purpose, and they were used as ornaments and barter goods on account of a progressive stylization. The stages of this evolution are apparent in Peru, where they developed side by side with battle-axes, heavy and large. Finally the thin light axes were designed exclusively as 'money tokens,' to be used in trade. This observation applies to the whole of America and not only to the Incas, for these articles have been found in Mexico, Brazil and Ecuador.[2]

The melting of metals was achieved by different processes. For copper it was sufficient to place the ore, already crushed, in an earthenware pot over a hot fire. Tin was added to make bronze, and clay or stone moulds were used to obtain the required object.

[1] R. Loredo: *El Reparto de los tesoros del Cuzco,* in *Revista del archivo histórico del Cuzco,* 1950, t. 1, p. 259.

[2] L. Baudin: *L'Empire socialiste des Inka, op. cit.,* p. 167.

The process was more complicated for silver which does not melt when heated. Lead had to be added and the two metals were then placed in huge round clay pots. These were very thick and about three feet high and fifteen inches in diameter, and filled with charcoal or dried llama dung. Holes left in the sides allowed the passage of air, but the ones on the side away from the wind were plugged with clay. Under each pot a light shelf held the embers which warmed the air entering the ovens. They were careful to choose high windy places to instal these primitive ovens, like the hill-side of Potosi. The melting metal was collected in a receptacle under the pot. Then all they had to do was to separate the lead from the silver by a succession of meltings which they did in their own homes.

The technique of metallurgy was carried on in several centres in Peru; at Nazca on the south coast, at Lambayeque and at Chavin in the north, and at Tiahuanaco.

Gold was found in mines, but more often in alluvium. The mines were shafts as deep as a man is tall, or narrow, low and dark galleries. The workmen dug in the earth with a wooden bar which had a copper end, and placed the gold-bearing soil in bags made from llama skins, and the contents were then tipped out on smooth slabs of stone. Water running in a thin stream from a little channel arranged for the purpose, little by little washed away the soil, leaving the metal behind. Guards posted at the entrance of the mine and around it ensured that no one fraudulently carried away packages of gold.[1]

METAL OBJECTS

Here we find again the mixture of primitive technique and modern processes which was so frequent in pre-columbian Peru. For if extractions were made by very simple methods, the manufacture of articles was equally complicated. The Indians knew about plating metal by hammering and inlaying one metal on another. They knew how to weld silver and inlay other materials into silver (for instance different coloured shells) and they were able to do embossing. Certain places were well known for their goldsmiths, not only in Peru, but in

[1] Pedro Sancho: *Relación para S.M., op. cit.*, p. 181.

countries where this art had developed before Inca times, such as at Chordeleg (Ecuador today), and in the Chibcha country (Colombia today).[1] In the latter the legend of the man or the realm of gold was born (El Dorado).[2] The story of Atahualpa's ransom helped to spread the legend of Peruvian gold in Europe.

Indian women in the Empire, in every walk of life, on feast days wore bracelets, rings, pendants, and above all artistically worked pins, as far as the regulations allowed. They generally showed better taste than their husbands and, as workers, showed themselves more skilled.[3]

THE ART OF EMBALMING

On the plateau, there existed one very special and complicated art: that of embalming. It was unknown on the coast, as the dryness of the air preserved bodies. In the damp valleys of the Corderilla, on the contrary, they used the balm of Peru and of Tolu, the menthol found in mint and sweet clover, alkalis, tannin and the soap found in the so-called Panama wood. Shrouded in cotton and surrounded by multiple layers of material which made it into a kind of parcel, the mummy was topped with a very rough human face in wood, metal or fabric. Because of the difficulties of this undertaking the process was only applied to the corpses of people of high rank.

TROPHY HEADS

Nazca craftsmen were particularly skilful in preparing trophy heads. The simplest of these 'curios' was obtained by drying

[1] In Ecuador, gold was inlaid in the teeth of certain people of high rank. Gold articles have been found half-way between Lima and Trujillo, others on the shore of Lake Titicaca. Holes bored in stone slabs at Tiahuanaco were prepared for the reception of nails with golden heads, so visitors are told.

M. Saville: *The gold treasure of Sigsig, Ecuador,* New York, 1924; Wendell C. Bennett: *Peruvian Gold, Natural History,* January 1932, p. 22; P. A. Means: *The Spanish Main,* New York, 1935, p. 103.

[2] At the time of his accession to the throne, the chief Chibcha de Guatabita on the high plateau, had to make a sacrifice to the gods by throwing gold into a lake. During the ritual ceremony which followed he was anointed with some sticky substance on which powdered gold was sprinkled, so that he shone as though he himself was made of gold. (P. A. Means, *The Spanish Main, op. cit.,* p. 105.)

[3] J. de Acosta: *Historia natural y moral, op. cit.,* t. 2, book 6, chap. 16.

the skin, emptying the cranium, and joining the lips with thorns; they were then attached to slings so that their owners could carry them about.

The same workers knew how to shrink them so that they could easily be suspended from clothing or weapons. In this case, the cranium was emptied through the neck opening and filled with warm sand; the face was rubbed over with warm, flat stones, and as soon as the sand had cooled it was replaced with more hot sand. This took two days and the head shrank without losing the likeness. The Jivaros of eastern Ecuador today practice a similar technique to produce their celebrated 'shrunken heads.'

THE PROVISION OF SERVICES

Instead of having to provide goods, the Indians could be called upon to provide services by leaving home and the family circle. They already did this traditionally by helping their neighbours, not as an act of mutual responsibility but out of respect for a custom based on the universal principle of reciprocity.

This co-operation, which took the form of equivalent services and counter-services, was called *ayne*. It is difficult to distinguish it from *minca* in the writings of modern commentators. Both consisted of collective work, but the first concerned an individual action, the mutual aid when it was necessary to build a home for a newly-married couple. The second related to a collective work for the common good, which required a division into teams complementary to each other, especially for public works. The collective having come before the individual, *minca* was not a generalization of *ayne,* it was rather that the one appeared as a special case of the other, though we cannot make any definite statement in this respect.[1]

As regards services to the State, specialization was highly developed, the principle being that each man was effective in the work for which he had shown the greatest aptitude.

[1] J. A. Fonvielhe: *L'Évolution juridique et sociale de l'Indien du Pérou, op. cit.,* p. 165; A. Sivirichi: *Derecho indígena peruano, op. cit.,* pp. 289 and 290; O. Nuñez del Pardo: *Chinchero, un pueblo andino del Sud,* in *Revista Universitaria de Cuzco,* 1949, 2, p. 201; G. Bedregal: *Nueva Organización de la comunidad indígena,* in *Revista Universitaria de Cuzco,* 1948, 1, p. 236.

In a manuscript from Indian archives, recently published, mention is made of the services provided for the Inca by the province of Chucuito. This district, which was of a certain economic importance because of its geographical situation (it was on the shores of Lake Titicaca), and on account of the density of its population, was one of the most prosperous in the realm. In 1567 the number of tributaries assigned to it, according to the estimate of competent people available, was 15,400. These tributaries were men between thirty and sixty years of age; the *yanaconas* and the *mitimaes* were excluded from this total and they were estimated at 1000 and were scattered as far away as Jauja, Pacari, Cuzco and even distant Quito. At the time of the Incas, according to the Spanish investigators, the tributaries of the province must have exceeded the figure of 20,000, but they had suffered heavy losses during the war between Huascar and Atahualpa. Besides this, a certain number of Indians had been sent to the Potosi mines, and others had fled into the mountains to escape this levy. From these 20,000 subjects of the Inca the following services were required: 3000 to be soldiers, an unlimited number to work on the construction of monuments at Cuzco, as servants for the Inca, couriers, guards for the *tambos,* young girls to serve the Sun, miners for the workings at Chuquiabo (gold) and Porco (silver), and finally men, women and children for sacrifices to the Sun.[1]

Let us examine some of these services. Those required for the roads were divided into two categories; the transmission of messages and the maintenance of bridges.

Messengers were used only by the government. They were chosen from amongst the most active and were specially trained from an early age. They lived in *chozas* or huts placed alongside the roads. According to the importance of the highway the rules provided that there must be four or six men at each relay. The system was as follows: two Indians always had to be crouched on the threshold, each one looking at one side of the road. As soon as one of them saw a runner, he went to meet him, then retracing his steps he ran alongside him to receive the oral message and sometimes the knotted

[1] M. Helmer: *La Vie économique au 16e siècle sur le haut plateau andin, op. cit.,* p. 137.

cord he was carrying. The new messenger then continued on his way alone as fast as possible towards the next *choza,* where in his turn he passed on the message in the same way. These couriers could be recognized from afar by the white plume they wore on their heads; and they announced their coming by blowing a trumpet. They were sworn to secrecy and were armed with a club and a sling.

The speed of transmission, thanks to this relay system, reached about 200 miles a day, according to the most reliable estimates. In two days the Inca received at Cuzco fish from Lake Titicaca, at a speed of about 190 miles daily.[1] The messengers, called *chasquis,* carried all kinds of small packets, such as snails for the Inca's table. Large parcels were entrusted to special porters, called *hatun-chasquis* (the 'big messengers'), each of whom walked for half a day.[2] All these workers were given their subsistence from public stores and their chief was a high official.

When the message was of particular importance, and emanated from the monarch himself, it was accompanied by a red thread from the *lautu* or a stick bearing marks whose meaning is unknown to us, but which appears to have been used by the Cañaris in south Ecuador.[3]

Near each *choza* a wood-pile was kept ready, which was lighted by order of a chief when an important event had just taken place—a rebellion or invasion—and each courier on watch along the road set fire in his turn to the one for which he was responsible. The fire signal thus spread to the capital, where it warned the Emperor and his council. Even before knowing the cause of this agitation, arrangements were made so that the army was ready to leave in the direction of the province where the alarm had been raised.

The bridge service consisted of the detailed supervision of

[1] Poma de Ayala: *Nueva Corónica, op. cit.,* p. 352; P. de Cieza de León: *Segunda Parte de la Corónica del Perú, op. cit.,* chap. 22; J. H. Howland Rowe: *Inca Culture at the time of the Spanish Conquest, op. cit.,* p. 231.

[2] There is some confusion amongst the chroniclers about the *hatun-chasqui.* He was either chief of the runners, or else a runner with a long stage.

[3] For appraisal of the speed of the runners and the recognition signs by sticks, see L. Baudin: *L'Empire socialiste des Inka, op. cit.,* respectively, pp. 197 and 125. On the Cañaris, G. Suarez: *Historia general del Ecuador,* Quito, 1890–1892, t. 1, p. 174.

these erections which were so exposed to the inclemencies of the weather, and to arrange for their immediate repair in case of need. The watchman always had to have with him wood and ropes for this purpose. He was sometimes charged with collecting tolls by setting apart some of the merchandise being carried. This was done for the bridge over the Mantaro to the south of Lake Bonbon.

Service in the mines was organized in rotation (*mita*), a system which was preserved by the Spaniards, but applied more or less as a punishment. Many abuses took place after the Conquest. In places where workings were carried on at high altitudes, where the cold was intense, work was limited to half-days (from midday to sunset) and only for four months in the year.[1]

The personal service of the imperial family involved a great number of people. An incredible throng of servants crowded the Inca's palace, 'with no other salary than their keep.' None of them entered the monarch's apartment unless called, and they had to enter barefoot.[2]

Certain ancient tribes provided special services suited to their skills. The Chumbivilcas sent dancers to Cuzco, the Collahuyas sent healers, and the Rucanas sent bearers for the imperial litter.

THE LICE TRIBUTE

A most extraordinary, but at the same time a most rational tribute, was exacted from groups of the poorest of the population, such as the Pastos, who lived in the southernmost part of the Empire. These poor people had to send to their rulers a horn filled with lice and counted by the taxpayers. We have already remarked on this when listing the conquests of the Inca Tupac Yupanqui. In this way no one could boast of escaping tax. The State made its impression on the most humble of its subjects and at the same time achieved a very salutary and hygienic piece of work.

[1] Pedro Sancho: *Relación para S.M., op. cit.*, p. 182.
[2] B. Cobo: *Historia del Nuevo Mundo, op. cit.*, book 12, chap. 36.

CHAPTER 15

ECONOMIC LIFE: BARTER

THE MARKETS

ALTHOUGH trade was very limited, it none the less played an important part in the Indians' life from a psychological point of view. It provided a memory of the past, of the time when it was far more extensive, because the uniform Inca system had not then been set up. Above all it brought a happy diversion into the monotony of existence. It was a great amusement and a great joy for a man, and still more for a woman, to go away for several days with a few neighbours, all duly authorized by their chiefs, to sell a few trifling articles in the market of the nearest town. Each town of any importance held a market three times a month.

The Indian who went to this gathering had to carry with him means of subsistence during his absence. He had not the right to be fed at the expense of the *tambos,* but he could exchange his products for others which suited him better, and spend a night there if necessary. Otherwise he slept under the stars with his head on a flat stone.

Sometimes the way was long and the load heavy, especially when carrying provisions and *chicha* for several days, but there was wealth in the town square, where often a feast day coincided with the fair, and singers and dancers and story-tellers spread an unaccustomed gaiety.

It is true that in this market without professional traders, exchange of merchandise was of little importance. It took place by barter, as it did before the Inca conquest and later under Spanish occupation. The Indian woman crouched on the ground, set out before her little heaps of grain, potato flour, *quinua* or pimento, and remained motionless as was her habit, happy to contemplate the scene of animation such as was unknown in her village.

Here is a passer-by looking at the produce exposed for sale. She crouches down opposite the seller and, taking from her bag the provisions she wishes to barter, she places a handful of salt beside a heap of pimento. The seller does not appear to have observed her tactics and continues to dream. The buyer adds another fistful of salt. This time the seller awakes from her impassivity, seizes what is offered to her and lets the buyer take what she proposed. The two sides to this bargain have not said a word, not even a polite greeting.[1]

This 'silent trading' sometimes lasted a long time, for the Indians were in no hurry. It was not always the same, for in spite of the uniformity of surroundings and of life, ancestral influences of unknown origin were maintained, and varied the psychology to some extent. The demands and reactions of the parties varied according to the groups to which they belonged. Everyone at Cuzco knew that the inhabitants of Aucaylly were obliged to calculate the terms of exchange with great care so as to obtain parity of value, taking into account the quality of each article, whilst the people of Chinchero bartered large quantities without bothering about anything else.[2]

Some did not rely on their personal skill and had recourse to scales. For a long time these were used on the north coast of the Empire where they were employed to weigh precious metals and were of the simplest design. The operator held them suspended by the middle of the lever which had a bag at each end. The article to be weighed was placed in one of these bags, the weights in the other. There was also a kind of Roman scale with one weight and one bag. Both these instruments were held in the hand. They were fairly sensitive and exact enough to give a high degree of precision, and this was necessary on account of the high value of certain heavy goods (precious metals) or by reason of their particular nature (poisonous medicinal plants). Weights consisted of stones chosen so as to obtain a range of multiples. A bag found near

[1] B. Cobo: *Historia del Nuevo Mundo, op. cit.,* book 11, chap. 8; R. Latcham: *El Dominio de la tierra y el sistema tributario en el antiguo imperio de los Incas,* in *Revista chilena de historia y geográfica,* January 1927, p. 247.

[2] J. M. Moscoso: *Los Ayllus reales de San Sebastian,* in *Revista Universitaria de Cuzco,* 1950, 2, p. 151.

Huacho contained two series of these weights, one of nine stones and the other of four.[1]

Some Indians, not being able to find the provisions they needed, accepted money tallies, thin copper axes, or shells of exquisite shades coming from tropical seas, which could be threaded and used as ornaments.

All the articles offered for sale were set out on the ground, and as the barterers crouched over their transactions the Indian who stood upright or moved around had an over-all view of the market, and could, if he were able, appreciate its picturesque appearance. The custom of doing business slowly enabled him to avoid injuring or crushing the merchandise spread out in all directions. He enjoyed this apparent abundance, made up of small contributions added together; an illusion of wealth which lasted for the space of one day.

Little llamas, offspring of the pair owned by each family as by right, lay motionless near bags of *chuño* and parcels with cords wound round them, like snakes, whilst their parents, used for the transport of all these marvels, passed in a dignified manner between rounded yellowish jars, and baked clay terra-cotta cups ornamented with hieroglyphic designs. Clients awaited their turn to seek advice from the healer surrounded by his packets of herbs. Ornaments of bird feathers in brilliant colours, which had come from the distant forests, brought an exotic note to the sandals and belts lined up in the dust.

The whole added up to very little. How could it have been otherwise, since this 'trade under a microscope,' as a contemporary writer expresses it,[2] was only the surplus obtained with great difficulty by supplementary labour or else due to exceptional weather conditions.

But there was a feeling of gaiety, the magic of bright colours, contact with human beings from other regions, the hope of dancing and drinking. There were few transactions for many people, no uproar, no discussions, only a light mur-

[1] E. Nordenskiold: *Emploi de la balance romaine en Amérique du Sud avant la conquête,* in *Journal de la Societé des Américanistes de Paris,* 1921. And by the same author, *The Ancient Peruvian System of Weights,* in *Man,* 1930, p. 155; C. Letourneau: *L'Évolution du Commerce,* Paris, 1897, p. 202.

[2] A report by Colonel Julio Guerrero, in *Revista Universitaria de Cuzco,* 1949, 2, p. 127.

mur which the llamas underlined with their heavy stamping. However, a fugitive impression of relaxation made the market a singular source of happiness. The rigid rhythm of daily life was momentarily broken.

FOREIGN TRADE

The Indians of the common people had no knowledge of foreign trade. This expression had for them only a very vague significance. Only soldiers had any precise conception as they went on campaign. The foreigner was the enemy they must fight, or else the barbarian whose country they could not think of occupying because it was too poor.

The nobility obtained goods from far-off countries by means of barter, especially if they lived in frontier areas, and the common people maintained relations with neighbouring foreigners which had been established before the Inca conquest, and were often very ancient.

The pilot Ruiz, one of the first of the Spanish conquerors, met on the Pacific, on his way to Tumbez, a raft crewed by Indians, subjects of the Inca, who sailed with a cargo of fabrics, mirrors, shells, precious stones and metals.[1]

Trade in recently conquered territories and all along the frontiers flourished until Inca regimentation stifled it, and little by little it lost its importance. It was not in the sovereign's interest to allow it to disappear, since he himself took advantage of it to obtain products unknown on the Andean plateau, and he also used the traders as willing spies. In the south of the Empire, the example may be quoted of the Pehuenches of the Mendoza *sierra,* who traded in salt, animal skins, dried fish, arrow-heads, and necklaces of green or blue stones, in sea-birds' feathers and edible seaweed.[2] For money they used little shells, pierced and strung into necklaces.

With goods circulated also news.[3] If the common people,

[1] J. de Sámanos: *Relación de los primeros descubrimientos de Francisco Pizarro y Diego de Almagro,* in *Colección de documentos inéditos para la Historia de España,* t. 5.

[2] With some exaggeration Ricardo Latcham writes that trade in South America had become international before the fifteenth century. (*El comercio precolombiano,* Santiago de Chili, 1909, p. 45.)

[3] It may be wondered if the Incas had any contact with the Aztecs, and if their predecessors had any with the Mayas or the Olmechs, who

settled on the land, knew little of the outside world, by contrast the Empire's neighbours, the nomads of the southern pampas, the indomitable Araucans, the natives of the Brazilian forests or of the western part of what is Ecuador today, were all of them familiar with the institutions and happenings of the Empire. The setting-up of this great monolithic State filled all those who heard about it with admiration or fear.

What filtered through in this way beyond the frontiers of the Empire was the echo of victories and triumphs, of marvels of architecture, of the perfection of statistics. Legends grew up which added further to this power and wealth. The intensity of the light shining forth from the Empire did not allow anyone to discern from the outside the precise and veracious details of daily life.

were more remarkable still, and only recently discovered. Probably they knew of their existence, but only had irregular and not very close contacts on account of the distance.

CONCLUSION

THE first obvious conclusion which emerges from our account is, once again, a lesson in relativity. Today we could no more acquiesce in the filth to which the Indian was perfectly accustomed than we could accommodate ourselves to the uniformity which suited him. Those who have no conception of liberty, nor of individual possessions, do not suffer by their absence, but we who have both could not dispense with them without distress or rebellion.

The Inca himself only sought an opportunist solution, the better to establish his authority, and he created an enormous administrative machine which adapted itself to the natural, historical and psychological conditions of his subjects. The secret of his success lay in this conformity.[1]

We do not enquire what would have happened if the Spaniards had not disembarked at Tumbez. One good man insists that the Inca government constitutes a stage on the road to liberty.[2] The individual ownership of property by the nobility brings support for this theory, but the tightening of the hold on the common people does not permit this to be maintained.

Seen with the eyes of a man of the twentieth century, daily life in the times of the last Incas gives the impression of having been organized once and for all as a piece of mechanism of gloomy perfection. The absolute and the permanent reigned without opposition. The common people had nothing to learn, nothing to foresee, nothing to desire. There was for them no inner withdrawal, no outer radiance. The Inca and his Council, and they alone, constituted the brain of this immense collective personality.

Such the Empire appears to us—gigantic, yet with everything localized, a grandiose moment of time which repeated itself identically, a dream come true of an endless immensity

[1] B. de las Casas, who always tends to exaggerate, states that the 'Indian Republics equalled and even surpassed all the republics of antiquity "in their good laws and customs."' (*Apologética historia sumaria, op. cit.*, t. 1, p. 681.)

[2] J. Guerrero, in *Revista Universitaria de Cuzco, op. cit.*, p. 153.

and of a duration without end. 'Wearying monotony and unconquerable sadness,' writes a commentator.[1] However the fifteenth century Indian drew certain advantages from this situation. He owed to it an orderliness, a security against famine and invasion, peace of mind, a settlement into total passivity. It was useless to bother about others, the State took charge of everything, of old people and the incapable. 'They do not know what charity is,' wrote Father Cobo, in speaking of the Indians, 'nor pity.' And he was astonished to see a woman pass near a child who had fallen over and was crying without even looking at him.[2] Polo de Ondegardo was indignant because he discovered that the Indians, finding one of their number with a broken leg, only reported the matter to the official concerned.[3] Nothing was more logical—the men were not to blame, it was the system which was responsible. But are we not right to repeat what Aristotle said of the communist city of Plato—here is an uncouth and unattractive society?

One might have thought at least that the Indian was happy, and many have thought so.[4] Durkheim imagines that the distinctive characteristic of the primitive is contentment, which enables him to describe civilized man as perpetually unhappy,[5] and Father J. de Acosta wrote that the Peruvian was both enslaved and happy.[6] But we do not believe that even at the price of his freedom the Indian could have acquired happiness.

No doubt happiness is a subjective acquisition; man is happy when he believes he is happy. But Indian psychology is complex. Security, mental inertia, freedom from the need for making a choice and from responsibilities, all combined to make a negative happiness. But to hold to this conclusion would be to ignore the predominance of mysticism in the mind of the inhabitants of the Andean plateau. Unhappiness overcome in the visible world at the price of liberty found another source in the beyond, as if it was inseparable from human nature and could be transposed but not eliminated. Happy the unhappiness which drew the soul of the Indian out of the drowsiness

[1] S. Lorente: *Historia antigua del Perú,* Lima, 1860, p. 332.
[2] B. Cobo: *Historia del Nuevo Mundo, op. cit.,* book 11, chap. 8.
[3] Polo de Ondegardo: *Relación de los fundamentos, op. cit.,* p. 87.
[4] We ourselves have thought this up to the present time.
[5] E. Durkheim: *La Division du Travail social,* Paris, 1893, p. 268.
[6] J. de Acosta: *Historia natural y moral, op. cit.,* t. 2, book 6, chap. 15.

into which the very perfection and severity of the Peruvian system threatened to plunge him—an unhappiness which, in the sphere inaccessible to human rationalization, of necessity and for always held the unforeseen hazards of birth, illness, accident and death.

INDEX